W9-CSF-880

Too Much Gold to Flush

The Gift of Infidelity

Pat Grissom

Permission requests should be directed to:
Patricia Ann Grissom
c/o Dedicated to Empowering Women, LLC.
P.O. Box 2235
Friendswood, Texas 77549
www.patgrissom.com

Disclaimer
The names of the people in this story have been changed to protect the innocent and the not so innocent.

Dedicated to Empowering Women, LLC. (DEW)
Cover & Layout Design - Ira S. Van Scoyoc
Copy Editor - Shirin Wright
Project Manager - Pam Van Scoyoc

Cataloging-in-Publication Data
Grissom, Pat.
Too much gold to flush : the gift of infidelity / by
Pat Grissom. -- 1st ed.
p. cm.
Includes bibliographical references.
LCCN 2012937377
ISBN 978-0-9853813-0-1

1. Grissom, Pat. 2. Adult children of dysfunctional families--United States--Biography. 3. Dysfunctional families--United States--Case studies. 4. Adultery--United States--Case studies. 5. College teachers--United States--Biography. I. Title.

HQ536.G75 2013   155.9'24'092
                                  QBI12-200014

First Edition

Printed in China

Dedicated to those for whom abuse has dimmed
the perception of your Inner Light.

Table of Contents

Introduction

Had I known what I was getting into, I doubt I would have gone there, but I sure am glad I did. ~Patricia Ann Grissom

Long, long, ago, in my early twenties, I stood chatting with a young mother after church while her two daughters, ages four and five, ran gleefully up and down the center aisle. She looked at her children and smiled. Then she offered a morsel that oozed with truth and remains ripe with wisdom today. "You know, before I had kids, they would never have done that." If someone had prophesied the story contained in this book, I would have vehemently denied the likelihood that I would follow such an insane course of action. Not me. I am a responsible, college-educated woman with a good head on my shoulders. When my marriage fell apart after only three months, I feared re-creating the same scenario further down the road of life. Therefore, I promised myself I would analyze the situation and understand what had happened, my part in it, and how to stop myself from traveling that path again.

My story covers the last five years, but it includes my other fifty-five years, since what I did during the events of this account hinges on who arrived on the scene, including the experiences I brought to the table. Two and a half years have passed since I spoke to my ex-husband, who, at this writing, resides in prison. It has taken that long to get the perspective needed to see what happened and where, when, and how I wandered so far off base to make such self-destructive choices. Why had I pursued a lifetime commitment with someone who repulsed others? What compelled me to ignore their reactions and my own gut instincts? In exploring this story, I gave myself permission to answer those questions and to mine all the gold this experience has to offer.

Writing this honest account of my part in this saga has felt like undressing in public, revealing aspects of myself that I neither want to see nor to show others. It has shown me fallacies in my thoughts and actions that I would never have seen otherwise. It has also revealed strengths that I did not know I possessed. I have seen myself shift from a victim in a self-made prison to the creator of an incredible life.

"All right, Mr. DeMille, I'm ready for my close-up." SUNSET BLVD, 1950.

Prologue

When I ask what my early life was like, Mother says she does not remember. Not, she cannot recall that far back; she literally does not remember the first year of my life. She had me seventeen months after giving birth to my brother. I was born right after my parents moved to a two-bedroom house with a bathroom. Before that, they had lived a couple of hundred feet from my grandparents' house in a one-bedroom with an outhouse. Knowing how overbearing my grandmother could be, and how easily intimidated Mother is, I can only imagine the hell she went through as a young mother with an emotionally unsupportive husband. Plus, this was a time before postpartum depression had been recognized as a legitimate medical condition.

At eighteen months of age, I received a twelve-inch teddy bear as a Christmas gift from a cousin, one of many, who had drawn my name in the family gift exchange. I doubt I had many toys, but the teddy bear's real appeal started after I discovered his silky stuffing via a hole next to his ear. I was hooked, and My Bear became a part of me. The smoothness of his filling between my tiny fingers lulled me to sleep at night. Mother said she often found evidence that I had been up in the middle of the night playing, so she probably welcomed something that would help me sleep. Of course the hole grew bigger, and My Bear began to leak, so Mother stuffed him with rags and sewed up the hole – to no avail. I would simply find another weak seam, for I could not drift off without rubbing his silky guts.

My sister was born when I was three, claiming much of Mother's time. As a result, I became even more attached to My Bear. Grandmother used to tell a story about the time I was in the hospital, and she and the nurses turned the room upside down looking for My Bear, who had somehow ended up behind the bed. According to Grandmother, I was in a virtual panic by the time they returned him to me.

With time, Mother tired of my dependency on My Bear. She had enough to do without adding my irrational attachment to a teddy bear to the mix. I begged and begged her to perform further surgical repairs, lest I lose all of My Bear's insides. While she stitched, she reminded me that I was too old for such things. Then she made me promise I would not work another hole in him. None of his original stuffing remained, she reasoned, so why did I continue to poke my finger inside him? But habits die slowly, especially when they are so well ingrained.

When I was four, we traded houses with my grandparents. They had a two-story farmhouse, and Grandmother, always the planner, had a vision of building onto our little house and making it big enough for them, which they eventually did. The day we made the big move, my siblings and I stayed at my aunt's house. That night our new home was a jumble of boxes and stuff. My Bear was lost in the mess. I thought I could not sleep without him, but I did. Knowing how I currently struggle to fall asleep, I can only imagine what a challenge it must have been then. I believed My Bear would surface once things were in order. But he never did.

I'm not sure if it was only a few days later or maybe it was weeks, but I remember deciding that he was on the top shelf of the living room closet. I managed to drag a dining room chair to the closet, but when I realized I couldn't begin to reach that high, I asked my parents to help me. Dad was watching TV, and Mother wouldn't be swayed from cooking supper. Again and again, I returned to the closet, convinced that My Bear was in one of the boxes on the top shelf, probably the small green one. It looked like a good fit for him. Though I could hear him calling to me, I could not convince my parents to help me.

The heaviness in my chest as I type these words reminds me of the helplessness I felt then, knowing that what I desperately needed was obtainable, but I could not convince the people at hand to help me. Connecting the dots between where I was then and what I grew up believing about myself, I can only surmise that many of my negative core beliefs solidified around losing what represented security at the time. The seeds of unworthiness and abandonment were already there, but losing My Bear created a shift, a marker of exactly when I decided it was not safe to have feelings. It hurt too much to love something dearly and then lose it. Along with that, I decided that I had to please others in order to get what I wanted. I could not be myself. I needed to be who they wanted me to be. So I started a lifelong obsession with trying to second-guess what others expected from me in exchange for them giving me what I so desperately wanted – attention, support, and love.

My Bear showed up again when I was in my forties. Mother gave him to me as a Christmas present. He was still in that little green shoebox that I had spied at the top of the living room closet forty years earlier. Ten years later, I was going through a grieving period after the guy I had been dating broke up with me. Finding it impossible to sleep, I got up in the middle of the night and ritualistically drained My Bear of his rag stuffing. Then I gave him a sudsy bath, gently dried him with a hair dryer, and restuffed him with fluffy white polyester. Associating him with loss, I cried as I stitched his gaping neck. Next I got out my journal and created a list of credentials for what I would demand in a man. No more dating guys who would break my heart. I had dealt with enough of that. Next time I would get what I wanted – a kind, sensitive man who would recognize what I had to offer and treat me well.

I began dating Rael (pronounced rail) a month later. When he lovingly delivered soup to my back door following my day surgery, I found that list of requirements, written just two months earlier. I e-mailed it to Rael, and he responded that what I was holding out for was such a close fit that he could have written the list himself. To add emphasis to his conviction that this was the Universe's way of showing us how fate had brought us together, Rael pointed out that I wrote this entry on the day he had attended his ex-wife's funeral. He said, as he drove away from the church, he had felt a burden of responsibility lifted from his shoulders. Jill had battled cancer for over a year, and while they were not together, there was a part of him that felt connected to her. His sales job concerning his qualifications to fit my requirements fueled my conviction that he was the person who could symbolically retrieve My Bear from the top of the closet.

Recently I made My Bear a coat of velvet with a satin lining. He sleeps with me again, and I drift off with the luscious feel of his coat between my thumb and forefinger. All the love I need is within me. I don't have to look for it outside myself. I just have to learn how to give it to myself. That is the real challenge – learning how to love myself.

We should say to each [child]: Do you know what you are? You are a marvel. You are unique… You may become a Shakespeare, a Michelangelo, a Beethoven. You have the capacity for anything.
~ Pablo Casals

Chapter One
Fall – Trying Out a New Swing

Love many, trust few and always paddle your own canoe.
~American Proverb

At fifty-four years of age and as a college professor, it would seem I had a clue about life in general or, more particularly, relations with men – but I did not. Several years earlier my thirty-two-year marriage had ended in divorce after my husband and I grew apart and our kids were nearly out of the nest. Full of trepidation, I decided to reenter the world of dating. Self-help books and women's magazines concurred that my maturity level when resuming dating would rank close to the maturity level I had attained when I left off that activity thirty-five years earlier. Do the math. Yes, I married at nineteen – young by today's standards, but largely acceptable back then.

Did I know what I was doing? Absolutely not! Clueless about where to turn for help, I asked my therapist, whom I will call Dr. Humor. Wit and comedy permeate his practice, from the notebooks of cartoons that lie in the lobby to the humorous stories he shares with his clients. When I related my dilemma, he told me the following anecdote:

"Early in my career, I worked with a college tennis coach, helping him address the psychological state of his players and how that affected their game. In exchange for my input, I received private tennis lessons.

Love as if you liked
yourself, and it may
happen.
                ~Marge Piercy

After assessing my swing, the coach showed me a different grip on the racket and a new posture to use as I moved through the swing. Then he told me to practice these until our next lesson the following week.

"When I played my regular tennis partner, I awkwardly tried my new swing, but it didn't take long for me to realize that I felt more comfortable with my old method. Under the stress of the game, I reverted to it and played as usual. At the second private lesson, the coach observed that I had not made the prescribed changes, so he redemonstrated the techniques. With my regular tennis partner, I once more attempted to implement the new swing, but again it felt like a handicap rather than an asset, so I again relapsed.

"At the third private lesson, the college coach said he could not continue to work with me if I refused to change to the new swing, so I promised to stick with the new technique – no matter what. At our next match, I told my regular partner I was learning a new swing and might not do as well as usual, but I wanted to stick with the fresh strategy. My partner delighted in my plan; in fact, he quite enjoyed trouncing me. The next time we played, my performance improved and within a month of using my new swing, I was consistently beating my partner."

My interpretation of this story was that I should date a number of guys without getting serious about any of them. By the time I had dated a dozen men, I would, supposedly, get comfortable with the whole issue of dating. Plus, I wanted to avoid the trap of falling head over heels for someone just because we had dated. Nor did I want to lose myself in a relationship, as I had in my marriage.

Rael was number eleven on the "dated list." I met Rael on an online dating site, the same place I had met the rest, except for the one introduced by my divorce lawyer. At the time, I marveled at the uniqueness of having the person who had helped me get out of my marriage act as matchmaker. Her candidate was above average, but in the end, he became one of the guys who took a number and moved on through my life.

Once we started dating, Rael and I discussed the fact that we had checked each other out on the dating site for about a year before we started exchanging e-mails. His two kids and an ex had kept me from what looked promising otherwise. For my part, I had frumpy-looking pictures. About the same time I posted better photos, he changed his marital status from divorced to widowed, which prompted me to send him a note asking why. He explained that his ex had just died, which, of course, elicited sympathy from me. It also made a difference in how I saw his situation – free of the typical baggage that having an ex entails. We e-mailed for a couple of weeks before he invited me to his Democratic house party for a showing of *An Inconvenient Truth* and *The Death of the Electric Car*. I asked Cheryl, a girlfriend, to go with me, lest this guy ended up being a pervert who had tricked me into coming to a house party minus the party.

About twenty people showed up. From his online profile, I knew Rael was vegetarian, so at the snack table, I consciously selected food that he would not find offensive. Yes, I was already monitoring what I did to please him – even before we started dating.

As I left that evening, Rael asked if he could call me for a date. I was not impressed with his looks, and we had talked only briefly because he had spent his hosting time moving from group to group. But I had this numbers thing going, and I was eager to get my dozen men dated. So I told him sure, and we agreed to meet a few days later at a restaurant close to my house.

The evening of our first date, I dressed in my typical first-date apparel, a long skirt with a fitted blouse. As I approached the entrance of the café, Rael was sitting outside at a table. He appeared distracted and pensive. Seeing me, he jumped up and declared, "You look beautiful."

His positive assessment of my looks started the evening on an optimistic note. Inside, we ordered at the counter before we sat down. I chose fish, thinking that would be nonoffensive to a vegetarian. When I hesitated over the wine list, and finally decided on the cheapest red wine on the menu, he declared I was only choosing it because of the cost. How did he know that? We had not had a conversation of substance, and he already perceived things about me that I had not shared. We sat down and began to talk.

While we talked, I noted one oddity about Rael. For no apparent reason, a wave of energy periodically moved through him, which resulted

> *Love yourself, accept yourself, forgive yourself, and be good to yourself, because without you the rest of us are without a source of many wonderful things.*
> *~Leo Buscaglia*

in his spasmodically jerking his head and shoulder together. Rael seemed oblivious to the involuntary contraction, so I discounted it as first-date jitters. His otherwise relaxed manner lulled me into a marathon conversation.

By the time the waitstaff began stacking the chairs on to the other tables and vacuuming the floor, I had shared too much about myself, including the fact that my parents had only been divorced for a few years, following a fifty-four-year marriage. When he asked me why they had separated so late in life, I replied that my dad was a recently convicted sex offender. Due to Rael's attentiveness, I had pegged him as a sensitive and caring person – a perfect match for what I wanted. Still, I was not sure I should test him with the details, so I hedged, saying I had already shared too much. In the parking lot, we stood by my car, and I gave him what I considered a safe kiss for a first date, an ounce of tongue.

The next day I received the following e-mail. Rael's words reflected many of my own feelings of attraction.

> *Conversation has a kind of charm about it, an insinuating and insidious something that elicits secrets from us just like love or liquor.*
> *~Lucius Annaeus Seneca*

To: Pat
From: Rael
Date: Tuesday, December 19, 12:36 PM
Subject: Our First Date

Hi Pat,

I truly enjoyed meeting and talking with you last night. We surely clicked. When I stood outside the restaurant waiting for you to arrive, I had one of those moments of dread flash through me that our meeting would go nowhere. I felt "my life is too complicated"; "I don't have enough time to give to a new relationship" – i.e., the fear that this is not going to work. Then, suddenly I see the waitstaff cleaning the restaurant, all the other patrons leaving, and I wanted to be with you much longer. That was three hours? No way, it seemed only minutes.

Driving home, I realized how much I miss having someone to talk with, someone to get to know, someone to excite and be excited about, someone who attracts me . . . someone like you. And in the parking lot...that little kiss... perfect! In your lips I felt no hesitance, no apprehension, no separation. To the contrary, I felt a total connection, as if I could fall into you through our kiss.

Thank you so very much. The pessimist in me thinks, "We're going to have a hard time meeting this standard in the future," but my heart thinks, "Wow, I can't wait to do this again." I look forward to talking and being with you again,
Rael

> *How delicious is the winning of a kiss at love's beginning.*
> *~ Thomas Campbell*

The next day another e-mail arrived, this one even more open and caring. I found his willingness to bare his soul irresistible.

To: Pat
From: Rael
Date: Wednesday, December 20, 7:07 AM

Good morning Pat,

I want to wish you a safe trip to Wimberley and Lubbock. Hopefully you read this before you leave, and if not, I hope you have Internet access on the road, and if not, "Welcome Home."

As I sit here this early morning, I notice a malaise creeping over me blanketing that wonderful feeling of exhilaration I felt while with you. Examining it, I guess I'm playing those same old messages I use to accept my aloneness. I have dread-messages playing in my head.

"Rael's a bad person." "Rael will never find love." "Rael only hurts those who care for him." As you talked about, I need to develop and practice some positive affirmations. "I deserve having someone special in my life." "I am worthy of Pat's love." "Me loving Pat is good for her." I'm sitting here feeling like Gollum in *Lord of the Rings, The Two Towers* when his child-self, named Sméagol, has an internal argument with his evil self named Gollum. He won that argument and Sméagol emerged, only to disappear when doubt challenged him. It is that, or maybe I just need a cup of coffee, ha ha.

I sure look forward to being with you again. I like how I felt when I was with you. I want, I need, I deserve to have someone to connect with and share life. I want someone to call when I have something wonderful to share or when doubt/fear challenges my affirmations and fertilizes my dread-messages. I want someone who loves me enough to share her wonders and trusts me enough to share her dreads. Jacob does that but on a six-year-old's level. I also need it on an adult level. I need someone wise and intelligent to see through my balderdash front I use to avoid my dread-messages, and to pull me back to my affirmations.

Oh well, I'm going to go make some coffee and get back to that exhilarating buzz of accomplishment. Today is Christmas shopping with the kids and cleaning a garage.

Talk soon,
love,
Rael

> *A baby is born with a need to be loved and never outgrows it.*
> *~Frank A. Clark*

I forwarded these and other e-mails I received from Rael to my friend Lilly, along with notes about how smitten I was with this guy who was not afraid to share his feelings. With Christmas only a few days away, I packed my car to drive to Lubbock to see my mom. On the way out of town, I called Rael to say good-bye. He asked me to stop by his house to meet Jacob. Wanting desperately to see him again, but hesitant, I admitted I had not put on makeup, and also that I had a dog companion, Poncho, that I was pet-sitting. Rael easily persuaded me, saying he would eventually see me without the façade of foundation and mascara, and I only needed to stay a little while before I took off.

Shortly after I arrived at Rael's home, he and I walked Poncho, staying within a block of his house, lest Jacob became alarmed if he could not find his dad. I did not realize it then, but at that point Jacob and Rael had only lived together about six weeks, following Jacob's mother's death from cancer in late October. Rael and Jill had divorced when Jacob was two. In the four years since Jill's moving out, Jacob had never spent the night with his dad.

> *"Why don't you come up sometime and see me?"*
> SHE DONE HIM
> WRONG, 1933.

Eager to let Rael know I found his short stature desirable, I commented on this. He replied that he was the "perfect" height because the average woman is a little shorter than him and the average man is a little taller, so he saw himself as the best of both. I was captivated by his positive self-image, although I also wondered if it was a front for insecurity.

When I stood in the driveway and told Jacob I had to go, he replied, "You just got here." He sounded like an adult, and I wondered if he was saying what he had heard his mother say.

In Lubbock, I shopped with Mother and found the perfect gift for Rael, a daily tear-off calendar with a "Bushism" on every page. Rael was/ is what my granddad once confessed to being, a Yellow Dog Democrat— he would vote for a yellow dog as long as it ran on the Democratic ticket.

While I drove back to Houston from Lubbock, Rael drove to Ft. Worth. We talked on our cell phones, exchanging pleasantries and anticipating our next date. He and Jacob rode with Jacob's half-brother, Christopher, and his step-dad, Richard, the man Jacob's mother, Jill, had married on her deathbed. Later, Rael revealed to me that Jill had done this to keep Rael from getting her first son even though she could not legally keep him from taking custody of his own child, Jacob.

> *The advantage of love at first sight is that it delays a second sight.*
> *~ Natalie Barney*

To: Rael
From: Pat
Date: Wednesday, December 27, 10:14 PM

To my cute, cute, clever guy,

What a lovely e-mail. And to think it has been sitting here waiting for me for over eighteen hours.

My only concern about the New Year's Eve get-together is that you might feel awkward being the only guy. It will be a small gathering – two other ladies and me. I am planning on making a broccoli dish that has sunflower seeds, Ramen noodles, green onions, and I'm not sure what else. The other vegetable dish I am making has a black-eyed pea base. It also has cilantro, carrots, celery, onions (you have to have onions in stuff to make it taste good – I'll also have breath mints available). I brought three jars of home-canned black-eyed peas from my mom's house. Those dried ones and canned ones you buy in the grocery store cannot compare with home-canned. I was raised on home-canned veggies. We always had a huge field garden where we grew green beans, corn, peas, okra, watermelon, cantaloupe, and squash.

Let me know when you get home. I love hearing from you. It was so nice to talk while driving, although we had to contend with poor connections and road noise. Hugs and kisses,
Pat

We continued to exchange e-mails while we traveled. Rael came to my condo the day after he returned home. We immediately began kissing. When we stopped to catch our breath, he commented that this was his favorite part of a relationship – the initial kissing stage before the real sexual stuff started. It comforted me to think he did not expect sex from the get-go. What he said and what he did were two different things because, within a few minutes, he had me pinned to the couch, rubbing his whole body against me in a motion that went beyond passion. His actions made me think of a ten-year-old at a school sports event. And how did I react? Well, I kissed him back with all the fervor I could muster, attempting to match his vibrating enthusiasm.

"Louis, I think this is the beginning of a beautiful friendship."
CASABLANCA, 1942.

Why, you might ask. Because I thought he expected me to. Too young to remember or comprehend the lesson being drilled into my head, I had learned that if a woman is attracted to a man, she must do what she thinks he expects or wants her to do – even if it is not particularly enjoyable to her. It is the cardinal rule I grew up believing about relationships.

To: Rael
From: Pat
Sent: Saturday, December 30, 10:02:55 AM
Hello Mr. Great Kisser,

I woke up at 8:00 this morning, of course, thinking of you. Hey, I went to bed thinking about you. I'm off to walk with a friend at 10:30. Just wanted to say last night was really, really nice. Thanks for being you – spontaneous, free, funny, zany, clever, affectionate, and open – a very nice combination of traits to find in a cute guy.

Love, Pat
P.S. I have beard burn on my face, a little reminder of our marathon make-out session.

Love takes off masks that we fear we cannot live without and know we cannot live within.
~ James A. Baldwin

To: Pat
From: Rael
Sent: Saturday, December 30

Good morning, Ms. Greatest Kisser in the World,

I never have stopped thinking about you. I feel like I'm still there in your arms. I can't stop smiling. I can't wait to see you again and hug you and be next to you and just be with you. I picked up Jacob and got to bed about 4:00. I woke at 8:30. At 9:00 a friend called me to come down to the Pearland Democratic headquarters to help move out the final furniture. Jacob went with me, and we had good ole donuts for breakfast. We stopped on the way home, and I bought all this food I plan on cooking today – a vegetable stew with okra and rice. I also bought some portabella mushrooms to grill.

I gave Jacob your present and all my spare change while in the car. He really enjoyed placing the coins in the device and watching them go to their respective slots.

I called and left a message. I'm sure you can hear the smile on my face.

Sorry about the beard burn on your face, but it surely is worth it.

I want to see you today, so I am going to call later and invite you over for supper tonight. Jacob will be here and maybe the three of us can play Uno or Skip-bo or watch a movie together.

Well, I have to find a sitter for tomorrow night, and start cooking.

Talk soon, love, love, kisses, hugs, caresses, love, love, Rael
P.S. Also throw in a little passion and desire.

In his e-mail, Rael says the beard burn was surely worth it – but for whom? His response should have clued me in on his narcissistic personality, but it did not. After a florist delivered a dozen roses of various colors to my condo, I called his home phone and left a blithering message about how flattered, overwhelmed, and awed I was by him. Then I sent the following e-mail.

To: Rael
From: Pat
Date: Saturday, December 30, 3:42 PM

Wow, double wow, no, make that a triple wow. In case you did not get my phone message, or to go along with my phone message: THANK YOU! You are one sweet, cute, boy. I am so impressed. If that was your objective, you accomplished it. I'm sitting here typing this in my birthday suit, having just gotten out of the shower, so I need to get dressed and out the door, but I just had to say it one more time. Thanks.
Electronic hugs and kisses, Pat

P.S. I can't wait to see you tomorrow night. If you are having second thoughts about leaving Jacob with Christopher, you could bring him and let him go to sleep upstairs. I have a few kid books, and I'm sure he has portable electronic stuff, Game Boys, etc.

P.S.S. Thanks again for the beautiful roses. I can't wait for you to see them. I can't wait to see you again.

All the beautiful sentiments in the world weigh less than a single lovely action.
~ James Lowell

> If somebody says, "I love you," to me, I feel as though I had a pistol pointed at my head. What can anybody reply under such conditions but that which the pistol-holder requires? "I love you, too."
>
> ~ Kurt Vonnegut

To: Pat
From: Rael
Date: Saturday, Dec 30, 1:28 PM
Subject: Wow, Great Phone Message

I just love your phone message. Those flowers truly left you speechless. If I knew you were going to be in your birthday suit, I would have delivered them myself. I just can't wait to see them tomorrow. I just can't wait to see you tomorrow. Gosh, isn't this fun, falling head over heels for each other. Pleasant dreams.
Your "lip" service man, Rael

The next evening Rael joined two of my friends, Cheryl and Lilly, and me for a New Year's Eve party. As we played card games, Cheryl, who had accompanied me to the Democratic house party at Rael's house, said something negative about dating. I honestly did not hear what she said, but it apparently offended Rael because he declared, "I would never ask you for a date." Throughout the evening, he had that nervous twitch that I'd seen during our first long conversation. Lilly and I talked about it afterward. As I recall these issues that put me off about Rael at the beginning, I am forced to ask myself what kept me so locked into the relationship. Attention and flattery, perhaps. He charmed me with his enthusiastic e-mails, phone calls, and apparent inability to get enough of me. It was what I had always wanted – someone who thought I had hung the moon.

As for his rude behavior toward Cheryl, I told myself that no one is perfect. It came with being human, right? Actually, Rael's rudeness was a stronger correlation to my father than I wanted to admit. I had witnessed my mother explain away Dad's insensitive behavior on numerous occasions. It did not occur to me that my oblivion to Rael's remark was reviving the behavior I had witnessed as a child. It felt too natural to question or even notice.

  **Family Reflections**

Now that I've introduced Rael, allow me to introduce my family of origin. There were four of us kids, all born before the first one went to school – two boys and two girls, with the boys being oldest and youngest, and us girls in the middle. Mother said she wanted girls and Dad wanted boys, so she seemed pleased with herself that she had finagled what they both desired. We lived in the Texas Panhandle, in Smyer, where, in 1930, my father and his sister garnered Grandmother the distinction of giving birth to the first recorded set of twins in Hockley County. During my formative years, the Smyer population sign touted 254 residents. I never figured out if that included my family since we lived five miles out of town and our mailing address was a rural route out of Lubbock. While I attended it, Smyer High School boasted around forty students, making my thirteen-member graduating class one of the larger ones. Remarkably, eight of us started first grade together.

My father farmed cotton with his father. And when Granddad retired after a heart attack, he remained closely involved in the production of the crop. I recall seeing my dad and Granddad in the spring, squatting among the cotton that had barely worked its way past the sandy surface. Each man scratched at the dirt and studied the red haze on the horizon, no doubt debating whether or not to spend the fuel or the labor on running the sand-fighter, a plow that broke the crust of the soil and, with some luck, would reduce the amount of sand that blew in the building sandstorm.

Periodically my dad talked about loading his sand-fighter on a flatbed trailer and hauling it up-country. He said he would know it was time to stop and put down stakes when someone asked him about that strange contraption he had with him – like Homer hauling his boat inland until someone asked him what it was. Dad never stopped talking about finding another way to make a living, and he adamantly discouraged us kids from following in his footsteps.

Illusion is the dust the devil throws in the eye of the foolish.
~ Minna Antrim

Nuggets of Gold

Since my original intention in writing this book was to learn from my experience, I decided to shake the sieve at the end of every chapter. Much of what I saw glistening among the dirt and rocks showed up early in the story, but that does not mean I learned the lesson right away. So don't hold me to automatically assimilating these gems of wisdom. The first truth that appeared is that, when I am trying something new, I need to make sure why I am doing it and what I hope to achieve. As I plunged into dating, I was determined to "try a new swing," as Dr. Humor suggested, but I lacked direction. Playing the numbers game seemed to satisfy the concept of persisting until I improved, although I had not established what enhancement in that area looked like. So the next time I decide to change my grip on a particular behavior, I am committed to determining what my desired result should be, and to define a more direct approach to achieving it.

> *Never dull your shine for somebody else.*
> *~Tyra Banks*

Next, I'd like to be myself. This goes hand in hand with defining my swing. That is what my new swing was supposed to have gotten me – the ability to be authentic in intimate relationships with men. Knowing what I think, what I like and don't like, being brave enough to stand by that no matter what – in other words, all that constitutes me, which is not who I was from the beginning of my relationship with Rael. So while I mention it here, I certainly do not give myself credit for having learned this lesson at this point in the story.

Lastly, save the family drama for after the let-me-get-to-know-you stage. I'm sure that Rael was attracted to more than the fact that my dad was a sex offender, but throwing that on the table in our first real conversation changed the dynamics of everything. It told him things about me that I did not need to tell him immediately. Plus, blurting out family history, especially when it is colorful and involves the police, drives away healthy guys, the ones I want to get to know better. At this point, I doubt I would have recognized or been attracted to a healthy guy. On the other hand, advertising my family history on the first date attracts men on the lookout for gals with vulnerable self-esteem who will fall for a little attention.

Life is change. Growth is optional. ~ *Anonymous*

Chapter Two
January – A New Year,
a New Love

Love is an irresistible desire to be irresistibly desired.
~Robert Frost

We were only a few weeks into the relationship and engaging in marathon kissing sessions. Fully aware of the dangers of having unsafe sex, I asked Rael to get tested for sexually transmitted diseases (STDs), and I agreed to do the same. We gave ourselves a month to get a clean bill of health before we had intercourse. To me that felt like a reasonable amount of time, but from the way Rael mentioned it in every conversation, it must have seemed like an eternity. Dr. Humor and I joked about Rael having a large wall calendar where he marked off the days.

Prior to the one-month deadline which sanctioned sexual intimacy, Rael was already talking about marriage. Like a smitten schoolgirl, in my journal on January 10, I wrote my first name and followed it with his last name. The next day, I had a medical procedure done, which involved grafting tissue from the roof of my mouth to my receding gums. Not major surgery, but not a stroll in the park either. After I returned home and slept off the anesthesia, I found Rael had left get-well gifts at my back door. I called to thank him, and later that afternoon, I opened this e-mail:

To: Pat
From: Rael
Date: Thursday, Jan 11, 1:28 PM
Subject: A Gentle Wake-Up for My Love

Slowly open your eyes my lovely Pat.
Let these loving words gently massage your heavy eyelids.
I hope you had a pleasant sleep and your mouth has no pain.
Our conversation at lunch just fueled my love for you and our relationship. It is so enjoyable to be able to talk to you about anything. You are so open and sharing and not afraid to share with me. It is wonderful. Thank you for accepting all of my love and for having patience as I shout from the roof, loud and often, about the great love I have discovered.
When I got off the phone earlier, I just wanted to rush to your house and hug you. I want to take care of you and nurse you and take away any worries and fulfill your every dream. That's how I feel every time I'm with you. I know it may sound corny or trite, but I honestly feel this way. I am just bursting to see you again. I do so love you, Rael

Love and respect
will make any good
relationship better.
~Stephen Ramjewan

His loving gestures made me think of a time a couple of months earlier, when I had wished for someone so sensitive and caring. My desire had prompted me to create a list of attributes I desired in a man. I found that entry in my journal and wrote the following reply:

To: Rael
From: Pat
Date: Thursday, January 11, 6:22 PM
Subject: Re: A Gentle Wake-Up for My Love - Thank you

Dr. Rael,

You are exactly what I needed to feel better. The flower is beautiful. The soup is delicious. The card is cheerful. And you are wonderful, sweet, caring, and sensitive – the best gift God ever gave me, the exact man I requested in my journal on Oct 22 of last year at 2:25 AM. Here is what I wrote at that time.

This is what I'm ordering up in a man:
1. Similar age.
2. Thin to medium build.
3. Physically affectionate.
4. Willing to commit to a relationship.
5. Open-minded – spiritually, mentally, emotionally, politically.
6. Easygoing – stays calm under pressure.
7. Likes me for who I am.
8. Interested in who I am.
9. Draws me out.
10. Encourages me to be me.
11. Appreciates beauty.
12. Thinks I am beautiful.
13. Takes care of himself physically and emotionally.
14. Good sense of humor.
15. Likes to travel.
16. Enjoys plays and movies.
17. Reads.
18. Eager to connect emotionally.
19. Emotionally healthy and recognizes that in others.
20. Views life as an adventure.
21. Positive attitude.
22. He has his own interests and encourages me to have mine.

The more connections you and your lover make, not just between your bodies, but between your minds, your hearts, and your souls, the more you will strengthen the fabric of your relationship, and the more real moments you will experience together.
~ Barbara De Angelis

23. Adores me and wants to spend time together.
24. Gives me the freedom to be independent.
25. Likes my friends and encourages my friendships.

I'll show you that page in my journal sometime. As I look back at it, I am amazed at how well you fit the bill. The only area that might be a little lacking is the traveling component, but I see you even getting interested in that. Reading back over this list revalidates the love I feel for you and the truth that you were drawn into my life through my intentions. It is my further intention to work toward making this relationship stronger and stronger with every passing day.

I love you and so appreciate all the incredible things you do for me – e-mails, phone calls, flowers, roses, stuffed flowers that sing, cards, and best of all, you being you – that is the best gift and exactly what I put on my wish list. Love, Pat

Love is of all passions the strongest, for it attacks simultaneously the head, the heart, and the senses.   ~ Lao Tzu

To: Pat
From: Rael
Date: Thu, Jan 11, 7:36 PM
Subject: Re: A Gentle Wake-Up for My Love – Thank you

I have to admit, it is almost freaky how well I fit your prerequisites for the man of your dreams. If I didn't know better, I'd say I broke into your house and found your journal, typed it out on your computer, and e-mailed it to myself. Seriously, I am so glad that you made that list for it has helped me find my perfect woman. Even when I read number 15, I thought almost exactly what you later wrote. Below are some of my comments (mostly humorous).

1. Similar age. *One month, five days older*
2. Thin to medium build. *Ah, so I lean toward medium*
3. Physically affectionate. *Affectionate, passionate, and all the other physical 'nates*
4. Willing to commit to a relationship. *Permanent and forever after*
5. Open-minded – *spiritually, mentally, emotionally, politically. Yeah, that's right, I'm a damn liberal Democrat*
6. Easygoing – *stays calm under pressure. And to think, my dad called it lazy and unmotivated*
7. Likes me for who I am. *And who you help me be*
8. Interested in who I am. *And who we are together*
9. Draws me out. *Ditto for me*
10. Encourages me to be me. *For you are far more than anyone I expected*
11. Appreciates beauty. *Especially radiant beauty*
12. Thinks I am beautiful. *Radiant beauty such as you*
13. Takes care of himself physically and emotionally. *And spiritually and psychologically and, with you, relationship-ally*
14. Good sense of humor. *And sometimes it's "bad," which is also good*
15. Likes to travel. *Travel to see you*
16. Enjoys plays and movies. *And even movies about plays*

If you treat your wife like a thoroughbred, you'll never end up with a nag.
~ Zig Ziglar

> *Inside myself is a place where I live all alone and that is where I renew my springs that never dry up.   ~ Pearl Buck*

17. Reads. *And writes, but no poetry*
18. Eager to connect emotionally. *I want to meld emotionally*
19. Emotionally healthy and recognizes that in others. *I do feeling-workouts three times a week*
20. Views life as an adventure. *Yet not adventure as a life*
21. Positive attitude. *Just so long as my blood work doesn't come back positive*
22. He has his own interests and encourages me to have mine. *I don't know. I'm losing interest in everything but you!*
23. Adores me and wants to spend time together. *Ah, duh! I want to spend all our time together.*
24. Gives me the freedom to be independent. *Absolutely, if you don't count being permanently attached to my side.*
25. Likes my friends and encourages my friendships. *Especially that one special friendship with that guy you know who lives over in Pearland with his 6-year-old son.*

Oh Pat, how can we not believe in God answering prayers? This is truly the result of a miracle. Not only do I have most of these characteristics, but these characteristics are your dream man, and you took the time to put them in your journal.

I know it is strictly coincidence, but you wrote your requirements for a man the night after Jill's burial. I'd been putting off trying to find someone until after Jill's passing. I felt somewhat guilty, but after all the tears at Jill's memorial service and laying her body to rest, I felt as if a weight had been lifted, a freedom to start a new life. After two years of dealing with her illness and the fears of a future without Jill in the boys' lives, the path was set, and I could begin traveling it. And that night you wrote about the man you wanted, the man I am, the man who had just begun his search for you.

Whoa, this is almost too strange for the cynic in me, but it's perfect for the romantic soul I've kept hidden, the romantic soul never before shared, the romantic soul that is yours and yours alone, my virgin romantic soul. I feel safe to release it into your hands. I feel relief. Thank you so much.

I love you like I've never understood love, Rael

> *We are all a little weird and life's a little weird, and when we find someone whose weirdness is compatible with ours, we join up with them and fall in mutual weirdness and call it love.*
> *~ Dr. Seuss*

In mid-January Rael said he had a gift for me, but he did not know if I would be pleased. When I saw that he had bought new locks for my condo doors, I was elated. At that time, not every lock had a key, and the keys I did have fit different doors, one at the front, and another at the back. Logically, I should have been leery of the guy I had dated less than a month replacing the locks, but I wasn't. In fact, I was flattered that he worried about my safety, but I also found the intensity of the relationship overwhelming. Soon after the situation with the new locks, I wrote this e-mail, which reflects the thoughts I mulled over most of that night:

To: Rael
From: Pat
Date: Tuesday, January 16, 4:14 AM
Subject: midnight wanderings/wonderings

*True love is not so much
a matter of romance
as it is a matter of
anxious concern for the
well – being of one's
companion.*
      ~ Gordon B. Hinckley

Rael, my man,

I woke up in the middle of the night, feeling a lot of fear, a lot of concern. It may have been where you were coming from when you had that dream about me being at your house, the couch, and me turning into someone else. I started typing on my laptop while snuggled up in bed. I tried to write without regard for what someone else (you) would think, without inhibitions. Since I am committed to making this relationship one of open, honest communication, I will share my midnight wanderings/wonderings. To do otherwise seems like keeping secrets. Besides, if this kind of thing is going to scare you off, I would rather do it now – before I get too involved. Now, that's a preposterous statement. I don't think I could ever get more involved, and I know I have never felt this way about anyone else. That in itself terrifies me. I get into that within my rambling writing. I love you, Pat

P.S. I had to reread it and edit it and then worry a bit about what you might think when you read it, so I send it with a little – no, a lot of – trepidation.

Attachment that I sent with this e-mail:

Middle of the Night Wanderings/Wonderings
January 16

My thoughts are consumed with Rael. Is it just chance that has brought us together or is there an omnipotent force at work here? Will it last? Do I have the right to question it, or will doubting the whole seemingly perfect situation make it disappear? Am I too focused on my negativity, my self-doubt, my past, my lack of faith, my preprogrammed limitation, or are the affirmations working? Am I actually bringing into existence what my heart tells me I have a right to create in my life?

My humanness looks for reasons why it cannot work.

1. Money – We have a totally different approach to spending money. I am conservative to a fault, frugal, hesitant, and, I have to admit, fear-based with my money. Rael, on the other hand, is free with his money, but it serves him well. He seems to have plenty, but then I'm not sure. He mentions not paying off his credit card for several months. I would never do that. I will and do pull out of my savings to avoid paying interest.

2. Jacob – He is a sweet, sweet kid, but he is a child, a huge commitment that I am not sure I am willing to make, and yet I have already made that obligation by falling in love with his dad. I see Rael being so free with him, so open about meals, bedtime, so eager to wait on him, so undemanding of any kind of responsibility with chores or expectations. He gives him constant positive reinforcement, which is good, but I worry that Jacob will never learn to be responsible. Maybe I'm too hard on Jacob, too demanding. Maybe I made my own children inhibited by my criticisms, and I don't want to see that.

3. Houses – I love my house. It represents freedom and the ability to do whatever I want, whenever I want. I don't have to have anyone else's approval on how I keep my house, how I decorate it, what I do with it in any way. This is my playhouse to use in any manner I

Of all the liars in the world, sometimes the worst are your own fears.
~ Rudyard Kipling

> *Love at first sight is possible, but it pays to take a second look.*
> *~ Anonymous*

see fit. I'm not sure I want to allow anyone else to live here, and I'm not sure I want to go to anyone else's house to live.

4.   Freedom – Marrying Rael would, in so many ways, limit my freedom. My programming tells me I would not travel like I do now, I would not come and go with the same freedom, and I would not make my own schedule without regard to anyone else. That is where Jacob comes in, along with my house and money. All of it is about freedom and that ability to choose what I want. But who is limiting me beyond myself? Why couldn't I have all the freedom that Rael seems to have? He is the one assuming the responsibility of a six-year-old, not me, and yet he seems much freer than I feel – or than I would feel in his situation, which is where I believe I would be if I married him.

5.   In my heart, I have already married Rael, but there is a part of me that is already resenting the restrictions. Was that what Jill was crying about on her wedding night? When I asked what moved her to tears, he said in a choked voice that he did not know. And then he added that she had wanted a child, and one of his requirements before starting a family was marriage. How deeply he had been hurt. How sensitive of him to share such a vulnerable time in his life. He must genuinely love me and feel safe with me to share such a painful episode of his life. Was she just as fearful as I? Is he attracted to us fear-based women, or are we attracted to him, but unable to give ourselves completely to marriage?

Could I? Could I give myself over to a relationship and still maintain who I am? Is that what all this is about, that fear of losing myself, that core belief that nothing good can come of living with a man? I fear all of it goes back to my father and those fears that caused me to create my survival strategies, the defense mechanisms that have caused me to seek out emotionally unavailable men like my dad. But here I am standing on the threshold of going into a relationship that seems totally fearless – at least, from Rael's perspective.

But can I operate in Rael's perspective? Isn't that another form of losing myself? This is about adventure. It's like jumping off a cliff, without a parachute and without a heavy-duty trampoline at the bottom. It feels like I am losing myself, and I am scared to death.

I love it when Rael tells me he loves me, when he approaches me with the eagerness of a child, when he offers uninhibited affection and love, when he does things for me with no agenda other than to make me happy, things like replacing my locks and leaving food and gifts at my back door after my oral surgery. It is so hard for me to accept, to comprehend that he is doing that without expectation.

I do love Rael, but I am scared to death at the same time. I fear allowing myself the freedom to fall over that cliff. It feels so scary, and yet it is what I have always yearned for.

Whatever creative spirit that formed me in the first place, give me the acceptance and belief that I have created this situation, that I have the right to be this happy. Resolve and quiet those fears that wake me up in the middle of the night. Help me to know that I am only limiting myself, that I do deserve and have the wherewithal to live this dream – that I am worthy.

True love comes quietly, without banners or flashing lights. If you hear bells, get your ears checked. ~ Erich Segal

Rael's reassuring reply came two hours later. Note the early morning time for both of our emails:

To: Pat
From: Rael
Date: Tuesday, January 16, 6:31 AM

Good morning Patty,

Thanks for sharing your midnight writing. I believe everything you are thinking is quite normal. These are such legitimate questions and during the "in-love" stage of a relationship there is little distance between legitimate questions and fear, little distance between perfection and "oh-shit." I think emotional highs, which occur when people are falling in love, are balanced with emotional lows, especially in our areas of existing issues. Howard Caesar gave a sermon about relationships and said we pick people as companions to help us work through our issues. If someone has an issue of being overwhelmed by a relationship, then they choose someone to overwhelm them. We both have our issues with relationships that we must address. Sometimes it will require you being balanced to steady me. Other times it will require my balance to steady you. And sometimes, guess what, neither one of us will be balanced, and we will fall and make mistakes.

I believe time will balance out our highs and lows and time will answer all of your questions. Reality, and lack of stamina, will ease the euphoria of falling in love. This is when we use our ability to love each other and build a relationship. Time is a gift I will give you. There is no rush. We have the rest of our lives to make a decision on what our relationship becomes. It's not like we need to get married to start a family or get away from our parents. We will marry when and if both of us are ready. I do not want another wedding night with tears of sorrow.

There are many things we must learn about each other, and I look forward to learning these things with someone as intelligent, open, and loving as you. Our love is but a seed that has produced a small stalk working its way to the surface. It has a long way to go before producing fruit. I write this with all of my love, Rael

To write a good love letter, you ought to begin without knowing what you mean to say, and to finish without knowing what you have written.
~Jean-Jacques Rousseau

Rael constantly expressed his adoration for me. From the beginning of our relationship, he opened the car door for me, and when he did, I kissed him before I got in – grateful that he showed me so much respect and love.

On the thirtieth day after our initial make-out session, Rael showed up at my home unannounced. I had just stepped out of the shower and stood on the other side of the front door with a puddle forming at my feet as I inquired, "Rael, is that you?" Dr. Humor had called it correctly. Somewhere in Rael's house hung a huge calendar with January 30 highlighted.

When a man opens the car door for his wife, it's either a new car or a new wife.   *~Prince Philip*

 **Family Reflections**

My family rarely went places together. By that, I mean my dad usually went separately, driving his pickup truck five miles to church or fifty miles to my mother's parents' house, joining us there. This gave him the latitude to come when he wanted and leave in the same manner. Plus, the noise level of four children must have bothered him. I have no memory of our having only one vehicle, but Mother says we did when we were young. Perhaps that is when Dad developed his aversion to traveling as a family. There were the rare occasions when all six of us ended up in the same vehicle. And I remember, with a knot in my stomach, the way he lined us up outside the car before a trip. Mother stood by silently waiting, too. First, he slipped off his leather belt with a swish, folded it dramatically, and then popped it loudly by moving it toward the center and then quickly out again. Next, he told us in no uncertain terms that he did not expect to hear a peep from any of us. While he threaded the belt back in place around his slender waist, he kept his eyes trained on us, saying, "And that means you. And you. And you. And you."

Under his icy surveillance, we silently climbed into the car, all four in the backseat. Five miles down the road, Ruth would whisper to Matthew, which led him to slap her knee, essentially telling her to shut up, and Morgan or me, or sometimes both of us, elbowing them lest we all get in trouble. At that point, Dad would swivel his long neck around, brushing his Stetson on the ceiling of the car, and glare. Sometimes he said it out loud and sometimes he said it with his eyes, *If I have to stop this car, I'm going to make it worth my while.* Either way, we knew he meant it, so we rode in stony silence after that.

I honestly do not remember Dad ever spanking me, but he must have. My cousin, who often stayed with me in the summer, says he spanked both of us, and she was scared of him as a kid. I was too, but I guess the final execution of his threats were something I have blocked

> *Parents are not quite interested in justice, they are interested in quiet.*
> *~Bill Cosby*

out, which makes me wonder what else I have blocked out about my childhood.

As I think back to how much I craved my father's attention, I understand why Rael's adoration was so flattering. On a deep level, he reminded me of my father, but at the time I did not give conscious thought to the idea. They were both free with their money, charming in order to get what they wanted, and they both had an immense amount of sexual energy. There was one vast difference between the two, though. Rael said he loved me.

In my thirties, I was going through a period of self-examination, which included going to group therapy where we talked about how crucial it was to a child to know that their parents loved them. One night, I called my dad long-distance, which in my household we did not do casually. In an emotional state fueled by days of pondering this act, I asked if he loved me. After some hesitation, he answered, "Well, yeah." I needed to hear the words, and I told him that it meant a lot to me to know that he did. Part of me was thinking that if I kept him on the line long enough, he would finally come out and say those three little words. He never did.

Some people never say the words "I love you."
It's not their style to be so bold.
Some people never say those words "I love you"
But, like a child they're longing to be told.
~ Paul Simon

Nuggets of Gold

Falling in love on the first date is highly unlikely and, contrary to popular belief, totally undesirable. If I think I am in love after the first date, I am probably mistaking initial attraction for the unhealthy part of me that is attracted to the unhealthy part of him. And what feels like love at this point is more likely lust. Whether it is coming from me or from the other person, to feel in love after one or two dates is more about being in love with the idea of being in love, which I have to admit I was. Until I know someone, I have no idea whether I am in love or not. In fact, thinking I am in love blinds me to seeing this person with any objectivity.

You, as much as anyone in the universe, deserve your love and respect.
~Buddha

In all matters, but most especially love, be honest with myself. There were things about this relationship that bugged me from the beginning, like the high-speed race toward physical intimacy, but I wasn't honest with myself about it. I let Rael take the lead on dictating the course of the relationship. I never considered it my responsibility to determine whether or not this was something I wanted. What I responded to was his overall enthusiastic need to be with me. It is difficult to see the situation in black and white when there are colorful distractions, like lots of attention, words of love, and generous gifts involved. Had I been totally honest with myself, I could have seen there was little to substantiate this overwhelming feeling of passion that had swept over both of us, except the dysfunction that drew us together in the first place.

Pay attention to key concerns or fears early in a relationship. It bothered me that Rael espoused the value of the kissing stage, but at the same time pushed me to see how far I would go, which I promptly justified as his overwhelming love for me. When I woke up in the middle of the night awash in fears and misgivings, my Inner Guide, that voice within me that knows the truth, was sending out smoke signals to which I needed to pay attention. I knew we were going too fast – emotionally, physically, mentally – and I had the right and the obligation to myself to put on the brakes, but I didn't. The difference between self-care and self-neglect is directly tied to my ability to pay attention to the warning signs and listen to my heart. If I ever fear I am losing myself in a relationship, I need to pay attention to what my emotions are telling me.

Your task is not to seek for love, but merely to seek and find all the barriers within yourself that you have built against it.

                              ~*Rumi, thirteen-century Sufi poet*

Jacob Sleighing

Angel in the Snow

Chapter Three
February – March, Red Flags Are Waving

The simple lack of her is more to me than others' presence.
~Edward Thomas

The following e-mail, written six weeks after we started dating, captures what we talked about at that time – marriage, going to New Zealand, marriage, where we would live, marriage, redecorating the house, and did I mention – marriage.

To: Patty Ann
From: Rael
Subject: Hi My Love
Date: Thursday, February 1, 8:03 PM
Hi My Love,

Sometimes not being with you is just overbearing. I sit here watching the clock, wanting to call you, but I know it is essential that you have time to do your writing. I'm so in love with you, Patricia Ann. I have felt all warm and cuddly inside since our telephone conversation this afternoon, when we talked about getting married and when we should do it. I look forward to working with you on all the details like living arrangements, financial arrangements, and all those other things. I want so much to take care of you, to cook for you, to work with you, to let you take care of me, to be with you at night, to go to sleep with you beside me and awake and reach over to you.

I looked on the calendar and tried to figure out when I should meet you in N.Z. I was thinking about being there on June 18th since that is our 6-month anniversary (a good day to ask you to marry me), but decided against it for two reasons. First, that is almost the end of your time there, and we would not see each other for almost one month, and, second, I would not be here for Father's Day. So now I'm thinking of flying there on either the 1st/2nd of June (almost three weeks apart) and coming back on the 14th/15th (two weeks before you return). Or I could come May 25th/26th. I'm thinking the first option because Jacob gets out of school on the 24th, and I'd be missing his first week of summer break. I'd rather not bring him with me for a variety of reasons. I don't think he'd enjoy what we would want to do; the expense; and (the most selfish) I want the time for just us to be together. Kind of a pre-honeymoon warm-up, ha-ha.

I also like sitting around daydreaming about what it will be like when we are married. If not for Jacob, I think your place is most excellent. I love your condo, especially the location. With Jacob, I'm thinking about this house. It provides lots of space too, so we can have a boys-type area upstairs and you can do your beautiful decorating downstairs. But first I would need to replace all of the carpet with tile. (NO CARPET!!!!) Or I could sell this place, and we could buy something else, but that almost overwhelms me. My initial thinking is that you keep the condo and rent it out. Then it will always be available if we want to live there. Then in eleven years, when Jacob is off to college (maybe he can graduate a semester early) and we are both retired, we can live anywhere. Here and other places. That'd be fun.

It is easier to guard a sack full of fleas than a girl in love.

~ Jewish Proverb

I do hope that you plan on continuing your summer trips even if I'm not able to accompany you. I think it is important for you to have this time to explore and experience these places. I'll do my two-week jaunts to join you. And soon, hopefully, Jacob will enjoy such travel.

Well, so much for daydreams. Back to the reality of watching the clock until I can call you. I'm thinking 8:45. Until then, take a long, slow, deep breath and open yourself up. I know you will be able to feel my love for you radiating out across the channels of energy that circumvent this world with all the extra love we humans are capable of when we let God lead us.

Your eternal love mate, Rael

Even though I told my friends I opposed the idea of marriage, I feared losing Rael, so after my initial resistance, I gave in to his enthusiasm about marriage. He had not officially asked me, but he often mentioned the idea.

Have you ever wondered which hurts the most: saying something and wishing you had not, or saying nothing, and wishing you had?
~Anonymous

My friends at the college where I taught teased me about how giddy I had become. When I talked with Rael on the phone, they could hear me laughing and giggling from their offices down the hall. Rael and I were in love, and we basked in the joy of it. I loved hearing from him. He called frequently throughout the day, and he e-mailed as often as he called.

Mid-February, we invited three couples over and had a vegetarian chili party. Rael brought Jacob, who immediately deemed the adult gathering boring. I did not have cable or the video games he liked to play, and the computer set-up Rael brought did not entertain Jacob for long. While the conversation continued at the table, Rael sat on the couch next to Jacob, reading him books and unsuccessfully attempting to entertain him. They left early in the evening.

Late February, we hit our first snag. I planned to visit friends in Colorado, but because neither Rael nor I thought we could endure that long a separation, we decided he and Jacob should come with me. I called my friends, Tonya and Owen, to ask if I could bring Rael and Jacob, to which I received the okay. Tonya picked us up from the Denver airport. Right after we entered our hosts' home, Jacob took possession of the television, turning it on without permission and then tuning it to a cartoon channel. Rael stood by with a look of pride on his face, probably because Jacob was asserting himself.

This incident reminds me of a similar time only a few weeks earlier, when I had accompanied Rael and Jacob to a store to purchase a vacuum cleaner. While Rael spoke to the salesman, Jacob played with, and practically dismantled, a nearby display. Afterward, Rael bragged about how take-charge Jacob had been – in spite of the salesman's efforts to rescue his merchandise. Rael did nothing to assist him. Father and son were still working out the basics of their relationship, since Rael had taken custody of Jacob only a few months earlier, when Jacob's mother died.

Compounding the situation was the fact that I was equally oblivious to how wrong Jacob's behavior had been until weeks later, when Tonya mentioned it. I immediately understood her point, but when I talked with Rael about it, he still saw nothing wrong with what Jacob had done. I have thought long and hard about why I had not recognized Jacob's behavior with the television or the vacuum cleaner salesman as wrong at the time, and the only thing I can surmise is that I did not question Rael's actions. It was a theme I had lived with all of my life. My mother constantly turned a blind eye to my dad's inappropriate behavior, and it felt natural to do the same thing with Rael.

Knowing Rael and Jacob were vegetarian, Tonya had stocked up on plenty of suitable food, but she did not have soy milk, which is all Jacob has ever drunk, besides water. She kindly allowed us to use her car while she taught at the local college, and we drove to the grocery store. Rael filled a cart with expensive items, and I wandered around, again unconscious of the rude behavior of my fiancé. Tonya had spent money and time purchasing vegetarian food for our visit, and Rael knew that. While he shopped, I walked up behind him and overheard him warning Jacob to avoid drawing my attention to the prices of the groceries since I

If we judge love by its usual effects, it resembles hatred more than friendship.
~Francois VI Duc de La Rochefoucauld

did not shop at exclusive grocery stores like this one; I was too cheap. A lump formed in the pit of my stomach to hear the man who supposedly loved me say something critical about me to his son, the child he wanted me to claim as a stepson. Unable to confront Rael, I turned away and acted as though I had not overheard him. If I had to pick a moment when I finally began to see that Rael's treatment of me was not always complimentary, this would be it.

When we traveled to Tonya and Owen's cabin close to Estes Park, Rael babied Jacob, pulling him in the sled and treating him as if he could not walk in the snow or, heaven forbid, pull his own sled. When Jacob came inside from playing, he threw his boots, gloves, and jacket in the middle of the floor, and then he plopped down in front of the television. Since they had come with me, I felt responsible, but I did not feel comfortable telling this little emperor what to do. My resentment growing, I trailed in behind Jacob, picking up and trying to pretend I wasn't mortified by both his and Rael's behavior.

Rael cooked soup, but he was not used to the difference in altitude, so it did not get done as quickly as he expected, and his meatless meal turned out yucky – that's a technical term for undercooked, bland, and unappetizing. Owen added chopped lunchmeat to his. *I wanted to, but I feared offending Rael, so I ate the soup and forced a smile.*

On our way back to Ft. Collins from the cabin, we discussed the two options for driving. When I suggested we take the longer, more scenic route, Owen and Tonya agreed. Upon hearing this, Jacob demanded to know why I got my way. Rael announced that I was the queen; whatever I wanted I got. My face grew hot as I seethed with anger, but rather than tell him I took exception to his remark, I said nothing.

Later Tonya told me she was also angered by his comment. I dismissed it as bad humor. Whether Rael meant it as a dig, or a lame attempt at support, it seemed to fuel the hostility that Jacob naturally had for me. Less than four months earlier his mother had died, leaving him to live with a father he had only known as a regular visitor. Then Dad started dating a woman whose mere presence threatened what little security he had built in his fledgling relationship with his father.

> *Love creates an us without destroying a me.*
> *~Anonymous*

Love is like water. We can fall in it. We can drown in it. And we can't live without it.

~Anonymous

Journal Entry   February 26

Jacob – what a smart little kid – in every way. He has Rael dancing around answering to his every shout and tantrum. He is the CEO of the McRael household. I'm not sure I could live and work in that environment. When he shouts, Rael jumps and runs. I know Rael doesn't realize what he is doing.

The things that bother me about that relationship are:

1. Jacob gets whatever he wants.
    —in a store, to eat, time-wise, when others are involved
    —Jacob's needs come first

2. There are no consequences —the idea of discipline is a foreign concept.

3. He is not expected to have manners.
    —say "please" and "thank you"
    —eat at the table and consume the same meal as everyone else
    —defer to someone else's wishes – even occasionally
    —he interrupts and shouts demands – like a mini-king who is only limited by size

4. He is treated like a baby – not expected to consider anyone else – Rael or anyone. No wonder he doesn't like school – or maybe he does. Maybe he enjoys the rules and limits, the consequences, the necessity of living in a community where he is

not king. It must be a lot of work to always be in charge.

5. He is not expected to do anything except eat, dress, and charm us with his intellect.
    —doesn't pick up after himself
    —leaves things wherever they fall
    —never puts away one toy before getting out another

All this must be terribly exhausting for Rael and for Jacob. No wonder he (Rael) needs a break from the child.

So what is my part in this?

I am the intruder – the person who could be a mom, but what would that look like?
    —a servant to Jacob – back-up gofer
    —a threat to his (Jacob's) intimacy with Rael
    —the police who comes in with rules and regs

Rael already has me set up to be the bad guy – the queen of "whatever she wants she gets" and "don't let Pat see these prices" (she's too cheap to spend money on you like I do).

> Love is like a virus. It can happen to anybody at any time.
> ~Maya Angelou

Two days after I wrote this journal entry (2/28), Rael called and said he would like to come over and bring dinner; he had something he wanted to discuss. I should have known something was amiss when he arrived with a fish entrée for me. After he wolfed down his food, he sat and waited for me to finish eating. When I asked what he wanted to talk about, he said we would discuss it when I was through. I urged him to go ahead and tell me what he wanted to say, but he refused. His face was taut with anxiety and the nervous twitch was back, along with an unusual, ominous somberness. The idea of confronting him about his lack of structure and discipline with Jacob occurred to me while I ate the rest of my salad, but from Rael's demeanor I decided it was not the right time. I wondered if he had come to dump me since I lacked the doting quality required to raise his son.

> To fall in love is to create a religion that has a fallible god.
>
> ~Jorge Borges

After I finished my meal, we moved to the couch, where Rael stonily shared an aspect of his history that would forever change my life. Starting in 1987, when he was thirty-five and his step-daughter Harmony was six years old, he had sexually abused her by masturbating in front of her. At that time he worked nights, and he was home alone with her. Marijuana was commonly used by both him and Harmony's mother. The abuse continued for six years. He did not say why it stopped, and I was too shocked to ask. With words that had obviously been rehearsed, he assured me that there had been no penetration. At sixteen years of age, four years after the abuse had ended, Harmony told her mom, Sandra, who immediately asked Rael to move out.

My immediate reaction was to recoil, but I also worried about Rael and how my response would affect him and our relationship, which I did not want to jeopardize. So I slid my foot down the couch and touched his leg with my toes. Dumbfounded by what I had just heard, I asked questions, which he answered, but what we both said is now a blur. Denial and fear took over. Rather than deal with my own emotions, I focused on Rael and how he was handling this situation. Was I being loving and supportive enough? Surely this was hard for him. What courage it had required to admit this to me. He didn't have to, but he did. This had to mean he truly loved me, and to make sure that nothing would jeopardize our future together, he was willing to tell me this, his deepest, darkest secret. Without knowing it, I slipped into an old pattern, a behavior I had seen played out throughout my life – make the abuser right.

Journal Entry   3:18 AM, February 28

I feel like I have been sucker punched – and I'm
hesitant to write about it here. Should I die in a plane
crash, someone would read this. And I can't tell anyone
without betraying a confidence. That's the part that
bothers me the most. I can talk to Dr. Humor, but telling
either one of my close friends feels like a betrayal to Rael.

The second part of this is that I think there is
something wrong with me that I am attracted to someone
who has this kind of disease. It is a disease, but it is
also a repulsive behavior. Is it my desire to complete the
relationship with my father? Was I somehow attracted to
Rael because of his past? Did I know on some level he
had this in common with my father?

I feel frozen – my emotions are so confused. I
don't know what to feel. Why am I attracted to someone
who could do that to a child? He was using drugs, but that
is only an excuse. How much of him is still working on
all that? He has taken an extremely terrible situation and
made it an opportunity for growth. He has grown. He is a
good person. I can't imagine him doing the things he told
me about. I want to cry, but there is a part of me that will
not allow me to go there. It feels too vulnerable. When my
throat tightens and my eyes burn with tears, I involuntarily
shove the emotions aside. Does all this bring up issues
about being molested as a child, memories I cannot
access, but which still haunt me by the impact of their
effect on my life?

This feels like one more reason not to love Rael,

All you need is love.
~John Lennon and
Paul McCartney

but it is, in fact, another piece of the puzzle that fits better than I want it to. His sickness fits my own, but does it fit the healthy or the still-struggling part of my inner child? He calls me Patty, like my dad did.

I am so jealous of people who have well fathers, who have fathers who have healthy boundaries, who are smart and able to do things, who have an interest in something besides sex.

How can I love someone who would do what he did to a child – drugged or not drugged? Does having a penis give him permission to hurt someone like that? And if I am married to him, how does all that affect me? Would it eventually repulse me as it did Jill? Is there some guarantee that he would remain faithful or loving toward me because no one else would have him if they knew the truth? Am I repulsed or attracted by this revelation, and how much guilt am I suppressing about either relationship – with him, and with my dad?

How much about this triggers the garbage from my past? When Rael told me, I had the sensation of someone twisting my gut. At the same time, it was essential to maintain physical contact – my toes stretched out and touched him where he sat at the other end of the couch. I was more worried about him and how he perceived I was taking this than about how I was feeling. I immediately started asking myself why I was attracted to him. What was wrong with me that I needed or/and was drawn to a child molester?

And why did I feel compelled to take care of his needs? What was it about me that felt so threatened by the situation that I could not admit how repulsed I was?

Who so loves believes the impossible.
~Elizabeth Barrett Browning

Am I still doing my co-dependence crap? Why was I more worried about what he thought about my reaction than about truly owning my emotions? My dad – Rael is my dad all over again. Are all men like that – or just the men I am attracted to? Should I give up the notion of getting away from it and just go with the flow? I am trapped in a house that I cannot escape. Every time I open what looks like an outside door, it lets me into another room. There may be an outdoor scene painted on the walls, but it is still a room with four confining walls that keep me from what looks like freedom – getting out of the house.

In numerous journal entries that follow my initial reaction to Rael's confession, I struggled with Rael's correlation to my father, and with my addiction to Rael and what that represented. In spite of knowing it was not a healthy situation, I persisted, just like someone hooked on heroin. Again and again, I questioned my sanity for staying in the relationship. In one journal I made a list of positives and negatives about continuing the relationship. At the bottom of the negative column, I wrote:

> *Love means nothing in tennis, but it's everything in life.   ~Anonymous*

- Falls in love quickly – will he fall out just as quickly?

- How will this affect my relationship with my children and future grandchildren, particularly my granddaughters?

- Is it love or a subconscious need to heal old wounds?

These three points seem significant since they are the key issues among many that I ended up facing. They also tell me that on some level I knew what was in store for me, but, driven by my compulsion, I plowed ahead.

Rael's identity as a pedophile repulsed me. How could someone do that to a child? At the same time, I wanted to believe that the therapy he had participated in enabled him to work through his problems. I tried to convince myself that since we both had the same spiritual beliefs, he was healed, or at least whatever demon had possessed him to act that way in his thirties had surely been banished by now. In spite of the research showing that while sex offenders sometimes learn to cope, they almost never lose the desire to offend, I dismissed the idea that Rael would ever commit a crime like that again. He had done that in his past, and he would never do something like that again. Never.

In hindsight, I realize our conversation that night was a turning point for Rael and me. Rather than serving as a signal to run away as fast as I could, it cemented me to him. At the time, I resisted the idea, but now I know that my overwhelming attraction to Rael was his likeness to my father – in ways that I had yet to fully grasp. My accepting him after he shared his secret told Rael things about me that I could never say with words. It gave him total control of the relationship, for if I could accept the fact that he was a pedophile, I would accept anything – anything.

If you haven't been loved by some significant other, you are in some deep trouble because it's very hard to replace.
    ~Jerry Parr, Secret Service during the Reagan administration

 **Family Reflections**

Recently someone explained to me what the term "objectified" meant, which is treating someone like an object, particularly a sex object, rather than a human being. I grew up being objectified, and it felt normal. When I hit puberty, Dad acted like an adolescent boy, referring to my bra as an over-the-shoulder boulder-holder. Since he was paying attention to me, I didn't mind.

The first time I remember seeing my father suffer real consequences for his immature behavior was the day I came home from school and saw that he had a whopper of a black eye. When I asked him what had happened, he said nonchalantly that some guy mistakenly thought he had been with his wife. I was around ten, and I wasn't entirely sure what he meant. Plus, I was hesitant to ask too many questions. He told me this without a hint of guilt, so I assumed that it had been a legitimate misunderstanding. Ironically, he almost seemed proud of his shiner – it got him noticed.

After I was grown, I decided this incident, along with countless others, laid the groundwork for why, throughout my school years, Mother and Dad had no friends with whom they socialized. When we were toddlers, they had periodically gotten together with a group of couples and played dominoes. At some point, though, Mother and Dad were shunned, and I would bet their outcast status had everything to do with the black eye or a similar "misunderstanding."

Family love is messy, clinging, and of an annoying and repetitive pattern, like bad wallpaper.   *~Friedrich Wilhelm Nietzsche*

Nuggets of Gold

If I think there is something wrong – there is. My Inner Guide had started screaming before Rael told me about his pedophile history, but as soon as the words were out of his mouth, I emotionally shut down. His failure to discipline Jacob and his comment about me in the grocery store were manageable issues that I should have addressed head-on instead of avoiding. But staying with Rael after I found out he had sexually abused a child for six years was an act of total and complete self-betrayal. I did not listen to that inner voice screaming at me. Instead, I told myself that Rael was a different man from the one who hurt that child. I said it so often and so fervently that I convinced myself of its legitimacy.

For me, saying no to an unhealthy relationship is ten times harder than saying yes to a healthy one. I know I was drawn to Rael because of who he is and the hole in my psyche that I yearned to fill. My relationship with him was my golden opportunity to learn that I have the right at any point to say no to a relationship. I not only have the right, but I have the obligation to say "NO!!!" when I am drawn to an addictive relationship like this one. Clearly, it hooked my old negative core beliefs about who I am, whom I want to please, and whom I deserve as a partner.

I am the one who has to set boundaries. I cannot expect someone else to do that for me. Being a pedophile is heinous, but tolerating that behavior means I was willing to forgo the boundaries that would have automatically kicked in if I had been thinking clearly, if I had healthy boundaries in place. Knowing about Rael's past was not enough to make me break off the relationship. This is where I failed myself.

Listen to my friends, family, and therapist. They have my best interests at heart. While I can see that now, I could not see that at the time. If those around me are telling me to stop and think about what I am doing, they probably have a reason. The greatest lesson in all this is to use my most valuable resources – my instincts *and* those people who can see things more objectively than I do. Part of drawing on this revenue is paying attention to what they say, which I did not.

     If you really put a small value upon yourself, rest assured that the world will not raise your price.   *~Anonymous*

Artist Painting Pat in
Maori Warrior Pose

Pat Taking a Mud Bath in a Thermal Pool

Waihi Beach

Pat Riding the Ferry

Chapter Four
March – April, Getting to Know You, Getting to Know All About You . . .

Be who you are and say what you feel, because those who mind don't matter and those who matter don't mind.
~Dr. Seuss

Rael's pedophile history lingered like an invisible elephant in the room, but I found it impossible to bring it up again for discussion. Rael acted relieved. He had told me, and I had not rejected him. Once when we drove into Houston to see a movie, he cruised through his old neighborhood and pointed out the location where he had participated in a weekly sex-addiction group and another place where he had attended family therapy. He said that many of their sessions were only attended by him and Harmony since Harmony's sister and their mother, Sandra, did not show up. He faithfully attended the sessions because he wanted to do what he could for Harmony, but her mother was probably too stoned to get herself there.

Like the good little girlfriend, I nodded in response to his explanation. Although I desperately wanted to believe that the mother's propensity to keep drugs around made her equally guilty, my inner voice wasn't buying it. So I tuned out the conflict in my head, and chose to believe that the past was gone. After all, I wasn't feeling anything, so it must be okay. This issue had played itself out in the past, and it would never rear its ugly head again.

I could not discuss the topic with Rael, but I did talk to my friends, and they collectively told me to run like hell. But I did not. When I told Dr.

Humor, he seemed to be genuinely saddened by my news. He told me he was sorry I had to go through something like this again, referring to my father and what the family had been through in recent years because of him.

Several weeks after telling Dr. Humor about Rael's history, I told him I had a deep-seated fear of losing Rael, that I felt like I was sixteen again, and I was terrified that I would never find anyone else. He chuckled and said that it might be hard to find another pedophile with a seven-year-old. While his point was not lost on me, I could not move out of my feeling of addiction. I truly felt helpless to pull out of the relationship. In fact, when Rael sat in the chair facing me at Dr. Humor's office and told me that we could still be friends even if we did not end up getting married, the idea terrified me. I could not imagine losing him.

> Oliver Hardy: "Well, here's another nice mess you've gotten me into!"
> SONS OF THE DESERT, 1933.

Rael and I were inseparable. Every weekend was planned around what we would do together. We planted a winter garden of kale, which did well, but when we planted tomatoes later in the spring they did nothing. Still, it was something we both enjoyed. One Sunday evening, Rael, Jacob, and I went to a restaurant that they liked because they could get veggie burgers. I ordered fish and chips, and when our meals arrived, Jacob asked what I was eating. I said it was fish, and Rael chimed in that I was carnivorous, so Jacob needed to watch out lest I eat him too.

Once more offended by a remark Rael made, I stuffed down the aching in my heart and went home without voicing my pain. All week I mulled over the exchange, determined to tell him how deeply he had wounded me. The following Saturday, we stopped to get something to eat after a movie, and he proposed that we share a vegetarian plate because he wasn't that hungry. I was ravenous, but I didn't want him to think I was a pig, so I smiled and agreed to his suggestion.

As we waited for our meal to arrive, I asked if he remembered the conversation the previous weekend about me being carnivorous and him warning Jacob to be careful lest I eat him. I told him it had upset me. He said he was sorry and admitted it was a poor attempt at humor. The matter didn't feel finished, but what else was there to say? Obviously, I had overreacted. After making myself miserable all week and finally getting up the gumption to say something, I ended up feeling I had made a big deal out of nothing. I ate my half of the vegetables, careful to leave the last bite because part of our dinner conversation included a remark by Rael that implied a person who did not clean their plate was somehow superior to one who did. I know you're thinking, what kind of idiot does this – not him but me, for buying his song and dance hook, line, and sinker, which I did. When I went home, I ate the equivalent of a full meal in the privacy of my own home.

Spring Break we went to Leakey, a town west of San Antonio close to the Rio Frio, a place Rael had frequented as a teenager. He gave me detailed accounts about him and his friends visiting there during his youth. I packed pimento cheese spread, but certainly not meat, not even tuna, after the "carnivorous" remark in the restaurant. While I ate the cheese spread with crackers, Rael remarked, "That stuff is gross." You can bet I didn't eat any more of it. His comment and my meek reaction testify to my growing need to please him – and his likely growing confidence that I would accept any kind of treatment he chose to give me.

In late spring, Rael bought a trampoline, and I tried my hardest to keep up with the boys – jumps, flips, somersaults, whatever Rael and Jacob did, I attempted as well. Remember I was fifty-four nearly fifty-five years old, certainly not a kid. Why did I do this? Because I thought Rael would be pleased. I wanted him to think I was the perfect mate for him, the perfect mom for his son. In hindsight, I ask myself why I wanted so desperately to get into this situation, raising a seven-year-old, which would obviously be a ton of work, at my age. I urgently wanted to believe that my experience and expertise as a mother made me indispensable to Rael. I wanted him to need me as desperately as I needed him.

Throughout our relationship, Rael periodically decided that he needed to give up caffeine. He prided himself on being able to go cold turkey, which fits his obsessive personality. He often repeated stories that had to do with compulsive behavior, like the time he went on a twenty-six-day fast. Another example of his ability to throw himself into something are

> Harry: "Yeah I called her up, she gave me a bunch of crap about me not listening to her, or something. I don't know, I wasn't really paying attention."
> DUMB AND DUMBER, 1994.

the numerous triathlons/iron-man events in which he ran, biked, and swam. He gave them up because others who participate are too compulsive. Hmmm. He became fixated on his current interest, which happened to be me at that time. I was his fascination, and I reveled in the attention. Thinking he could not live without me, as he often said, fed my need to be needed.

He had other quirks, like his issue with milk. I like milk and consider it healthy, but because he had read a book that convinced him it was full of pus and bacteria and fundamentally harmful, he tried to dissuade me from drinking it. Jacob had never drunk cow's milk. His standard breakfast was Lucky Charms cereal and soy milk. The kid also had cavities in his baby teeth, and he was shockingly small for his age.

The nervous tic I noted on our first date vanished except in stressful situations, but other habits surfaced. While driving, Rael clutched the hand-hold above the car door and chewed on his arm. He also adjusted himself no matter who was present. When he commented with pride that his nine-year-old was starting to emulate him in this behavior, I realized Rael was not oblivious to his own actions. My friends noticed and commented, and I agreed the habits were peculiar, but a few silly idiosyncrasies were not going to keep me from pursuing the relationship of a lifetime.

Rael told story after story about his escapades with drug use in his twenties that had continued into and through his thirties, but while I knew him, he was clean. When we went out on Sunday evenings, he often had a mixed drink while I had a glass of red wine, and we enjoyed having a margarita with Mexican food once a week or so, but otherwise he rarely drank alcohol. I was much more likely to have a glass of wine in the evening.

Right after we started dating, Rael grew a beard. I asked him to since that was less abrasive to my face than stubble, and I found it handsome. He is bald on top, and when we met, his hair was cut short. But he did not cut it after that, so by the time we separated two and a half years later, it was down his back. After it got long enough, he secured it in a ponytail.

I included Rael in all of my social functions: a play that I attended

> *We are always training people how they need to be with us by how we respond to their behavior. . . . What you tolerate will happen again. . . . and again. . . . and again.*
> *~ Katherine Woodward Thomas from* Calling in "The One"

with a friend, another friend's Eagle Scout ceremony for her son, and the party a co-worker gave for everyone in our department. Although I was busier than I wanted to be, I did take time to see a few girl friends without Rael. Of my three children, my middle child – the one who was not married or dating – gave me the most grief about my dating Rael. He did not like him, even though I thought they would have much in common, like their love of movies. Since I was in my rationalizing mode, I figured Drew's dislike of Rael stemmed from the fact that I was replacing his father.

Throughout our get-to-know-each-other phase, I focused on what I wanted to see, which was that he said he loved me, and acted like he did. I tried extremely hard not to think about what he had told me about his past; when I did think about it, I told myself that the past was gone – it was not who he was now. An incident from that period makes me realize how blind I had become. We were sitting around the living room at a Democratic group social when a five-year-old girl engaged Rael in a teasing/chasing sort of child's game. He reluctantly interacted with her, but when he could, he did his best to avoid her.

Listen to the whisper before it becomes a scream.

~ Oprah Winfrey

Later, on the way home, he remarked that the little girl seemed to be attracted to him. He said that he could not help that these little girls were coming on to him. Rather than him being attracted to them, they were responsible for his attraction to them because of their behavior. As I look at it now, I realize how narcissistic and distorted his thinking was, but at the time, I slipped into the logic I had been raised with, my "mother mentality." What harm had taken place? After all, nothing had come of it.

Grasping at anything that supported the idea of maintaining my relationship with Rael, I told myself that forces both of this world and beyond supported my union with him, even the wishes of dead people I had never met. As bizarre as it sounds, I believed that Jill, from her grave, had attracted me to this situation; she wanted me to mother Jacob, and she had somehow participated in bringing Rael and me together.

Toward the end of the spring semester, I began wrestling with two commitments I had made. First, I had agreed to fly to New Zealand and house-sit for Mel and Jane, who owned a bed-and-breakfast which was not active during the off-season, when I would be there. Second, I had said I would fly to North Carolina as soon as I returned from New Zealand to teach summer school at a community college. I had looked forward to the trip to New Zealand for a while, but the teaching gig in North Carolina appeared on my calendar when a friend convinced me to join her in accepting an offer made by a mutual friend. The closer my departure date for New Zealand loomed, the less I looked forward to immediately traveling to North Carolina once I returned to Houston. I was dealing with guilt about leaving Rael to go to New Zealand, and I did not think he would appreciate me fulfilling my commitment to be gone another six weeks on top of that. After researching the cost of housing and realizing the pay would be minimal, I used that as my justification for nixing the deal to teach in North Carolina.

Summer – New Zealand, Here I Come

Turn your face to the sun and the shadows fall behind you.

~Maori Proverb

If I had not committed to traveling to New Zealand before I met Rael, I probably would not have gone. I had, though, so as soon as I finished the spring semester, I left, feeling apprehensive about traveling that far on my own. During my layover in Los Angeles, I entertained the idea of extending my stay in New Zealand, totally ignoring my recent plague of guilt over deserting Rael for a month. Because I had canceled my trip to North Carolina, I had additional time before I needed to return to teach a summer class I had picked up at my regular job. Rael planned to follow me to New Zealand in a few weeks, so it wasn't like I wouldn't see him all summer. Before I had time to talk myself out of it, I changed my return flight to two weeks later. Standing at the ticket counter while the agent rescheduled my booking, I dreaded the idea of telling Rael what I had done. At the same time, I knew postponing my return to Houston bought me that much more of a reprieve from the emotional baggage our relationship had already acquired.

My first e-mail to Rael upon arriving in New Zealand:

To: Rael
From: Pat
Date: Wednesday, May 16, 9:06 AM

Good morning here, good afternoon there, my dearest, Rael, love of my life, I must apologize for not being totally present last night when you called. I was thrilled to hear your voice, but as you said, I was mentally exhausted. Plus, I was concerned that Jane was ready to eat, and I was holding them up. She prepared a lovely meal, with lots of nice vegetables - many of which they had grown - eggplant, bell peppers, roasted potatoes, English peas, summer squash. After supper, I took an incredible hot bath and then fell into bed and slept soundly until sometime in the night when I got up to use the bathroom. I was awake for an hour or so then, but I did not turn on the light to check the time because I was determined to go back to sleep and sleep until daylight, which I did. I awoke again at 7:20, got up, and dressed more warmly since I was cold most of the day yesterday. (They don't use heaters the way we do, so bring lots of warm clothes.)

I hope you are not too upset that I will be staying two weeks longer. I thought, since I was not going to North Carolina and have looked forward to this trip for so long, that I would stay as long as I could and still get back in time to teach that class at San Jac this summer. What I earn will help me get a little ahead starting the school year.

I love you and miss you terribly. I am so looking forward to having you here and sharing time.
Love,
Patty Ann

Traveling is like gambling: it is always connected with winning and losing, and generally where it is least expected we receive, more or less than what we hoped for.
~ Johann Wolfgang von Goethe

To: Pat
From: Rael
Date: Thursday, May 17, 11:00 PM

Hi Patty Ann,

Just got off the automated phone service to make the first available afternoon appointment to get my passport. It was June 1st at 12:00. Ouch! So I got back on the phone and changed my appointment to the first available morning appointment, which ended up being May 25th. That gives me one week to get my passport. If this fails, I'll have to hijack my Southwest Airlines flight if I plan on making it to NZ. (Uh, Homeland Security, that previous sentence was a joke.)

I just called you on the phone, but no answer. Should I bring an answering machine with me? That's the trouble with staying with old farts, they don't believe in modern technology like answering machines and clothes dryers.

So wish me luck on obtaining a passport.

Love,
Rael

In traveling, a man must carry knowledge with him, if he would bring home knowledge.
~ Samuel Johnson

Notice I did not mention meat at the meal in my first e-mail – I did not want Rael to think I had "fallen off the wagon." In a phone conversation, I had told Rael that Jane used a clothesline rather than her dryer, which was considered a luxury in New Zealand, thus the comment above about modern technology.

To: Rael
From: Pat
Date: Sunday, May 20, 10:57 PM

Dear Rael,

      I had an exceptionally enjoyable birthday. It got off to a fantastic start by hearing from you, which has become the highlight of my days here. Not that I am not enjoying myself - I simply love to hear your voice.

      For lunch I had arranged to meet a lady - Tineke, who is a Dutch friend of Jane's - at the RSA (Royal New Zealand Returned and Services' Association), which is a service organization like the Moose Club. I got lost, and by the time I found Tineke, she had met up with another friend, Rose. They said that the RSA in Waihi did not open for meals until 2:00 and suggested we go to Waihi Beach to the RSA there to eat. I was all for that, and Rose has a car, so we were in business. We drove there and had a fabulous meal. Then we did a bit of driving around, stopping at a place called The Porch, where we had coffee and tea and a bit of dessert. We walked on the beach, and I collected shells. I will take you back there when you get here.

      Today I found myself leaning toward Rose and Tineke and concentrating with all my might to catch half of what they were saying. They are both Dutch, and add to that forty years of living here, and you've got a bit of a different accent. When I told her you were coming to join me here, Tineke asked me if I love you. I said yes. Her husband died six years ago. She is an artist who lives alone. I saw some of her artwork at her house when we

The whole object of travel is not to set foot on foreign land; it is at last to set foot on one's own country as a foreign land.
~ Gilbert Keith Chesterton

dropped her off there. It is unique. I may buy something if I have money left when I get ready to leave.

We, the three of us, talked a lot about love and marriage. Rose is going through a divorce. This is her second marriage. She seemed a bit depressed. I'm glad she got out today instead of sitting home feeling sorry for herself. The consensus of the discussion was that it is marvelous to find someone you love at any point of your life, but especially after you are old enough to appreciate it, which is where I am with you.

I'll close with those three magic words - pass the salt - no - I love you, Pat

They change their climate, not their soul, who rush across the sea.
~ Horace

My e-mails were strategically written to remind Rael of my undying love for him – even though I was halfway around the world and even though we would be separated for the better part of the summer. My insecure self clung to Rael in spite of his sexual history, fearing he would forget about me in my absence or, worse, find someone else. So I wrote to him daily, and I made sure I was home when he planned to call, which was usually twice a day. In the morning, it was no problem since he called when I "should be" woken up, which he usually did. While I was still groggy with sleep, he was getting ready to leave his office at the end of the day. Then he called before going to sleep, about 1:30 p.m. for me.

While I looked forward to talking to Rael, I also grew to resent him determining when I needed to wake up, and expecting me to be home in the afternoon. Actually, he was never insistent on this point. Instead, I was the one who obsessed over making it easy for him to reach me. I fell into the trap of thinking that I needed to accommodate him in order to keep him interested in me. After all, he would endure a six-week separation, not all at once, but in two three-week periods, separated by

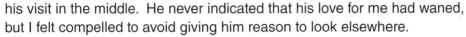

his visit in the middle. He never indicated that his love for me had waned, but I felt compelled to avoid giving him reason to look elsewhere.

When Rael came to New Zealand, he fearlessly rented a car at the airport and drove ninety miles to Waihi. Always the organizer, he arrived with a three-ring binder containing maps of how to get to every destination on our trip to the South Island.

The first night in Waihi, Rael became chilled and could not stop shaking. He got out of bed and was standing there naked, which struck me as funny, so I laughed, which hurt his feelings. His indignation made me laugh even harder. Surely he was trying to amuse me; otherwise, he would get under the covers. Right? Apparently not. I realized he was genuinely shivering and offended, so I coaxed him back to bed. After that, we used the space heater at night, even though I knew Mel and Jane would be aghast at the idea of using electricity when we could bundle up.

> *Only the traveling is good which reveals to me the value of home and enables me to enjoy it better.*
>
> *~ Henry David Thoreau*

Assuming the role of hostess, I worried when Rael seemed bored or tired. If I couldn't keep him content in this idyllic spot, then I would never feel secure in the relationship. My stay in New Zealand offered the perfect setting to go into even deeper denial of the issues Rael had told me about three months earlier – you know, the topic I didn't want to hear about in the first place, the issue that I told myself over and over again was a nonissue. While I entertained him there, I never allowed that unmentionable topic to enter our conversations.

After spending several days in Waihi, we drove to the south end of the North Island. Late in the day, we saw our first traffic light of the trip. This tells you how sparsely populated the North Island is, and an amazing fact is that it holds three-quarters of the country's population. After we left a visitor's center, we were running late getting to the family in my travel club with whom we were scheduled to spend the night. Rael drove like a madman, over curbs and going the wrong way on the roundabouts. After that, I insisted on driving.

We spent most of our time looking at the various sights. For lodging, we primarily stayed with couples from my travel club, the same group that had given me the connection to Jane and Mel, as they were members as well. A couple of nights we stayed in hostels. Wherever we went, people were friendly, especially after they heard our Texas accents. Since it was winter there, the tourist areas were not crowded.   Upon returning to Waihi, we hiked around the city and took a trip to the beach. Rael's time there seemed to fly by.

I have been a stranger in a strange land.

~Exodus 2:22

    Rael brought an answering machine with him, and we left it for Jane and Mel to use. They returned after I had left, so I'm not sure what they thought of it. I can imagine the odd responses they must have gotten to Rael's voice, with its distinctly Texan accent, asking the caller to leave a message.

    Early in my visit to New Zealand, Tineke invited me to attend a meeting of her art group, where the members showed the paintings they had done since their last get-together. For the next get-together, everyone agreed to bring a self-portrait. It had been years since I painted, but I was eager to renew this interest, so I committed to complete the assignment.

    Needing photographs to work from, I took digital pictures of myself, loaded them on my laptop, and then painted from that. The paper I had purchased was one-fourth the size of a full sheet of watercolor paper, so I laid three pieces together, each one going horizontal, and used it as one long vertical piece. While Rael and I were visiting the South Island, one of our hosts showed me a trivet made in the shape of the Chinese symbol for marriage. He mentioned it because Rael and I were talking about getting married. I liked the lines and shape of it, so I traced around the metal trivet. When I started painting, I thought of it. Since my time there had been preoccupied with thoughts of whether or not I should marry Rael, I decided to experiment with masking my face with the symbol. I did several paintings, some with the symbol overlay and some without. To show them at the next art group, I strung them together, using string taped on behind the paper to hold them together. The group seemed properly impressed, and I was pleased with the results – two long portraits, one with the symbol and one without.

    After I returned home, I framed these two paintings and hung them above my couch. The vivid greens and purples expressed my strong emotions and desire for passion in my life, and my serious, pensive expression reflected the dilemma that I wrestled with throughout my time in New Zealand. I knew I loved Rael, but I was not sure I was ready to commit to marriage and all that this particular union would entail. The painting with the Chinese symbol overlay, which strategically covered my eyes, now seems to be prophetic of how much the idea of marriage clouded my thoughts and vision.

Eventually, I bought two of Tineke's paintings, one for me and one for Rael. Mine, *The Queen of Hearts*, is one of my favorite possessions. She is a constant reminder of my fantasy summer in New Zealand.

My plane landed in Houston in the wee hours of the morning and, as he had promised,   Rael was there to greet me. When we got to my condo, I found all kinds of "welcome home" greetings, yellow ribbons trailing from the oak tree out front, homecoming ribbon streamers on the front door, and fresh flowers – purple, of course.

Journeys end in lovers meeting.   *~ William Shakespear*

Family Reflections

The summer of 1963 my sister and I went on a forty-day journey with our grandparents, pulling a travel trailer with a pickup that carried a shell over the back. While my grandparents rode in the cab of the pickup, Ruth and I lay on the bed at the back. The shell leaked close to the front, so more than once we found our pillows soaked when we went to bed. There was room for one kid up front, but I usually opted to ride in the back. From the Texas Panhandle, we made a loop through Kentucky and then Michigan, visiting aunts, uncles, and cousins along the way. When we were one night from home, Ruth cried herself to sleep while I celebrated our last day on the road. That summer taught me that I liked the idea of expanding my boundaries, realizing that people live differently elsewhere, and that diversity is good. Also, that summer awakened within me the love of travel and adventure.

     In December of 2000, I flew to Dallas and joined my parents and Ruth, who were driving to Georgia to celebrate my brother Morgan's fiftieth birthday and his college graduation. We also planned to see my other brother, Matthew's, new home. The day after the graduation, a snowstorm kept us from going anywhere. While we stayed at the house, Dad watched the weather channel. The next day, instead of going to Matthew's house as planned, Dad decided to leave a day early. I pleaded with Mother to join me in refusing to let Dad change our plans, arguing that it meant cutting the trip short for everyone. True to form, Mother did not challenge him, so I sulked in the backseat of the pickup as Dad drove three hundred miles out of his way to take me directly home rather than go back through Dallas. Somehow this change in itinerary justified his decision to disrupt what everyone else wanted to do.

A vacation frequently means that the family goes away for a rest, accompanied by a mother who sees that the others get it.
~ Marcelene Cox

Nuggets of Gold

Be brave. Do things that look scary but will allow me to fully participate at the same time. Before going to New Zealand, I wrestled with the idea of driving on the left-hand side of the road. Could I do that? Would I find myself mired in one traffic blunder after another? I worried about it to the point of clouding my excitement about taking the trip. When I finally did find myself behind the wheel, I found it entirely manageable – certainly not the giant challenge I had imagined. There have been other occasions that I let my fear keep me from speaking up in a crowd or doing a bungee jump or parasailing. The bungee jump and the parasailing are inconsequential, but not speaking up when I have something to say weighs in as highly regrettable, for those are times when I squelched who I was out of fear. Those are opportunities I cannot reclaim, and their memory is a reminder of a great truth: it is up to me to allow my light to shine, rather than hiding out for fear of being wrong.

Be present in the moment. My time in New Zealand was fantastic, and the thing that made it so great was that I had anticipated it and knew that it would only last for a given amount of time. Isn't that life in general? None of us will live forever, so why not make what we have right now the best day ever and appreciate it for all of the gifts that it brings? That attitude of being present and appreciative allows me to be in a not-so-good-place and still see the beauty that is present.

Being in a state of deep appreciation is a surefire way to keep us rooted in the present.
        ~ Rick Foster and Greg Hicks from Choosing Brilliant Health

Pat Grissom, *Self-portrait*, watercolor with
Chinese symbol for marriage overlay

Pat Grissom, *Self-portrait*,
watercolor

Chapter Five
Fall – Return to Reality, Both Personally and Professionally

The bigger the summer vacation the harder the fall.
~ Anonymous
(probably a teacher)

Within days after returning home, my department chair contacted me, asking if I would take his job, so he could move into the dean's position. After negotiating two course releases rather than the one initially offered, I reluctantly agreed. No one else wanted the job – for good reason. Along with accepting the position, I claimed the former department chair's larger office. One evening I let my night students go a few minutes early, with the stipulation that they swing by my old office and carry a box from it to my new office just down the hall. Several men in the class made quick work of moving the major items like bookcases and a mini-fridge. So in less than thirty minutes I "shifted," as they say in New Zealand.

I had been home only a few weeks when I wrote the following letter. It focuses on Jacob, rather than addressing my growing concern about my relationship with Rael. He and Jacob were out of town visiting Jill's family. Not only did I chicken out on confronting Rael in person, I also didn't even e-mail it to him. Instead, I left it in his clothes closet to find when he returned home.

Dear Rael,   August 4

You are in Illinois, and I am here dog-sitting, cat refereeing, and acting as consult for my friend who, after only a couple months post-wedding, has become totally disenchanted with the idea of marriage. What lesson is in this for me? What am I not looking at that I should open my eyes to? I want our relationship to work, but I also know that I am the world's greatest denier of what I do not want to see. I spent thirty-two years thinking if I tried hard enough, I could force myself to be something I was not. The last four years have been all about me – what I want from life. Ideally, I would have done that before I got married at nineteen, but I lacked the maturity at that time. Now I am looking at marriage again, and this time I want to keep my eyes open and enter it knowing what I am getting into.

The issue that comes up for me again and again is Jacob. He is a sweet little seven-year-old boy who has no boundaries or expectations placed on him. He is in charge, and you are his primary means of getting whatever he wants, whenever he wants it. When he does want something, he bellows out orders, and you immediately attend to his needs. He does not know how to say "please" or "thank you" to you or anyone else. He thinks that every time he goes into a store that has toys, he should get one, even though he has more toys than any child could play with in a lifetime. And he does not care for or value what he has because he knows there is always more available the next time he goes somewhere. He does not have any responsibilities – no chores, no requirements that he pick up after himself, no accountability whatsoever. I do not see him as the problem. He is only reacting to his raising.

I am reading *Boundaries with Kids*, and I agreed with what the authors say. Yes, children need to have consequences for inappropriate behavior. Yes, raising a spoiled, self-absorbed child is only setting them up for failure in relationships as an adult. Yes, children need to know what is expected of them, and they need to learn responsibility and the joy of working toward a reward. So why am I reading the book, instead of you? You're the one raising Jacob and none of these concepts seem to concern you. I'm not saying you don't care – quite the opposite. I believe that your interactions with Jacob are based purely on your love for him, but I also think that your fear of him rejecting you paralyzes you from setting limits, making requirements, or creating and enforcing consequences. You argue that vegetarian is healthier, and yet you let Jacob fill his body with Doritos and Chips Ahoy! cookies. I've never seen you use any kind of discipline with Jacob except when you blow up at him verbally.

We talked about this before, and I saw tears in your eyes when you responded with a plea for me to help by offering some kind of guidance. I was flattered by your faith in me, but the assignment feels daunting, knowing you probably wouldn't support me. It's been too long a time since I dealt with a child this age, and Jacob is not mine. The patterns are already set – by his mother, whom I never met, so I don't know how she dealt with him, and by you, and that has only been since you took over full-time parenting in October of last year. He is still young, and you have not had this job long, so all of it is up for review

> *Raising a kid is part joy and part guerilla warfare.*
> *~ Ed Asner*

Respecting yourself means listening to your body and emotions continuously. Then acting beyond a linear logic to achieve one's goals.   ~Anonymous

and revision, but it has to be something you want to alter because you see the need to change. If it is working for you, who am I to throw a wrench in the works?

Who am I? Possibly your wife at some point, and at the same time Jacob's stepmom, and responsible by association for the lessons he learns while growing up, and to some degree accountable for how he turns out. I know myself well enough to know that long-term I would not be happy in a household where the child is in charge. When we have gone on trips together, I have come home feeling resentful of the way Jacob ran the show, and you catered to his every wish. I know you get good feedback from his teachers about his behavior, so he has the ability to be part of a group and live with boundaries and rules. In fact, I think he is looking for order in his life. He wants to know the limits. The real issue is, do you have the desire to create and enforce those limitations and guidelines?

While talking with my friend about her conflict with her husband, I told her that any change from him has to be motivated by his own desires, not her expectations for him. The same is true in this situation. I can write letters all day long, and we can talk about it until we have exhausted the subject, but ultimately any lasting change will occur because you think it is worthwhile and in the best interests of all concerned, including you. Otherwise, any kind of resolution we come to on this topic will be gradually forgotten – like your plan to eat meals together instead of separately or in front of the TV.

I realize that Jacob is going through an enormous adjustment period after losing his mom. You are too. The nonconfrontational part of me says just wait and maybe things will get better. The realistic side of me says if I don't address these issues now, I will be just like my friend in a year or two, wanting things to be different, but feeling powerless to make that happen. I've worked too long to get where I am now to go back into a relationship in which I feel powerless. I love you, and I love Jacob. I want the best for both of you – and for me, which means we have to agree on and implement a workable strategy for parenting Jacob before I can become part of your family. As we discussed before, any changes that take place after we married, Jacob would associate with me and resent me as a result. Plus, I'm clear that things will not change once I become a permanent resident at your home. Why would they? If I was okay with how they were going in, what leverage do I have for change once I am part of the situation?

What do I suggest as a means toward this end? There are some terrific books out there. I have a couple that I've bought since knowing you. The one I am currently reading has enough valid core ideas to make it worth reading. Going to a counselor together (you and me or you and Jacob or both combinations) and/or on your own is also an approach that might help you sort out how you want to proceed. Because what I am asking you to do is going to take some time and energy on your part, I think you might also want to look at where you are spending your time now and how much time you have to give Jacob once you get all of your other commitments satisfied. When we spoke on the phone, you mentioned joining the board of your community association. They would be lucky to have you since you are an organizer, but I wonder how

The tools we are given from which to create are our thoughts, beliefs, assumptions, actions, decisions, and words.
~ Katherine Woodward Thomas from Calling in "The One"

> Many people go throughout life committing partial suicide – destroying their talents, energies, creative qualities. Indeed, to learn how to be good to oneself is often more difficult than to learn how to be good to others.
>
> ~ Joshua Liebman

much time that will leave you to spend with Jacob. I have been guilty of overfilling my schedule with commitments when I did not want to address other parts of my life. Could that be part of your motivation to take on another job outside your family?

I wrote this because I love you, and I want our relationship to grow, to flourish, and to endure. It is also a compliment to you that I feel I can tell you what is in my heart, and I believe you will listen and respond with honesty and openness.

Love,

Pat

To: Patty Ann
From: Rael
Date: Thursday, August 9, 5:30 PM
Subject: Letter about Raising Jacob

Hello my love,

Tonight I found your letter to me that you hung in my closet. Thanks for taking the time to express your thoughts and share your apprehensions. I realize that I am not setting boundaries as I should, and I appreciate you taking the time to express what you see happening.

I don't totally agree with some of your interpretations, and these are topics we should discuss. Maybe I'm being delusional, but I surely don't see him as a spoiled, self-absorbed child. Maybe you are right that I never use discipline with Jacob. I just don't see it that way.

I see the need for change and improvement. I realize some of the reason for my lax attitude with Jacob is laziness, some fear, and a lot is lack of motivation in that it is not as important for me. I agree Jacob likes boundaries and operates well under them. These are all things I would like to discuss with you when we have time together.

I'd like to write more, but I feel a little overwhelmed by it all at the moment.

Just got off the phone and feel much better,

I'll talk soon, I hope,

Love always, Rael

In our phone conversation that left him feeling "much better," Rael congenially agreed that he needed to change, that he certainly could improve as a parent. In return, I quickly accepted his promises, fully believing that he loved me so much that he would do what was obviously the right thing for Jacob's sake and in order to keep me. In the above e-mail, Rael says as he is signing off, "I'll talk soon." It is a small thing, but suggests his need to control.

> Children today are tyrants. They contradict their parents, gobble their food, and tyrannize their teachers.
> ~ Socrates

As a result of my letter, Rael purchased the two childrearing books I suggested. Starting with *Boundaries with Kids* by Henry Cloud and John Townsend, we read the chapters independently, and then we discussed them. Gradually, we moved from a neutral point of view to me defending the book and him tearing holes in their strategies. About halfway through it, I tired of the process and gave it up as nonproductive. Rael had a degree in psychology, and if he had used it for nothing else, he knew how to wear me down, playing a mind game of persuasion and manipulation. The idea of tackling the second book fell by the wayside.

During this period, Rael attended several therapy sessions with me, which offered an opportunity for him to perform and play mind games. He reveled in showing me how psychologically superior he was to Dr. Humor, while I sorted out my allegiances to two men for whom, I would later realize, I had formed the same codependent relationship I had had with my father. I desperately needed their approval, which ended up costing me the ability to be myself or to be honest in my relationships, particularly with men.

> Life is like Sanskrit read to a pony.   ~ Lou Reed

Since I seemed well entrenched and Jacob certainly offered no attraction as a means of funneling his need to focus intently, Rael needed a distraction. Therefore, he accepted the position on the homeowner's board that I had urged him to decline. The Democratic Party had begun revving up for the election, so he became heavily involved in that as well. Together they filled his need to follow an obsession – or two.

A couple of incidents, both of them involving Jacob, added to the emotions that ran high that fall. The first one happened the day we took a trip to a park in Baytown. Rael had recently purchased a canoe, and he wanted to show Jacob and me some of the waterways around the area where he grew up and currently worked. We had barely lowered the boat in the water when Jacob started whining to go home. I suggested we keep going, but Rael patiently cut the canoe trip short. On the way back to Rael's house, we stopped to get drinks. Jacob refused to go inside the store. When I tried coaxing him out of the car, he curled up in a ball on the floor of the car and lashed out at me. In retrospect, I suspect that Jacob was jealous of the attention Rael gave me instead of him. In a clueless manner, I became outraged, demanding Jacob apologize to me and behave like a little boy instead of a wounded animal. Jacob remained crouched on the floorboard while Rael and I argued in front of the store. I raised my voice more than I ever had with him. Then Rael and I went inside. Jacob stayed put. End of problem.

I had trouble sleeping that night. Rael blamed the thirty-two-ounce soda that I had drunk – and I did as well. Now I realize it wasn't just caffeine that kept me awake.

The second incident happened at an amusement center where we planned to bowl. Rael had forgotten his wallet. So rather than drive an hour back to his house, he asked if I minded paying the entrance fees. I happily agreed, since he always paid for everything when we went out. Once we had finished bowling, Jacob wanted to play at the machines. That entailed buying a $20 card that lasted about thirty minutes. If it had been a birthday or a reward for making excellent grades, I could have justified the money, but it was just a typical weekend, which meant we went somewhere and spent $50 or more appeasing Jacob.

When Rael asked if I would buy the $20 game card, I said sure, but I resented the expense. Afterward, I was naïve enough to expect a simple thank-you, but that didn't occur to either Rael or Jacob. At home by myself that night, I struggled with my indignation that a grown man could not say "thank you" and that he would raise a child who did not know how or when to acknowledge a gift. Finally, I phoned Rael, telling him that I expected an acknowledgment. When he pooh-poohed my request, I told him that I was sincerely hurt by his reaction. Even after we talked extensively about the situation, I don't think he ever heard what I tried to tell him – that modeling saying "please" and "thank you" and teaching a child to do the same are fundamental aspects of parenting.

Not only is life a bitch, but it is always having puppies.
~ Adrienne Gusoff

As I look back at that time, my heart goes out to this seven-year-old who had lost his mother one year before that. Regrettably, I now realize how I too felt the need to compete for Rael's attention. Part of my issue with Jacob stemmed from my own desire to have Rael to myself as I had in New Zealand. Along with both Jacob and my immaturity lay the fact that Rael had not developed as a parent, for he did not fill that role from the time Jacob was two until he lost his mother when he was six and a half years of age – well over half of the kid's current age. Rael said that, even prior to their separation, Jill had expressed anger that he spent so much time doing the things he wanted to do, like gardening, rather than helping her with Jacob and Christopher, Jacob's half-brother. I knew from the get-go that Jacob would make or break our relationship, and I can easily see why he resisted developing an attachment to me. We both wanted to own Rael.

Plagued by my enduring contradictory feelings about Jacob and Rael, I spent hours composing another e-mail only three weeks after the letter I left in his closet.

To: Rael
From: Pat
Date: Monday, September 24, 5:32 AM

You are the sweetest, most generous, most loving man I have ever known. Having followed your rule of saying something positive before I launch into the meat of the letter, I will go on to say that I know this letter will impact our relationship hugely, and I write it after many hours of soul-searching and deliberation.   I have tried in my typical wholehearted way to build a relationship with Jacob. While I know myself well enough to realize I can endure just about anything for an indefinite period of time, I choose to not live with a child who knows no boundaries, a child who is in charge, a child who is treated like a peer rather than a seven-year-old boy who needs direction and guidance.

I have tried to approach you about this a number of times, and you have deflected my efforts to actually talk about the issue – having a heated discussion in front of a convenience store immediately following an incident does not qualify as truly addressing the issue. I've thought of all kinds of explanations, like the same boundary issues that prompted you to abuse Harmony are still in place. Not in a sexual way, but whatever caused you to do that then still paralyzes and blinds you to what you are doing now. Nothing I have said is going to change the situation. Only you can start setting boundaries with Jacob.

The bottom line is, I cannot marry you. You've never officially asked me, but before you go to the trouble of putting together a tremendous production – the answer is no. I love you, and it hurts to the depths of my being to say this, but it's better to be honest now than to wake up six, seven, eight, nine years from now and realize that I am miserable. In ten years, Jacob will be in college, but what will have happened to our relationship in the meantime? I truly love you, and I want the best for you in every way, but I cannot allow that love to be clouded over while you refuse to address an issue I cannot tackle on my own.

Patty Ann

We're terrified that we'll find out that our worst fear is true – that we are really unworthy of love.
~ Katherine Woodward Thomas from Calling in *"The One"*

I e-mailed this letter early in the morning and spent the rest of the day at school waiting to hear from Rael. When he called me that afternoon, he was obviously upset, and by the time we hung up thirty minutes later, he had me back in his fold. It took little to persuade me that he would go back to giving me unlimited attention, that he loved me, and that he desperately needed me. All of this answered a deep-seated need I harbored. A part of me knew I should not give in to the magnetic force that drew me to him, but I could not ignore his addictive charm. My letter, journal, and e-mail clearly expressed my doubt, but when I finally mustered the courage to confront Rael, it took little for him to convince me that things would be different; he valued our relationship, and he would do whatever it took to keep me.

That fall semester, following Dr. Humor's advice, I signed up for a painting class at the college where I taught. If I had not, I'm sure my recently renewed interest in watercolor would have taken a backseat to the more pressing matters dictated by my new position as a department chair. But since the class was part of my weekly schedule, I got back in the groove of painting on a regular basis – at least during those few months. For Christmas, I gave each of my children large paintings – collage composites of my favorite photographs of them, bridging the years from early childhood into their late teens. At the end of the semester, I painted at Rael's house, trying to finish these paintings. Jacob showed an interest in joining me, so I gave him paper and paint, and we worked together, each of us lost in our creative worlds. Later, Rael told me what a magical time that was to see Jacob and me sharing something that we both seemed to love so much. Of course, Rael's observation endeared him to me, thus further cementing my growing need for him.

> Learning without reflection is a waste, reflection without learning is dangerous.
> ~ Confucius

  I have often described myself as a retreat and workshop junkie. Nothing gives me more pleasure than to escape the workaday world and spend a few days at my favorite retreat center, the Cenacle Retreat House on the west side of Houston. Several weekends a year, I volunteer as the "helper," which entails ringing the bell for meals, assisting the presenter with their needs, and helping with problems that arise. The grounds are gorgeous, and I've pounded many a tennis shoe on the nearby walking trail. Along with the beauty and peace found there, the food is fabulous. And I love to eat. The chef at that time loved to season the food, and the greeting I got from Rael upon returning home after attending a retreat was a negative comment about my garlic breath. Of course, he didn't start making these comments until we were well established as a couple. Ultraconscious of what he said about me and too intimidated to do what I wanted in spite of what he said, I gradually stopped going to the Cenacle even though it is one of my favorite places in the whole wide world.

  Before I stopped going, I sat with Sister Mary and told her about Rael. Yes, I told her about his incestuous relationship with his stepdaughter. Sister gave me that worried look she gets when she doesn't want to say something, but she knows she must, and then she informed me that people who commit sexual crimes typically don't get well. I told her I was familiar with the research. What I did not say was that even she could not sway me from staying in the relationship. Her sentiment simply added to the number of people who tried to dissuade me.

In mid-October, Rael and I participated in a vegetarian cook-off in Austin, Texas. Rael had done this with Diane and Misty the previous year, and he was eager to rekindle the feeling of camaraderie he had experienced then. In fact, the picture that had attracted me to him on the website was taken at the previous chili cook-off. I eagerly bought props for the Hawaiian theme that his group had chosen. Diane lived on the west side of Houston, so we picked her up on the way to Austin. We would meet Misty there. On the way, we stopped and bought a basketful of groceries to add to the truckload of supplies that we were hauling with us.

We stayed at a hotel a few miles from the zoo, where the chili cook-off would set up at the crack of dawn, Diane in one room and Rael, Jacob, and I in another. Rael paid for both rooms, along with the entry fee for the cook-off, and the groceries. We went to a dinner that night, where I met many of the other cook-off participants. A few doors down from the restaurant, we bought two large bottles of wine. That night Diane took the remains of our wine and hers back to her hotel room. The next morning, she was hungover and totally wasted.

We wanted to get to the zoo to claim a shady spot and to start cooking, but Diane forgot the onions and carrots in her hotel room. Rael volunteered me to drive back to get the vegetables. After some confusion about where we could set up, the two guys, Rael and Misty's boyfriend, and I unloaded the truck while Diane and Misty stood by, waiting for us to finish. By then I understood that the day focused on Diane and her fabulous recipe and Misty and her great body, both obvious assets to a successful chili cook-off. What did I have to offer except my go-along-to-get-along demeanor? While they cooked, drank the beer that I bought from a nearby stand, and laughed and played, I stood back, took the occasional picture of their frivolities, and felt sorry for myself. Loading looked like unloading with the film running in reverse.

On the way home, I sat in the front seat with Rael while Diane rode in the back with Jacob. We stopped at Olive Garden to eat. Again, Rael paid the entire tab. As we started out the door, Diane went into the restroom, so Rael, Jacob, and I sat in the lobby and waited and waited for her. When she finally came out, she appeared to be in worse shape than

A hangover is the wrath of grapes.

~ Bumper Sticker

that morning. Back in the car, she initially made fun of Jacob, and then she lambasted Rael when Jacob got upset and started lashing back at her. Thankfully, Diane fell into what I suspect was a drug-induced stupor, so we drove the rest of the way home in silence.

That should have been enough. I should have seen the writing on the wall and realized I did not want to be with someone who would ignore me around his friends. The next day, when I told Rael how upset the whole experience had made me, he said how much he valued his "go-with-the-flow girl." Once more his vote of confidence coerced me to let go of any ill will toward him and blame everyone else, including myself.

Within that same week, I found a bag from a jewelry store containing a receipt for a ring on the nightstand on my side of the bed. Since confrontation is not my strong suit, I wrote a note asking him why he left this out where I could see it. I left the note and the receipt on a decorative pillow on Rael's side of the bed. I don't know about you, but I see a pattern – write a note and say what I do not have the guts to say to his face. Weeks later, I found the note and the receipt beneath the throw pillow, which had been tossed on the floor. Since Rael never acknowledged my note, he probably went to bed in the dark and never saw it. And I never mentioned it.

For Halloween, we spent days creating a spook-house on the front porch of Rael's home from the plethora of Halloween decorations that he had accumulated over the years. On the big night, I donned a witch's outfit while Rael and Jacob dressed as pirates. With a shrill cackle, I invited the little ones to come in if they dared to fetch a piece of candy – but to be careful lest they leave minus a few fingers. All three of us enjoyed the evening immensely. For once I maintained my authenticity and things went well. Does that mean I should be more witchlike?

The first day of November, I had a second oral surgery identical to the one I had in January, but this time no gifts or soup appeared on my back step. When my friend Lilly pointed out the difference in Rael's behavior over the ten months that had passed, I admitted I had noticed the change, but I rationalized he now understood it wasn't that big a deal.

Intelligent people realize that unhappiness comes from within, and while an event may be irritating, one can change his reaction by his definitions and verbalizations of the events.   ~Albert Ellis

Funny, how easily I could justify and explain away his behavior.

On November 11, Rael took me to a swanky restaurant that overlooked Clear Lake. Several years earlier, Lilly and I had discussed how this day would be the perfect day to get married since it had so many of my favorite number, one: 11/11. Seated by a window with a great view, Rael acted a bit nervous, and then he sort of blurted out the question, would I marry him. I had shared with Rael the conversation Lilly and I had had about the significance of the day, and to his credit, he remembered.

This was the first time someone officially proposed to me, and I said yes – because that is what I do. My first husband and I sort of agreed on the idea of marriage over the first few months we dated, and we married after six months of knowing each other. When I said yes to Rael, because I thought I should, I was also thinking, *You could back out. You don't have to marry this guy.* During the meal, he excused himself for an extralong restroom break, and when we got back to the car, I found on my seat a real rose encased in 14-carat gold, thus preserving it. I got roses two more times, once on Valentine's Day and then for my birthday.

The day after I got the engagement ring I wrote the following:

> *Each of us, to experience peace, must recognize that we have a choice as to whether we view our identity as small and severely limited or as unlimited as love.*
> ~Dr. Gerald Jampolsky

Journal Entry   November 12

Yesterday I got a ring – an engagement ring. It seems odd and scary and impossible and extremely nice and comforting that someone loves me enough to do that for me – that someone loves me and wants me to be a permanent part of his life and wants me to help him raise his child and wants to share everything he owns and knows with me.

A little over two weeks later I wrote this:

Journal Entry   12:40 AM, November 29

I'm scared –

1.   . . .that I'm convincing myself that I am in love with Rael.

2.   . . .that we are too different – moneywise, basic philosophy.

3.   . . .that I can never truly embrace vegetarianism.

4.   . . .that I would never feel truly comfortable with Jacob.

5.   . . .that there is a price tag attached to all of it – a cost I can't define.

6.   . . . .that I'll feel trapped in a marriage.

7.   . . .that I am feeling myself pushed from behind about the whole idea of marriage.

8.   . . .that I am more excited about going back to New Zealand than I am about getting married.

9.   . . .that I'll quit writing and painting.

10.   . . that with time his past – Harmony and being a pedophile – would be huge.

11.   . . . that he doesn't have a clue what he did to that little girl (Harmony).

12.   . . . that he is as insensitive as I want to believe he is sensitive.

13.   . . . that I am stretching to believe that Jill brought us together.

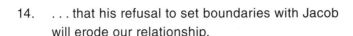

14.　. . . that his refusal to set boundaries with Jacob will erode our relationship.

15.　. . . that there is not enough of me to be a good wife and do all the other things I want to do.

16.　. . . that I am not strong enough to walk away.

17.　. . . that I will cling to the relationship past the time of it being healthy for me.

18.　. . . that I want the relationship to prove my worth.

19.　. . . that I am still stuck in that idea that I am nothing without a man.

> *Other people's opinion of you does not have to become your reality.*
> *~ Les Brown*

As I go through these old e-mails and journals that chronicle the events of our courtship, I clearly see the self-destructive course I chose, after repeated hesitation. Ultimately I could not let go of that irresistible force that pulled me along, my need to feel loved and validated. The fears and concerns that I explored in my journals and letters to Rael validate my apprehension, but I did not have the self-esteem or courage that I needed to follow my inner truth – the voice in my head that repeatedly urged me to end the relationship.

For Christmas gifts, Rael and I cooked up several batches of organic apple and strawberry preserves. We covered the lids with holiday fabric tied on with a ribbon. While Mother, who drove down for Christmas, sat in a patio chair, Rael and I rebuilt the fence around my patio. Wearing an old pair of lace-up boots discarded by one of my sons, I helped Rael haul off the old fencing. I assisted him in manhandling the auger to dig the fence posts through the thick and massive roots of the giant oak tree. We erected the posts and hammered the boards in place. It felt satisfying to work this project together, even though I doubted I would have time to enjoy the fence at the condo because I had decided to move in with Rael.

A sense of melancholy prevailed as I gifted my children with the paintings I had done. It would be the last holiday in my condo. I felt less and less available to them, for although we had not set a date, I had chosen to marry Rael and give my time and devotion to him. That's what one does in a marriage, right? My Christmas present to Rael was extravagant and defied logic – a 42-inch plasma TV. My mom recently reminded me that when she accompanied me to the store to purchase the TV, I declined the salesman's offer for free interest for a year, saying I did not want to find myself still paying for it if we broke up prior to paying it off. I had grown up in a household focused on the television, so why did I promote the same thing in my own home?

It's good to have money and the things money can buy. But's its good, to check up once in a while and make sure that you haven't lost the things that money can't buy.   *~ G. H. Lorimer*

 **Family Reflections**

If Dad was in the house, the television was on, and he controlled which channel we watched. His favorite shows were Westerns and cartoons, but it didn't matter, since he had already seen everything – multiple times. Having the TV on and knowing he chose the channel – both before and after the advent of the remote – seemed to give him a feeling of control. Mother and Dad struggled to pay the bills, and since my dad was a cotton farmer, there were years he did not make a crop. But I bet we had the first color TV in a five-mile radius. (Our closest neighbors were a mile away.) And we were also the first family in our community who had two televisions in one household. As luck would have it, we won a TV at a Lion's Club fund-raiser.

We watched television during meals. It sat on top of the refrigerator three feet from the table. Conversation during the meals was prohibited because it kept Dad from hearing the TV. Talking during commercials was okay, unless it was a "good one." While my kids were growing up, I forbade television within eyeshot of my dining room table. I used to get absolutely livid when I walked into a restaurant and saw a TV mounted on every wall. Now, that is so common that I am forced to ignore it. I do not watch TV. I have one, and I watch movies occasionally, but I do not have the time or the inclination to watch TV in the evenings. And, truthfully, I do not miss it.

The answer to life's problems aren't at the bottom of a bottle, they're on TV!
                                                    ~ Homer Simpson

Nuggets of Gold

No is always an option, even if I've already said yes and/or I am halfway through the agreement. I can always find something else to do. No one forced me to unload and reload that truck for the chili cook-off. I did that out of my own sense of victimhood, so from now on, I am not a victim. If I am in the middle of something, and it ceases to meet my expectations, I have every right to leave. And if I can't physically leave, I need to make sure I always have a decent book with me.

> *Missy: "I hear they've got an assertive training class for Southern women. [looks puzzled] Of course that's a contradiction in terms."*
> FRIED GREEN
> TOMATOES, 1991.

If I ask someone to change several times, and they say they will, but they don't, they are not going to, and I owe it to both of us to leave the relationship. I knew this truth going in; in fact, that was part of the reasoning that I gave Rael about why I wanted to address the issues that bothered me before we got too far into the relationship. And yet, I did not honor my instincts by following up with my side of the deal. I did not say, "Okay, I see that this does not mean that much to you, so I'm out of here." Instead, I stayed, and by staying, I told him that he did not have to change because I would not insist on it. As my brilliant mother-in-law used to say, "If you tell a kid you are going to chop off their arm if they do that again, you'd better be prepared to get out a hatchet." If I wasn't willing to follow through by gathering up my marbles and going home, I should have never brought up the subject.

My voice of truth speaks to me, but I have to be willing to listen to it in order to benefit. My journal entries are tangible proof that I knew more than I was willing to admit to myself. That wise voice was intent, and it was not quiet. Sometimes it woke me up in the middle of the night. Sometimes it kept me from falling asleep. No, this voice was not that subtle, soft-spoken whisper of a demure child. This voice screamed at me – but I drowned it out with my addictive need for my relationship with Rael.

I should never say yes to a proposal of marriage because I think I may not get another offer.   If I never got married in the first place, it would not be the end of the world. I can say that because I have experienced marriage, and I have three terrific children as well as grandchildren, so I can be exceedingly cavalier about all that. Nonetheless, no woman needs to get married. We are past the day when a woman is dependent on a man for an identity, financially or culturally. Some of us want the experience of having kids, and I am extremely glad I have been blessed with that joy, but not at the price of my own self-respect and dignity. How much honor is there in marrying someone because I don't think anyone else would have me – for me or for him? Regretfully, that self-defeating thought motivated me to say yes to Rael's proposal.

No one can figure out your worth but you.   ~*Pearl Bailey*

Chapter Six
Winter - A Move, a Trip to the Emergency Room, and Two Deaths

Every issue, belief, attitude, or assumption is precisely the issue that stands between you and your relationship to another human being; and between you and yourself.
                                        ~ Gita Bellin

Over the month of January, I gradually moved my things to Rael's house, one pickup truck or carload at a time. Rael found this method annoying and tedious. Several times he offered to hire a moving company and do it all at once. That made sense, but I preferred to do it in pieces. Plus, I could not justify spending the money on something we could do ourselves, so I gradually let go of what felt like my freedom, one trip to the condo and back at a time.

When I integrated my dishes with Rael's, he teased me about stacking my serving bowls and leaving space in the cabinet. I had limited cabinet space in the condo, and it didn't feel right to sprawl out in this new setting. Plus, I hesitated to "take over," lest I become the pushy girlfriend. While cooking our first meals together, I self-consciously bumped into Rael, and he assured me this awkwardness was natural – part of the process.

We continued using the upstairs bedroom Rael had slept in since Jacob moved back in over a year before that. Rael said Jacob felt more secure with us upstairs. In the next year or so, we planned to move downstairs to the master bedroom and make one of the upstairs bedrooms into a studio for me, perhaps the one Jacob used for a short time after we painted the walls blue, then embellished them with fluffy grey and white clouds. I could see myself continuing to watercolor paint or constructing stained glass panels there. When I moved into my condo, I had the almost new, top-quality carpet removed from one of the upstairs bedrooms to convert it into a studio. I even assembled my monster workbench in it, but I never found the time or the motivation to organize and use it. My dining room table ended up being my primary work space for the paintings I had done the previous fall.

We are, each of us, our own prisoner. We are locked up in our own story.   ~Maxine Kumin

Also in January, I started a series of workshops based on my affirmations. Two other ladies and I planned to meet at the condo every seventh Saturday for seven sessions. I thought of our seminars as a pilot program to work through what it felt like to design and stage something like this on a grander scale. Having only two other people involved made it more flexible and doable.

Rael decided we needed to take a family trip over the Martin Luther King holiday. After researching options, he settled on Ogden, Utah – a town that offered enough touristy things to do without all the hype. Two days before our departure, I got a phone call from my brother telling me Dad had been hospitalized. The plane tickets had been purchased, and I told myself there was nothing I could do in Lubbock for him. I wonder now if I wasn't more concerned with disappointing Rael.

Since he and Mother divorced, Dad had neglected his health; or rather he had missed Mother taking care of him. For a few months after he and Mother separated, Dad stopped in at Mother's house almost daily with one lame excuse after another. When she finally made it clear they were finished, he found a girlfriend and quit pestering Mother. I don't think the girlfriend doled out his pills or monitored his diet. In fact, they ate most meals out.

Dad spent his days "checking on the crops." And once a week or so, he drove one hundred miles to New Mexico to buy a lottery ticket. The previous October Dad had pulled out in front of another car and caused an accident. At that time, I suggested he accept in-home care, but that meant relinquishing his driver's license, which would happen right after hell froze over. Gradually losing the ability to drive probably triggered his rapid decline.

On our trip to Ogden, I felt guilty for playing while my older brother Morgan and his wife Allison had driven from Birmingham, Alabama, to help Dad. While we frolicked in Ogden, building space-cadet snowmen complete with vacuum cleaner parts we found in the trash, I thought of where I should be – in Lubbock, helping make decisions about Dad's care. The second day in Utah, we rented snowmobiles – something I had always thought looked like a world of fun. Like many forms of entertainment, it's most appealing when one is an onlooker. I managed to get mine stuck in a snowbank, and Rael spent the better part of the afternoon getting it unstuck – twice. After we had checked in the snowmobiles, Rael realized he had lost his video camera out of his pocket. While Jacob and I waited in the rental car, Rael backtracked and looked for it, to no avail.

By the time we got back from Utah, Dad's health had further disintegrated. My dad died a week later. I felt guilty about not going to see him. From my office, I e-mailed Rael telling him the situation. When I got home, Rael had already told Jacob, but neither of them said anything to me after I walked into the house. Instead, they stared at me expectantly. I retreated to the bathroom and worked on crying, more out of a lack of a relationship with my father than about sadness for his death. After a few token tears, Rael, Jacob, and I went out to eat, but neither one of them said a word about my father's death.

Rael did not offer to go with me to the funeral, but he did indicate that he wanted to send flowers, so once I arrived in Lubbock, I e-mailed him the location of the funeral home/mausoleum where my father would be entombed. Long before he died, Dad had made arrangements for his remains to lie on a mausoleum shelf rather than go in the cold ground. Rael's flowers never showed up, and when I asked him about it upon my return home, he said he had forgotten to order them. Clearly, I had moved down on the priority scale, but once more, I did not say or do anything to indicate I was deeply offended and hurt by his thoughtlessness.

While we were in Lubbock in January, my brothers, Morgan and Matthew, looked for a key for Dad's house, but when they could not find

I cannot give you the formula for success, but I can give you the formula for failure – which is: try to please everybody.
~ Herbert Bayard Swope

one, they decided to replace the locks. Morgan had a hard time with the procedure, and at the time, we attributed that to the stress of Dad's death. Later that year, we realized this was our earliest indicator of a serious health issue for Morgan.

Over Spring Break, my siblings and I returned to Lubbock to finish cleaning out Dad's house. Initially, Jacob and Rael planned to accompany me, but honestly, I did not want to deal with them as well as with the emotions that were sure to accompany the situation, so we decided they would fly up at the end of the week and drive home with me. Also, a friend I had planned to spend the night with on the way to Lubbock indicated that I was welcome, but Rael and Jacob were not. Again, her reaction to Rael should have been a glaring indicator of reality, but I refused to pay attention to what my friends and even my journal was trying to tell me. When I called Rael from Lubbock and said I would just as soon drive home on my own, he said, "Great, I'm up to my chin getting out the vote for the Democratic primaries."

Before I left Lubbock, my brother Morgan and I had an odd conversation about a stained glass panel that had belonged to Dad. It was a portrait of his father that I had built for Dad on his sixtieth birthday.   While we were driving, Morgan and Matthew had batted back and forth the idea of alternately keeping the stained glass panel at each of their houses. A few days later when Morgan began packing up to leave, he put the stained glass panel in his car. I asked him why, and he referred to the discussion that he and Matthew had had. Clearly upset, I told him that I thought they were just kidding. He asked me what I wanted him to do with it, and I said it should go back in the window in Mother's house, where it had been before Dad and Mother divorced. Morgan said there wasn't a chain to hang it there, so that was impossible. Confused by his childlike logic, I said I would hang it myself. After he leaned the panel against the wall in that room, I asked him if he was upset by my request.   He said flatly that he wasn't, which further baffled me since I was distressed enough for both of us. Once more, I would look back and see the indicators of what Morgan was unknowingly battling and would eventually kill him.

"What we've got here is failure to communicate."
COOL HAND LUKE,
1967.

April the first, I went to the doctor for another round of antibiotics. It was at least the third bladder infection I had suffered from since I started dating Rael. And it would not be the last. After picking up the prescription, I stopped by the condo to get something to drink while I took the first pill. Sitting in the hammock in my backyard, I studied the new fence, nostalgic for the time when I lived there. I already felt imprisoned by the choices I had made. My soul tried to tell me I was not yet locked in, but I couldn't listen; I was too invested in getting what I thought I wanted – someone who loved me. Rael said he loved me, and initially he demonstrated that, although his expressions of love had begun to seriously wane.

On the way home, I had an allergic reaction to the medication and began laboring to breathe. At the time, I was on my cell phone talking to my friend Lilly, and when I told her what was happening, she advised me to go to the emergency room. I thought of a clinic that Rael and I had used several months earlier, when Jacob's temperature spiked one weekend. I drove the several miles to the clinic, filled out the paperwork, and then called Rael. They had given me a shot of Benadryl by the time he got there with Jacob in tow. When he saw that I was not in crisis, he took Jacob across the street to feed him at a pizza place they frequented that offered a decent vegetarian meal. The doctor was getting ready to release me when Rael and Jacob returned. He drove home and left me on my own since I seemed to be fine. I was already feeling melancholy, so his eagerness to leave as soon as possible hit a raw nerve.

I called Rael as I stopped at a pharmacy on the way home to get a different antibiotic for the bladder infection. He asked if I would pick up Jacob's brand of ice cream, Blue Bell's Cookies 'n Cream. It was the only type or brand he would eat, and he had to have some before he went to bed. At home, I decided to put on a happy face, so I came in the back door, singing a little ditty and announcing that the ice cream truck had arrived. Rael came downstairs from where he had been working at his computer and said, "I've never heard you sing before." He was obviously pleased, and after a short conversation while he put the ice cream on a cone, he returned to the political stuff on the computer upstairs. While I sat alone at the kitchen table and ate leftovers, I spiraled to a new low. I took a

Some days there won't be a song in your heart. Sing anyway.

~Emory Austin

tub bath and went to bed.

The next morning, I walked my usual three miles and pondered the situation. It seemed ridiculous to go on like this, so I decided to move home – this simply wasn't working. Rael had his keys in hand and had started out the door to drive to work when I announced my intentions. Frustrated, he said this made two times that I had threatened to call it quits. After I told him what had upset me, he got all teary-eyed and told me that he could not read my mind, and I had to tell him what I expected. We held each other and cried together and vowed to each other to be better communicators. I left that encounter feeling guilty for legitimate reasons. I had not said what I needed and held firm to that. Rather than fortify my self-esteem, this experience eroded what little self-worth I still clung to. I used it to criticize myself, rather than lovingly ask myself what I wanted. Of course, my Inner Guide had tried to tell me to do exactly what I desired to do – move home. But that little girl who desperately wanted love and approval could not or would not listen.

Never be bullied into silence. Never allow yourself to be made a victim. Accept no one's definition of your life; define yourself.
~ Harvey Fierstein

One Friday morning when I woke up Jacob for school, he informed me that he did not have to go that day. When I called Rael to verify this, he said that he knew it, but he assumed I would be there to babysit. He also knew I had therapy every other Friday, but he had not bothered to get a babysitter. Frustrated, but determined to make my appointment, I took Jacob with me. When I told Dr. Humor what had happened, he suggested Jacob could read in the waiting room while we had our session. Seizing the opportunity, I said I wanted him to join us.

Dr. Humor spent the first half of the session trying to put Jacob at ease, which meant getting the child to at least sit down. Still standing, Jacob answered his questions as minimally as possible, but gradually Dr. Humor elicited from Jacob an admission that he chose vegetarianism because he did not want to hurt anyone. Then Dr. Humor asked Jacob what he thought I would like to ask him. I was totally dumbfounded when Jacob replied that he thought I would like to know why he was mean to me. Dr. Humor connected the dots and asked Jacob if he was mean to me on occasion. When Jacob admitted he was, Dr. Humor returned to Jacob's explanation that he was vegetarian because he did not want to hurt anyone.

That night Rael and I lay on the bed with the bedroom door shut, and I related what had been said in Dr. Humor's office. He quietly listened, and then responded that I was not required to love Jacob. I said that I did, although I privately wondered how honestly I had spoken. I went on to tell him that I very much wanted things to work out between Jacob and me. I'm not sure if the session with Dr. Humor had an impact, or maybe Jacob had listened at our bedroom door while Rael and I talked, but after that, I sensed a positive shift in Jacob's attitude toward me. Nothing monumental, but a shift nonetheless.

Mother and I had taken several trips together since she and my father divorced, and with my pending marriage to Rael, I felt the need to plan one more – just in case it did not work out for Mother and me to do that again once I married. In May Mother and I flew to Niagara Falls. After we toured there, we took a train to Montreal, where we picked up a Canadian cruise ship that took us to Nova Scotia and then around to Bal Harbor, Maine, before we ended the trip in Boston. Rael called my cell phone every night. The whole time we were gone, I talked nonstop about Rael. I am sure Mother grew sick of hearing about what he would buy in any given store we shopped or what he might say about the attractions we viewed. I felt guilty taking a trip without him, and now I feel badly about having treated Mother so thoughtlessly.

I had my birthday while we were gone, but I came home to no present. Disappointed, I told Rael I wanted a birthday present since we had agreed we would say what we needed. He gave me another rose encased in 14-carat gold, like the one he gave me with my engagement ring.

In my absence, Rael had the sunken floor of the living room raised, which meant hauling in seven loads of cement to fill the space. This was the first of our long-range plan to remodel the house. The overall goal was to transform the house from his house into our home.

> *In order to believe he is loved, the wounded child behaves the way he thinks he is supposed to…. Gradually, the false self becomes who the person really thinks he is. He forgets that the false self is an adaptation, an act based on a script someone else wrote.*
> *~John Bradshaw*

Summer

The first part of June, my brother Morgan came home from work and tried to tell his wife Allison a story, but it came out jumbled. He couldn't put the details in order, but more than that, he did not seem to understand that what he was saying did not make sense. She took him in for a CT scan the next day, and when the doctors didn't get back to them immediately, Morgan and Allison optimistically assumed the best. Perhaps the doctors chose to give Morgan and Allison a reprieve before the final verdict. Two weeks later, they delivered the diagnosis – Morgan had an inoperable tumor between the two hemispheres of his brain.

He had a hard time communicating, but Morgan did tell my other brother Matthew that his primary concern centered on who would take care of Allison – his wife – my sister-in-law of thirty-seven years. They had one of those marriages I found easy to envy. She called him her cabana boy because he would do anything for her.

> *Chains do not hold a marriage together. It is threads, hundreds of tiny threads which sew people together through the years.*
> ~ Simone Signoret

That summer, Rael decided that a camp trailer was the answer to our vacation dilemma, which I did not know existed – the dilemma, that is. Remembering previous ill-fated camping experiences in my first marriage, I voiced my concerns, but my objections fell on deaf ears. This would be different, he argued. Rael could afford the trailer because Jill had designated him a beneficiary on a life insurance policy. I'm quite sure she did not realize she had left it that way, but he ended up with the money nonetheless. Rationalizing that he had given her $30,000 for her part of the house when they divorced, he used that amount to remodel the house and pay for the trailer. To his credit, the rest of the $100,000 went in the boy's trust fund – at least, that's what he told me.

The trailer had an incredibly loud AC, and an oven that never worked after the time the salesman demonstrated how to use it. I did not like the TV addiction that followed us on trips and prompted Jacob to sit and watch a movie he had seen countless times rather than go outside and play. And I hated the cramped quarters and lack of privacy, especially for sleeping. With each trip our paraphernalia grew, eventually including three bikes, a canoe which rode on the hood, and a rack that Rael constructed out of PCP pipe, and several pieces of bulky lawn furniture. Setting up and packing everything before we drove home, along with cleaning up the trailer once we got back, became a prominent part of how we spent our camping time. Based on my history with travel trailers, I started off against this idea, but once the deal was done, I decided to hunker down and focus on making it a positive experience.

We took monthly trips to state parks, and in July we took a two-week trip back to Leakey in Central Texas, where we had spent Spring Break the previous year. Toward the end of our trip, I lay awake throughout the night. The longer I lay there, the clearer I became that this was not me. What was I doing spending my summer vacation in a camp trailer? What was I doing raising a seven-year-old? At the first light of dawn, Rael rolled over and asked me what I was thinking. I told him he did not want to know. That got his attention. Then I proceeded to tell him about my nightlong pondering. Of course, true to form, he convinced me that things would be different from that moment on; I would call the shots – some of them at least. Like so many times in the past, I capitulated while fully embracing the new-found attention that Rael lavished on me at that point.

While I rejected the idea initially and never found myself excited about the business of taking vacation and weekend trips in a camping trailer, there were the positive points to the whole thing. First and foremost was the opportunity to get out in nature. We took canoe trips and rode bicycles throughout the state parks that we visited, managing to average one a month. Our philosophy was, if we were going to have this thing and pay for storage, we might as well use it. I shot some of my best photographs while we were camping. And we got to see some seriously cool wildlife. At Caddo Lake State Park, containing the only natural lake in Texas, we were able to get close enough to a pair of beavers to video them before they slipped into the water. At Brazos Bend State Park, we watched alligators sun themselves in the early spring. It touched me how much Rael appreciated nature. He loved to set up the feeders and see what types of birds he attracted. Most of all, camping took me out of my routine, and while I resented the time away from my writing, it proved to be

> *Travel has no longer any charm for me. I have seen all the foreign countries I want to except heaven and hell and I have only a vague curiosity about one of those.   ~ Mark Twain*

the most quality time we spent as a family.

I was the official babysitter that summer. Early on I decided Jacob and I would take a weekly field trip, but I also vowed to make it educational as well as fun. We toured the Houston Zoo, the Museum of Natural Science, the Children's Museum, and the San Jacinto Monument. On the first trip, I succumbed to Jacob's pleas for a souvenir at the zoo gift shop, but when he settled for a cheap gadget, I decided that in the future if Jacob needed a souvenir, he could ask his dad in advance for the money. They both knew where I stood, but even when Jacob remembered to ask, Rael never remembered to give him the money. Rael probably saw no benefit to doling out money if he didn't get the thrill of being the hero when Jacob spent it.

For Father's Day, I started a collage/painting for Rael along the same order as the pictures I had painted for my kids at Christmas. I searched his computer and used the pictures I had taken of him to create a composite design that included him, Jacob, Christopher, and me. The largest part of the painting featured a tight shot of Jacob and me on either side of Rael. On the big day, I gave him the painting, which I had barely developed past the initial stages, and vowed to finish it as soon as possible.

Also that summer, Rael promised Jacob a weekly allowance of $20, which I thought was exorbitant and told him so. He asked how my kids had acquired money for toys or the things they wanted. I told him they received a modest allowance, and they had to work for that. The rest came from doing jobs for the neighbors or getting gifts for their birthdays. Rael gave Jacob the money only once, although Jacob kept a running tally of what his dad "owed" him.

Several weeks into the allowance program, Jacob convinced his dad to take him shopping. This was the only time Rael gave him the money. At a pet store, they bought a gerbil and all of the accessories, including an array of plastic housing compartments that were connected by tubes. When Jacob played with the gerbil, he was supposed to do it behind closed doors because our three cats also wanted to play with a gerbil. At one point, the cage door was left open, or the cats got in and opened it, but either way the gerbil escaped, and we could not find it – until the rodent

Children will not remember you for the material things you provided but for the feeling that you cherished them.
   ~ Richard Evans.

turned up dead. I found him, and when I showed Jacob that his pet had died, he refused to look at the body. He continued staring at the TV, his primary method of filling the majority of his waking hours before and after school and all weekend.

I took the dead gerbil downstairs and told Rael, who asked if Jacob had seen it. I said he had avoided looking at it. Rael dropped the gerbil in the kitchen trash. That made me think about how Rael and Jacob had acted when my dad died, and I wondered what had transpired when Jill passed away. Had Jacob been my child, I would have insisted he see a counselor after his mother's death, but Rael reasoned that he and Jacob had talked and shed their tears, and they were through with that. When the subject came up, Rael told me about bringing the crowd to tears and laughter at Jill's funeral. Mr. Grandstand. He never missed an opportunity to step into the limelight. While hardly the epitome of compassion, with his college degree in psychology, Rael certainly perfected the art of psychological manipulation and maneuvering.

Throughout the summer, I attempted to write, but between swimming lessons and everything else involved in supervising a seven-year-old, I didn't get much done. One afternoon when I was hiding out in my room in front of my computer, Jacob asked if I would type some of the things he had written. I'm a sucker for that kind of request, so I did, and we printed it out. He was thrilled to see his words in print. Along with what little writing I got done, every seven weeks I continued doing my workshops on affirmations, which I had started back in January. We held these at the condo, which was empty except for a couple of beds and a few pieces of Rael's furniture that we had stored there when we brought mine over to use instead.

Bolstered by Rael's support following the camping meltdown and burned out with babysitting nonstop, midway through the summer I hired a teenager to take care of Jacob on Fridays, which became my day to play. She watched TV downstairs while Jacob did the same upstairs. He never got out of the house. And he did not have any friends, except one boy four years older than him. Several times I expressed my apprehension to Rael about Jacob not having friends his age, but Rael either dismissed my

They say such nice things about people at their funerals that it makes me sad that I'm going to miss mine by just a few days.
~ Garrison Keillor

concern or pointed out that my best friend was thirteen years younger than me. My reply that the difference at my age had less significance fell on deaf ears.

My commitment to Rael and Jacob left me little time for my friends and family. My children required little of me, but I still wanted to spend time with them and with my friends. I felt limited, so I ended up giving in to Rael's urgings and shortchanging my other relationships. Before I met Rael, I talked to Mother every evening while we walked in our respective neighborhoods, each of us communicating via our cell phones. Now, I talked to her weekly, and even then it was not an in-depth conversation like the ones we had before. It did not feel right to put my needs and wants above those of Rael's and Jacob's.

When I wrestled with my relationship in Dr. Humor's office, he agreed that Rael needed me. He said I was Rael's Big Oil, the place where Rael had worked for twenty-five years, the stable, consistent force that he returned to between bouncing from one obsession to the next. Because I wanted to believe that Rael loved me and was devoted to me, I interpreted Dr. Humor's comment as encouragement and support, not the warning that I can now see he meant. We discussed a future scenario of me escaping the Texas heat by taking Jacob off to the Northwest while Rael stayed in Houston. My appeal was not only as a reliable entity for Rael to return to when he tired of his latest frenzy, but as a caretaker for Jacob. I did not admit it to Dr. Humor, but I assured myself that I never had to worry about losing Rael since I believed no one else would accept his sexual history. Also, I doubted he would risk losing me to pursue someone else. Where else was he going to find a Stepford wife like me?

We are so accustomed to disguise ourselves to others that in the end we become disguised to ourselves.
~ François Duc de La Rochefoucauld

Phase two of the remodeling job included the kitchen and putting down tile throughout the bottom floor. This took most of the summer. Rael hired the same guys who had raised the floor to do the tile, but when it came to tile work, they were inexperienced and it turned out badly. In several places the tile was not level – to the point of stubbing an unsuspecting toe. I had scheduled an appointment for the tile company to come back, but Houston evacuated for hurricane Ike that day, and the contractor never found time to return.

We painted the woodwork with white enamel and the living room mint green. On the wall where Rael had installed the new TV above the fireplace, I did a faux finish that Rael proudly showed to others. When he had the trees trimmed in the front yard, I saved three long branches to use for curtain rods on which I draped a purple gauze fabric. Rael teased me about my unorthodox decorating, but I also think he secretly liked my originality.

My brother's tumor grew rapidly, and by the time I traveled to Birmingham the first week in August, he was bedridden. Mother and Allison had begun a bedside vigil. Earlier on the day I arrived, the doctor had put in a shunt to drain the tumor. Morgan never regained consciousness after that. They moved him home that weekend. When the healthcare workers asked for a medical history, Allison said he had never been sick. I returned to Houston while Mother stayed there to help Allison. They took turns sitting with Morgan. He lived until the end of August. A group from their church offered love and support throughout the ordeal. I kept contact via phone, each day hearing the details of his steady decline.

Toward the end of Morgan's illness, Rael and I stood in the kitchen as I told him that Morgan's body had begun shutting down. I will never forget his gleeful expression and his sing-song voice as he said, "Bye-bye, Morgan." My face stung as if he had slapped me, and again I said nothing, this time as much out of shock as habit. He did not offer to accompany me to the funeral, nor did he mention sending flowers or donating to the charity the family suggested. Instead of honoring my true feelings by questioning why Rael could not show me love and compassion during this sad event, I once more justified his actions by telling myself this was how he dealt with death, especially the death of someone he did not know. Nowhere in that reasoning was me taking care of me. Instead, I reverted to what I knew best – how my mother had reacted when my father did something harmful; I stuffed down my emotions and plodded forward, numb to my feelings.

A psychological script is a person's ongoing program for his life drama which dictates where he is going with his life and how he is going to get there. It is a drama he compulsively acts out, though his awareness of it may be vague.

~Muriel James & Dorothy Jongeward

 **Family Reflections**

I was sixteen and seeing a therapist, which in 1968 in Lubbock, Texas, was pretty darn progressive. My shrink was a graduate student at Texas Tech University, and our sessions were part of her training, so it cost nothing while satisfying a growing need I felt to make sense of my world. During one of our conversations, Valarie asked me what emotions I felt concerning the topic we were discussing. I honestly had no idea what she meant. She offered suggestions like sadness or anger. Still I scanned my brain for a viable answer. My family did not talk about our emotions. We didn't communicate that much to begin with, and if we were going to carry on a family discussion, feelings wouldn't make the list of possible topics.

Once, in my twenties, my father and I were riding the hospital elevator down after visiting my grandfather, who was dying of cancer. When I started weeping, my father told me to suck it up. In hindsight, I can reason that he did not want to deal with his own emotions, so it was easier to forbid me to set in motion what might eventually prompt him to cry as well. I'm sure he was terrified of what might happen if he gave himself permission to cry, but that hardly justifies the way he treated us kids.

When my brother-in-law died in his early thirties, after a year of fighting throat cancer, he left Ruth a widow at twenty-nine, with a ten- and a twelve-year-old to rear on her own. She fell into a deep depression. Six weeks into her mourning, she accompanied Mother and Dad to the airport to meet my plane. When we got back to my parents' home, Ruth retreated to the bedroom. A few minutes later, my father told her to "suck it up," get off that bed, and come to lunch. You may doubt his ability to be so callous, but what troubles me more is how we as a family reacted. We silently passed the black-eyed peas while the TV blared in the background.

> *Having a family is like having a bowling alley installed in your head.*
> *~ Martin Mull*

Since we were all so well trained by then, none of us seemed to have the foggiest notion of defying Dad and doing what seems only natural and humane – reaching out to Ruth.

Rael reacted differently; he ignored the situation or used inappropriate humor, but his behavior did not vary that much from Dad's. Neither one of them was in touch with their feelings, nor did they reach out to the people they supposedly loved. Identifying my emotions during every phase of this story has proven to be one of the most challenging aspects of writing it. This deep excavating has also given me the greatest gifts – for where I thought I felt nothing, I have found a sensitive and caring woman.

From the earliest age most of us had our feelings—of curiosity, excitement, joy, fear, sadness, and, especially, self-protection anger— shamed. In order to defend against the painful feelings of shame, we learned to numb our feelings. ~John Bradshaw

Nuggets of Gold

Putting up with disrespectful treatment because I did not want to appear "too demanding" or "too needy" is the ultimate disrespect for myself. When I failed to show up for myself – when I got sick and Rael was not there for me, when my father died and Rael was not there for me, and when my brother died and Rael was not there for me – not only did I give him the clear message that it was okay to treat me that way, but I also reinforced my belief that I did not need respect nor was I worthy of it. Although Rael lacked the wherewithal to give me what I needed, I owed it to myself to recognize the need and respond appropriately.

Our purpose is found each moment as we make choices to be who we really are.
~Carol Adrienne,
author of The Purpose
of Your Life

I am at fault for not speaking up for myself. This goes hand in hand with self-care. It is another form of self-nurturing. Slinking off in the corner to pout only makes the situation worse. I end up feeling sorry for myself and everyone else is clueless since I have not said anything. I must be brave enough to speak my truth, listen to the words that come out of my own mouth, and take appropriate action – no matter what that involves, which in this case would have meant calling it quits. I give myself permission to speak, knowing that what comes out is not always as articulate or clear as I would like, but if it comes from my heart, it will be the truth and that is the only requirement.

I should take my own needs seriously. It is too easy to discount my needs as unimportant, insignificant, or not pressing. By doing that, I disrespect myself. The lowest times of life are the hardest times to see our own needs, but they are the most crucial for learning to practice self-care. Of course, all of this stems from growing up in a household where emotional needs went unrecognized. Taking care of me is my responsibility, and it is not fair to expect others to do it for me. If I show the people around me how to practice self-care, they may try it on themselves, and hopefully they will treat me with the same compassion I have offered myself. If I don't take my needs seriously, who else will? Others may offer sympathy and compassion, but in the end, I am the one who has to live with me, and if I am not there for myself, I have lost everything.

Self-esteem is the ability to value one's self and to treat oneself with dignity, love, and reality.   ~Virginia Satir

After

Before

Chapter Seven
Fall – Living in Sin

I do not know how to distinguish between our waking life and a dream. Are we not always living the life that we imagine we are?   ~ Henry David Thoreau

September we attacked the master bathroom. Considering the whole remodeling job, this aspect of it offered the greatest challenge. Many drawings and much discussion of options and possibilities preceded the actual work. We officially started the weekend we rented a steamer and took off the vinyl-coated wallpaper. By Sunday night, we were both so tired we could hardly carry on a coherent conversation.

While in New Zealand, I had admired a home that had an open shower (no door and only the existing walls enclosed it), so we incorporated that into the plan. The floor tile that we put down in the rest of the house was too slick to use in the bathroom, so we began a search for tile with a flat finish that would coordinate with the tile on the bedroom floor.

Rael and I were driving all over Houston on one of our tile quests when I saw storage buildings and remarked, "It's stupid that people have so much stuff that they have to rent a storage building to store what won't fit in their house."

Rael immediately shot back, "Says the woman who stores her extras in an empty condo."

His remark prompted me to consider the possibility of selling my beloved refuge. I had lived in it since my divorce five years earlier, and it symbolized my freedom. But he was right. Why was I hanging on to it? I had accepted his proposal of marriage, and we were discussing wedding dates, so allowing it to sit empty was a waste. I decided to sell it.

> *A home is not a mere transient shelter: its essence lies in the personalities of the people who live in it.*
> *~ H. L. Mencken*

Late August I called a friend in real estate to list the condo, and we scheduled a date to get together and do the paperwork. The day I was supposed to sign the papers, Hurricane Ike came barreling toward Houston. Rael convinced me to travel with him and Jacob to Ft. Worth, where we rented a hotel room and enjoyed a fun weekend, visiting the zoo, touring the city, and eating out. The storm did hit Houston, and rather than return to a lack of electricity, which meant no air-conditioning, we elected to stay a few extra days.

We were driving home and gawking at the incredible destruction when my friend Candy called and said their house had been badly damaged by the storm. She asked if her family could use the condo while they repaired their house. I agreed without hesitation; it was a good excuse to not sell my condo, which I was only doing to please Rael. Cleaning the numerous branches from the yard and repairing our fences temporarily side-tracked us from working on the bathroom. When we returned to it, Rael began reworking the piping for the tub and the shower while I began constructing a 5' x 4' glass panel to fill the window opening.

The design was of a dozen beveled roses climbing up a wall. It had been years since I worked with glass. Initially I doubted my ability to execute such an elaborate and large design, but I had told Rael I could do it, and I did not want to disappoint him. As I scored, broke, and sanded the individual pieces of glass, I found my old rhythm, and I loved it. Part of my pleasure came from creating something memorable for my new home. This part of it only I could do. My unique contribution made Rael's house feel like my home.

In October, I invited my kids over, and we celebrated Rudd, my older son's, twenty-ninth birthday. For the first time, I cooked meat in the house – a big skillet of chicken fajita. The meal was a tremendous success with all involved, except Jacob and Rael, who complained that Jacob was not used to the strong odor of meat cooking. Silently, of course, I took exception to his comment since we frequented restaurants that served meat.

The last significant challenge of the bathroom was maneuvering the claw-foot tub past the door frame, which took considerable juggling, manipulation, and temporarily taking off the cast-iron feet. We had batted back and forth the placement of the tub until Rael hit on what we ultimately agreed upon – setting it in the middle of the floor at an angle.

Each weekend during the bathroom remodel, we celebrated making it through two days of backbreaking work by going out to eat Sunday evening. When we ended up with the same waitress several times in a row, we began sharing our trials and tribulations. During one conversation, she referred to us as a married couple, and I corrected her. Rael chimed in that we were living in sin. Jacob sat there not saying a word.

My kids came over for Drew, my second son's, birthday the week of Thanksgiving. Again, I cooked a large meal, but in direct response to Rael's comment about meat odor, this time I used tofu to make the lasagna. After the meal, we set up the tripod and took group pictures with some of us in the claw-foot tub and some of us standing behind it.

As the weeks passed, it was harder and harder for me to keep my regular Friday night date with my friend Lilly. Either Rael had planned something like a camping trip, or he wanted us to participate in a Democratic group activity. I resented his intrusions on my friendship, but rather than confront him about it, I complained to Lilly. Truthfully, I wanted to keep everyone else happy, but I rarely considered what I wanted.

One weekend that fall, I babysat my granddaughter, Lace, who was a couple of months old. Although I had managed to shove aside the fact that Rael had admitted to previous pedophile behavior, that weekend I thought of nothing else. I watched him like a hawk. The night we kept Lace it occurred to me that with time I would see less and less of my kids because I could not risk allowing my grandchild or future grandchildren to

> *There is nothing like a dream to create the future.   ~ Victor Hugo*

spend time alone with Rael. I would never forgive myself if they suffered what Rael's stepdaughter had endured. Looking back, I see that some part of me knew I was choosing Rael over my own children, but I felt powerless to do otherwise. Even as I assumed this addictive role, I could not see how self-destructive my relationship with Rael had become. Nor did I want to face what it was doing to my relationships with my children and my friends.

> *Each of us in this culture, this twisted, inchoate culture, has to choose between battles. One battle is against the cultural ideal, and the other is against ourselves.*
>
> *~Sallie Tisdale*

My friend Tonya from Colorado called in November. She wanted to know if I would like to travel with her to South Africa. The idea of exploring South Africa had never occurred to me, but I love to travel, so I am usually game to try anything; the more exotic and out of the ordinary, the better. Even though I agreed to go, I also knew I would need to work the date for our trip around getting married, going on a honeymoon, and being home in the summer to take care of Jacob. As my college semester ended three weeks before the public school year, I decided that that block of time would be ideal for traveling to South Africa. When I told Rael my plan, he replied that he thought we would go on our honeymoon then. After juggling the dates, he and I decided to schedule the wedding the weekend before Spring Break, which gave us enough time to go on a seven-day cruise around the Hawaiian Islands, a trip I had long dreamed of taking.

Along with deciding when we would get married, we discussed whether or not I would change my last name to his. I did not want to since I had used Grissom for thirty-seven years. Rael argued that it was my ex-husband's name. He said that if Grissom was my maiden name, he could understand me keeping it, so after much discussion, I did what I typically did – I conceded to his wishes. While it would be a lot of paperwork and aggravation initially, long-term it added to the proof of our union.

For Christmas that year, I gave Rael a video camera, replacing the one he had lost while digging my snowmobile out of the snow back in January. It had been a year full of losses. The new year offered the promise of new beginnings, like our pending marriage.

Family Reflections

I spent a sizeable portion of my free time during my elementary school years constructing the perfect playhouse, using stray boards and bricks I found around the farm. First, I staked out a space next to one of the several barns, so the designated building made up one wall of my new home. After assessing my materials, which consisted of anything not nailed down, I drew up plans. Then I set to work, often pushing myself so hard I found it necessary to go inside and lie on the couch until my stomach quit hurting. Once I had completed my project, I let it stand for a few days before I tore it down and started over somewhere else. Rarely did I actually play in those playhouses. Occasionally, my father would tire of the constant eyesore and tell me to "get rid of that mess." When he did that, I elevated my construction obsession to tree houses – until I thought enough time had passed, and Dad might not notice me building another playhouse.

My playhouses were not just an at-home project. I also worked furiously on them when we drove fifty miles to my maternal grandparents' every other Sunday. We stayed the whole day, which gave me lots of building time. Lacking anything else to do on the remote, sandy farm, my cousins and siblings also got involved in the playhouse projects at our grandparents' house. Between visits, Granddad left our playhouses intact. Granddad's farm had one particular tree that worked well for tree houses. As a team, we once constructed a three-story tree house. This took several trips and the engineering skills of several different families. As an adult, I look back and think with pride, *I was just a kid, but I still did that*.

There is no doubt in my mind that my original need to construct playhouses came from my general unhappiness with my family. If I could not have what I wanted within the confines of the house in which I lived,

> *The man who has a house everywhere has a home nowhere.*
> *~ Marcus Aurelius*

perhaps I could find it in a house I built for myself. Of course, as a child I was never able to construct a loving home for myself, so I built one playhouse after another until I thought I had grown too old for such things. Funny how I believed that I had outgrown my childhood compulsion and methodology for "fixing" my life.

I have been very happy with my homes, but homes really are no more than the people who live in them.   *~ Nancy Reagan*

Nuggets of Gold

Never again will I put endless hours of work into a house unless I have my name on the title. I truly enjoyed the creative process of remodeling Rael's house, and I have to admit my relationship with Rael was at its all-time best while we worked together on the house remodeling, particularly the bathroom. One of my greatest investments in the relationship was in the effort and talent I put into the bathroom, particularly the window. If I could go back and undo it, I would make it a legal relationship before I put large amounts of time and/or energy in a home we live in together.

> *When you make a commitment to a relationship, you invest your attention and energy in it more profoundly because you now experience ownership of that relationship.*
> *~ Barbara De Angelis*

Never again will I change my name because it is what someone else wants me to do. From a purely feminist point of view, I would love to do away with the whole practice of women changing their last name when they marry. Nine times out of ten, women are the ones who raise kids in a single-parent household, and they are the ones who will more than likely end up marrying again and once more be faced with whether or not they should change their last name. I know it would get complicated, and in the '60s and '70s we tried the idea of hyphenating maiden names with spouses' names, but that didn't resolve the issue. I daresay few men have been faced with the dilemma of giving up their last name when they elect to get married.

Never again will I allow someone to dictate what I can or cannot cook in my own home. This is a two-way street – like any other aspect of a relationship. I should have been clearer about my rights as a member of the household, to cook what I think is appropriate for my friends and family. On the other hand, Rael should have encouraged me to do that, but neither one of us was psychologically evolved to that point. Ideally, I will use this experience as a reminder to check in with myself about what is prompting me to do whatever I am doing, making sure I am not operating out of fear or intimidation created by the situation.

Chapter Eight
Spring – Get Ready, Get Set, Get Married

Love is temporary insanity curable by marriage.   ~ Ambrose Bierce

After returning home from another trip to Ogden, Utah, we began preparing for the wedding. Rael suggested we have it at home because this was where Jacob was born – in the master bedroom with a midwife in attendance. Where Jacob's mother had him, and how that figured into my wedding to Rael escaped me, but I did not dare utter that aloud. Rael wanted Jacob to feel comfortable and at ease at the wedding, which I had to admit made sense. Plus, the price was right, and it was available, so we decided to have it at our house. Once we settled on the idea, I rationalized that it seemed right to stage it at a location we had worked so hard to transform into something we both loved.

We decided to hold the ceremony in the backyard, using my new stained glass panel in the bathroom window as a backdrop. Rael designed and built an arbor that framed it. We then planted mandevilla vines at either end and filled the flower beds with a variety of tropical flowers and bushes. I repotted all of my plants, outlined the patio with hanging baskets, and strung white Christmas lights on the grapevines and on the bushes that surrounded the patio.

We created our own wedding invitations and debated how many invitations to send out. My guest list was much longer than Rael's. Looking over his names and mine, I realized he had few friends – at least the kind he deemed worthy of inviting to the wedding.

Since right after my divorce, I had worn a wedding ring on my right hand. It reminded me of my commitment to myself. It was a rose-gold ring I had inherited from my uncle, who had bought it fifty years ago with the intention of proposing to the woman he was dating, but they broke up before he asked her. The fact that it had never been used as a wedding band and once belonged to someone I loved made it seem like the perfect ring to go with the engagement ring Rael had given me. We must have discussed this early on for he had my engagement ring made out of rose-gold as well. Ideally, using my wedding ring along with the engagement ring Rael had given me symbolized continuing to take care of myself in the marriage.

My vision of Rael's ring included three strands of rose-gold braided together, signifying the union of the three of us – Rael, Jacob, and me. Rael took the lead on having the ring made up since he wanted to use a jeweler close to where he worked. Since I wasn't there to describe it to the jeweler, I sent a model of what I had in mind – three cords braided together. I drove over to see the waxed ring before they cast it and was disappointed – the jeweler had twisted three strands of gold, rather than braid them. The final outcome, which I did not get to see before the casting, was braided, but it also turned out quite bulky and heavy. I never thought it was particularly attractive, but I didn't have to wear it, and Rael approved it. Its extra bulk added to its expense, but Rael paid for it, so. . .

The trouble with some women is that they get all excited about nothing – and then marry him.

~Cher

To further sanctify our union, we decided to design a pendant for Jacob. After much discussion about intertwining circles, we finally settled on an infinity symbol weaving through a circle, thus joining the three of us in a unit that would last forever.

A few days before the service, I touched up the woodwork in the master bathroom because I hoped our guests would want to see the results of our hard work. Never mind that they would have to walk through the bedroom that still served as a studio/storage area/guest bedroom. My wedding day, I furiously worked the carpet shampooer as I moved up the stairs to the den. The caterer commented that I was not the typical bride. I had to admit I was not.

La Vern, my cousin and lifelong friend, who is a Unity minister, agreed to officiate the wedding. This would be my last marriage, and I wanted it to be particularly meaningful, so, of course, Rael and I wrote our own vows. I had a hard time pinning him down on the final wording. The day before the wedding, LaVern and I sat in the kitchen, trying to firm up the service. I asked Rael to sit with us and give his input, which he did reluctantly while expressing a need to wrap up last-minute details. After some discussion, he grabbed his keys and stood in the back doorway, ready to go pick up four-dozen folding chairs from the rental shop. His parting words were: "Three months from now no one will remember what we said."

The day of the wedding ceremony, I ceremoniously shaved my legs. Most brides don't consider that anything out of the ordinary. In fact, it is standard hygiene for most American women. Early in our relationship, Rael had asked me to not shave my legs. He said it was more natural, and he bragged that Jill, Jacob's mother, had not shaved her legs for two years in order to please him. Well, I certainly wasn't going to be outdone by someone I had never met.

Thirty minutes after the starting time printed on the invitations, I leaned over the claw-foot tub and peered through the beveled glass window. While music from the '60s and '70s played in the background, thanks to my son Drew, who had downloaded all my favorite music onto CDs, I watched the crowd gather and settle into the chairs. I wondered if they could see me from their perspective as well as I could see them from inside the bathroom. Rael walked in and said we needed to start. I was nervous, so once more he and I rehearsed the greeting that we intended to offer our guests as soon as we walked "on stage." I allowed him to lead me though the house to the back porch.

As we stepped in front of our guests, Jacob, who sat on the front

Love is a great beautifier.
~ Louisa May Alcott

row, announced, "It's about time." Everyone laughed.

My son Rudd operated the video camera behind the crowd during the ceremony.

Rael and I fumbled through the greeting, significantly shortening it from what we had originally planned. LaVern gave a brief introduction and an opening prayer. Then she gave the following homily:

> *Marriage is the triumph of imagination over intelligence.*
>
> *~Anonymous*

Homily

Before I start lecturing these two on the seriousness of marriage, I want to take a moment and share with all of you how deeply honored and joyful I feel to be the one conducting this ceremony. Many of you know that Pat is my cousin. Since we were born only six days apart – and, yes, she is the older one – we have been bonded almost since birth. We claim each other not only as best friends but also as spiritual "twin sisters." I have always thought of Pat as strong, confident, and assured – despite anything she has ever said to the contrary. Knowing that Rael sees those attributes in her also and desires to honor her as the wonderful individual that she is makes it easy for me to welcome Rael as my "honorary" brother-in-law.

Then she launched into the standard wedding spiel about the holy union, which is sacred and not to be entered into lightly, and only under the guidance of infinite wisdom and divine love. She went on to talk about the deep, implied trust of love. Furthermore, she said that by marrying we agreed to be a light and a tower of strength for each other. She charged us with believing in each other to the utmost. Also in keeping with my previous conviction, she reminded us that it is necessary to honor and respect your love of self.

During the wedding vows Rael and I read the pledges we had written to each other:

Pat's Pledge:

Rael, on our first real date, the first words out of your mouth were, "You look beautiful."

A month or two into our relationship, I had day surgery and you left soup, a card, and a flower at my back porch. That night I looked back in my journal and found a list that I wrote before I met you of more than twenty qualities I wanted in a man. You matched every one of them, except the desire to travel. Not long after that, you insisted on changing out the locks on my doors at the condo since I didn't have keys for all of them.

When you power-washed the driveway at your house, you wrote "I love Pat" on the street for the world to see. Then you followed me to New Zealand, traveling and at the same time demonstrating to me your incredible organizational skills since you showed up with a notebook of detailed maps for every location we planned to visit while you were there.

You gave me carte blanche to redecorate the bottom floor of the house, which opened the door to raising the sunken living room with seven yards of concrete, moving walls, lengthening walls, and putting up with gauze and timber rather than standard curtains and rods. You designed, executed, and survived the remodeling of the master bath, and in the process gave me something I have always dreamed of – a claw-foot bath tub.

You've taught me to enjoy camping. You made friends with my man-hating cat. You welcomed my children

> Getting married is a lot like getting into a tub of hot water. After you get used to it, it ain't so hot.
> ~ Minnie Pearl

into your life, and you've given me the opportunity to parent a young child again. While we share so much, you have also given me freedom to follow my own interests and dreams like writing and traveling with or without you.

Lastly, and most of all, I love you for allowing me to be part of your life, which means giving me the privilege of being around someone who is almost always positive and happy, someone who dares to examine the norm, someone who stands up for the rights of others, and generously gives of himself in every aspect of his life.

Rael McRael, for these reasons and many, many more, I pledge my love to you from now and forever more.

The chief reason why marriage is rarely a success is that it is contracted while the partners are insane.
~Joseph Collins

Several of these comments elicited laughter from the audience, particularly the one about Rael not liking to travel and then following me to New Zealand. And, in retrospect, I have to admit my statement about giving me the "opportunity to parent a young child" did not come from my heart, but from a desire to say what I thought he wanted me to say.

Rael's Pledge:

Patricia, since you have come into my life I have begun to realize my most valuable possession is my time. More important than everything I own, of a of my accomplishments, and even my job is the time I get to spend with those I love, and especially with you and with Jacob. And I want to make a commitment to share with you this most valuable possession. I will give my time to you enjoying activities and experiencing adversity, listening to your dreams and your frustrations, sharing your joy and your sorrows, working projects as well as just doing the chores, traveling to faraway places or just sitting quietly.

I have also come to appreciate you for how much we are alike and for how much we are different. You have shared yourself openly and you have accepted me for my strengths and my many weaknesses, past and present. I feel like I have gotten to know you so well, yet I realize there is so much more you will share if only I listen with not only my ears, but also my heart and my soul. It seems like you have given up so much to be with me while I have done nothing but receive. I cherish our future together and give thanks to the blessing of having you as my partner in life. Pat, I love you.

> *Let there be spaces in your togetherness.*
> *~ Kahlil Gibran*

While rereading Rael's pledge to me, I realize that he pledged me nothing. It is a mini essay on what he is getting out of the relationship, but he says nothing about what he is willing to bring to the table.

Ashley, my daughter, read my reading selection – without having a chance to practice. Plus, she came to the wedding between two sixteen-hour evening shifts. AND she had a baby in arms (Lace) who was ready to breastfeed at the same time as Ashley's part in the ceremony. Therefore, I held a crying baby while her mother beautifully read the poem entitled "On Friendship" from *The Prophet* by Kahlil Gibran. Because Rael did not ask anyone or maybe he could not find a willing friend, he read his own reading. I do not remember the name of it, although I do recall it had something to do with death, which puzzled me. Of course, I did not question or challenge him on the issue.

When we exchanged rings, LaVern stated that the ring I wore

on my right hand symbolized a commitment I had made to take care of myself or, in a sense, a marriage to myself. She went on to say the ring on my left hand symbolized a commitment Rael and I made to become husband and wife and to take care of each other.   And I wanted to combine these two commitments by symbolically joining these two rings. When I placed Rael's ring on his finger, LaVern explained that the braided strands of gold symbolized the entwining of our family – Rael, Jacob, and me.

LaVern asked Jacob to step forward, so we could fasten the pendant around his neck. While we did this, she told our guests that the circle interlaced in the infinity symbol represented the never-ending circle of love shared by – again, Jacob, Rael, and me.   To further symbolize our commitment to each other and to our newly bonded family, we lit a unity candle. The wind sabotaged our efforts to keep all three wicks of the pillar candle lit, but the significance was there nonetheless.

Next, LaVern asked Rael and me to turn and face the people who had come to honor and celebrate our union. She asked them to pledge to encourage us and love us, to give us their guidance when asked, to support us in being steadfast in the promises that we had made. Once they collectively answered, "We Do," she pronounced us husband and wife. We kissed, and she presented us as Pat and Rael McRael.

LaVern closed the service by reading the Apache Wedding Blessing. She then concluded the ceremony by asking our guests to join Rael and me in a joyous celebration inside. Rael and I walked down the aisle and greeted the guests. Soon after we started visiting with everyone, Jill's sister Sarah, who had cried throughout the ceremony, approached me and apologized for ruining my wedding day. I assured her she had not. She and her husband Wade left right after that.

After the ceremony, while the photographer took group shots, I noticed she turned her camera at an angle. My camera has an orientation feature so pictures automatically appear upright. I thought

When you make the sacrifice in marriage, you're sacrificing not to each other but to unity in a relationship.
~ Joseph Campbell

she must be reading the light meter and assumed the pictures would surely turn out straight. During one of the group shots, Rael asked the photographer why she held her camera like that. A flicker of confusion passed over her face before she set up the next group and took the picture – again cocking her camera at a sharp angle. Apparently this is an extremely 'in' technique – or it was a couple of years ago – so my wedding pictures are trendy or cockeyed, depending on your point of view. When I looked back at the pictures and the video, I noticed that Rael's sleeves hung past his fingertips and I wondered why he hadn't seen to having his jacket altered during all his wedding preparations.

The caterer prepared a beautiful spread of food – all of it vegetarian. We handed around champagne in glasses imprinted with the word "Obama," as well as his likeness. After the toast, we urged our guests to take the glasses lest they find them in their Christmas stockings.

Many terrific friends showed up to wish us well. Since we both had put so much effort into the preparations for the big day, we went to bed exhausted – and relieved to have that part behind us. We already lived together, so the marriage changed little in our lives. It just made everything official. And it gave me a new name, which I immediately began changing on my bank account, credit cards, driver's license, at work, and on my social security card.

Honeymoon

The following weekend we left on a seven-day Hawaiian cruise around the islands. We flew into Honolulu, and the first night there, we stayed in a hotel and walked along Waikiki Beach. The next day, we took a long hike along the shore to Diamond Head. Outside the hotel, we waited for our taxi and saw a limousine parked out front, which we were informed was ours. We posed for each other and took pictures

It's easy to enjoy each other while on a vacation to Maui. The key is to find someone you can have fun with during the six-hour flight over there.

~ Tom Arnold

throughout the short ride to the ship.

Hawaiian dancers entertained us while we stood in line to get on the cruise ship. We had a balcony cabin, something I had never experienced before, but it was compact, like any other room on the ship. Part of what you pay for with this luxury is the privilege of announcing to the rest of the table at dinner that you are staying in a balcony cabin. We never sat with anyone else, so we had no one to brag to. One night we were seated at a small table next to another small table. Rael seemed to think the couple sitting at it was staring at us with disdain. He asked in a half joking/half challenging way what they were looking at. The woman said she thought my necklace was attractive, and that seemed to appease Rael, although he did comment later that they were "really snooty." For the evening meals, I ordered fish without qualms since I no longer needed to be different than who I was to catch this man. I had him, and I quickly settled into a newfound level of security; I was in this marriage for the long haul and Rael needed me, not so much for himself, but he certainly needed a mother for Jacob.

The last night on the ship, we feasted our eyes on the Na Pali Coast State Park located on the north shore of Kauai. From the ship's deck, we saw the vertical undulating waves of land that make up this impressive and inaccessible coastline. Our last day in Hawaii, we got off the ship at Oahu, where we had started seven days earlier. Renting a car, we drove to the north side of the island and snorkeled. I was disappointed we did not go to Pearl Harbor, but Rael said he didn't want to glorify war. We probably would have gone if I had insisted, but as usual I let him take the lead, and we ended up going to a stupid movie instead.

Mother had stayed with Jacob in our absence, and when we got home, we showed him all the loot we had bought, including a conch shell that we had watched a man cut to make it "blow-able." I could get more noise out of it than Rael, but he wanted to buy it, so we considered it his souvenir. I had bought plenty of necklaces and earrings to remind me of our trip.

Life on board a pleasure steamer violates every moral and physical condition of healthy life except fresh air. It is a guzzling, lounging, gambling, dog's life. The only alternative to excitement is irritability.
~ George Bernard Shaw

Finishing the Spring Semester as Mrs. McRael

On April 6, Jacob had his ninth birthday, which prompted us to hold a small party for him. I made a list of who gave him what, and, being the diligent mom, I insisted that he write thank-you notes to everyone who had given him a gift. He opposed the idea, and Rael fanned the flames of his resistance by telling Jacob that he had never written a thank-you note in his life. Rael's comment made me think of my recent suggestion that he help me write thank-you notes for our wedding gifts, and his refusal, saying that the invitations had said "no gifts," so people shouldn't expect a thank-you note. After some coercion, Jacob wrote the notes. He did a fantastic job, adding pictures and creating his own unique wording for each one.

Heading into summer, I took the attitude that since I was now officially part of this family, I would start asserting myself, and I signed Jacob up for Summer Y-camp at the YMCA two days a week. I chose the days when they had field trips. Neither Jacob nor Rael was impressed. In fact, Jacob hated the idea, and Rael bent over backwards to keep from upsetting or challenging Jacob. His policy on parenting was "keep the kid happy." With memories of the previous summer and feeling overwhelmed with responsibility, I held firm. Once I got back from South Africa, I planned to be the mother that Jacob desperately needed, which included limiting the amount of television he watched and making sure he had plenty of opportunities to play with children his own age. Taking him to the Y twice a week seemed to cover both of those objectives. Besides, I wanted time to write, shop – anything but stay home with a child who refused to go anywhere unless it had to do with electronic entertainment.

In spite of what I said in my pledge to Rael at our wedding, I already dreaded full-time motherhood and working my schedule around Jacob – like I had the summer before – but I no longer had the option of walking away. I had taken the giant step. We were married, and I had committed to Jacob as well as to Rael. Jacob needed a mom, someone who would act on his behalf. And I was the woman who would do it – as soon as I got back from South Africa.

> Anna Harrison: "You never asked me if I wanted a new mother. You never even asked me if I liked her!"
> STEPMOM, 1989.

 **Family Reflections**

My senior year of high school, Wayne, my first real boyfriend, gave me an engagement ring for Christmas. He did not ask me to marry him – just handed me the small box. At that time, I had no concept of refusing a gift like that – sort of like I didn't think I could turn down Rael's ring nearly forty years later. If a guy wanted to marry me, why wouldn't I say yes? He must love me or else he wouldn't propose marriage. Besides, graduation loomed on the horizon, and I had no other prospects for a husband – what most girls of that era desired at that point in their lives.

I tenaciously pursued my relationship with Wayne in spite of my dad's efforts to dissuade me. While Dad didn't take an interest in us kids, he also didn't like the fact that I had a boyfriend who consumed my attention. To discredit him, Dad made remarks about his weight. He also threatened to read the letters Wayne mailed me weekly since he lived thirty miles away, and it was long-distance to talk on the phone. The biggest loss for Dad was losing control of me and what I did. In hindsight, I see that Wayne held limited potential as a provider. He barely passed his high school classes. Number one, he lacked intelligence, and number two, he worked full-time as a roustabout the second half of that spring semester. His dad worked the oil fields, so Wayne took a job there when it opened up, perhaps realizing it was the best he could do career-wise. When Wayne failed to show up to take me to my senior prom because he didn't get home from work in time, my dad offered to take me. In retrospect, I have to give my dad credit for offering, although I did decline. Who shows up at their senior prom with their dad?

Wayne broke up with me graduation night. I had just gotten back from our senior trip, where I had forgone the joy of carousing at midnight with the gang because of my engagement. Facing a fate of spinsterhood at nineteen, I fell into a depression. It quickly dissipated when I started

Most of our assumptions have outlived their uselessness.
~ Marshall McLuhan

dating a number of guys and realized I had more going for me than I thought. Three months later, Wayne showed up, riding a motorcycle. I went on one date and burned my leg on the tailpipe. Riding the bike thrilled me, but I soon realized that reuniting could be disastrous, and I nixed his next request to get together. His mother called me on the switchboard where I worked as a telephone operator while I attended college, and told me I had wrecked Wayne's life.

Years later, I learned that he had spent time in prison for sexually molesting his stepdaughters.

Nuggets of Gold

A life spent making mistakes is not only more honorable but more useful than a life spent doing nothing.
~ George Bernard Shaw

Getting clear about what I want in a wedding or any other ceremony is much more important than following the book. Honestly, I would not change anything about my wedding, except make sure the photographer and I were on the same page as to the orientation of the pictures. The wedding reflected what I wanted and what Rael and I had agreed upon. The location had meaning for both of us; the ceremony was unique, meaningful, and a composite of Rael, LaVern, and my ideas. Loved ones attended. The food turned out great. Even the weather cooperated.

Honeymoons are a great way to start a marriage. Whether or not the marriage lasts, the honeymoon should offer some fond memories, and mine does. I did enjoy the trip and the time we had together. I'm glad we did something that was special to both of us. Like the wedding itself, I will always have these memories as a pleasant reminder of the time we had together.

Giraffe

Elephant

Kiwi Fruit

Jackass Penguins, Mother and Chick

Chapter Nine
Week 1: May 15 – 21:
South Africa, Here I Come

I'll be back."

~THE TERMINATOR, 1984.

My plane departed Houston at 6:25 PM. On the way to the airport, Jacob quizzed me from the backseat of Rael's car. He loved to see if he could stump me. "What kind of car are we driving?" he asked. I drew a blank. For days after that I obsessed about how stupid Rael must think I am that I could not remember the name Prius. My head buzzed with all the details of leaving the country and my husband of two and a half months (nine weeks; with one of those spent in Hawaii on our honeymoon).

At Heathrow Airport in London, I wandered around until I found a couch in a busy hallway. I would board another plane in eleven hours, and I wanted to take advantage of the opportunity to lie down and stretch out. Paranoid it would disappear while I slept, I made an uncomfortable pillow out of my backpack. When food became more enticing than the fitful sleep I managed amidst the constant movement of people, I explored the shops and bought an egg salad sandwich because Rael would approve. In the same shop, I bought a postcard – Michelle Obama with the Queen – for Rael.

In Johannesburg, the airport looked like a sea of people.

Tonya and I looked for each other for thirty minutes. I was concerned because I had no way to call her international cell phone, but with relief, I finally heard her call out "Biker Babe," a name we had adopted for each other after inadvertently becoming part of a biker rally during a visit to Galveston. Before we flew to Cape Town, we found a café where I ordered rooibos tea, a popular herbal tea in South Africa. Tonya had spent the previous night at a bed-and-breakfast in Johannesburg, where the owner advised her to buy a money belt because theft was a real issue, so we found a shop in the airport that sold them.

During our flight to Cape Town, I conked out after drinking a glass of wine. As soon as we stepped into the airport lobby, we spotted a man holding a sign that read "Pat & Tonya." Our first host couple had hired Howard to pick us up and deliver us to their house. On the way, he pointed out what he called a township. In the States, we would call it a slum. They stretched for miles.

After meeting Rhoda and Samuel and their son Henry, I took a heavenly shower. They provided a wonderful supper of cheese, tuna, homemade bread, guacamole, and cape gooseberries on vanilla ice cream for dessert. Then I got on the Internet and e-mailed Rael.

> *Every year it takes less time to fly across the Atlantic and more time to drive to the office.*
>
> *~Anonymous*

To: Rael
From: Pat
Date: Sunday, May 17, 8:30 PM

Dear Rael,

     We made it to our first destination – Rhoda and Samuel, an awesome couple. He is taking off from teaching to work on a book about Jews in SA. He teaches history at Cape Town University. Their son, Henry, lives at home and is in medical school at the same university.

     I've had a shower, and in the last two days of mixed

up days and nights, I've gotten several naps along the way. I'm not numb from lack of sleep, but I am looking forward to stretching out in a real bed and hopefully getting a full night's sleep. It is 8:22 here, which is 1:22 p.m. for you. Miss you bunches and love you more than words can convey. Pat

P.S. Please call Mother if you get a chance and let her know that I got here okay.

P.S.S. If you want to call, use the Penny Talk # at the top of the list in the kitchen, posted on the inside of the door. When it asks for the number you want to dial ...

For my part, I travel not to go anywhere, but to go. I travel for travel's sake. The great affair is to move; to feel the needs and hitches of our life more nearly; to come down off this feather-bed of civilization, and find the globe granite underfoot and strewn with cutting flints.
~ Robert Louis Stevenson

We had some confusion about getting the rental car, which I thought would be delivered to the house. After calling and sorting it out, we headed out, with Tonya driving on the left-hand side of the road – most of the time. At our first stop, we were approached by a man wearing an orange vest who said he would guard our car. We declined the offer, thinking it was a racket, but we later learned from our hosts that the orange vest indicated he had invested in it and was authorized to stand guard. We visited a colony of jackass penguins that numbered two to three hundred in population. Their name must derive from the braying sound they make when courting – how charming. Then we drove to a point along the coast where the Indian and Atlantic Oceans come together. We ran out of sunlight on the way home and got lost twice.

During supper at a seafood restaurant, we enjoyed a long conversation, during which I confessed my guilt about being gone from home. Back at our hosts' home, Rhoda offered a cup of tea, but Rael called, and I ended up talking to him while the tea grew cold. Afterward, I apologized to her, and she said she understood. When

I checked my e-mail I found the note Rael had referred to in our conversation. True – I had not been gone long, but its brevity bothered me. I thought back to my trip to New Zealand and remembered the numerous lengthy e-mails, we exchanged. That was at the beginning of our relationship. Now that we were married, things were different. We had a new security with each other.

Life, as the most ancient of all metaphors insists, is a journey; and the travel book, in its deceptive simulation of the journey's fits and starts, rehearses life's own fragmentation. More even than the novel, it embraces the contingency of things.
~ Jonathan Raban

To: Pat
From: Rael
Date: Monday, May 18, 9:13 AM

Hello my love,
     The training on Saturday was productive. I spent most of Sunday trying to download Star Wars: Clone Wars for Jacob. Otherwise, I was totally lazy. This morning I picked tomatoes and bell and banana peppers from the garden. I had some for lunch today. Tonight we need to go to the store and clean up for the maid. How is Cape Town? I assume it to be a small city, but it should be very pretty, being on the coast. I'll call again soon.

Love, Rael

To: Rael
From: Pat
Date: Monday, May 18, 9:45 PM

Dearest Rael,
     Cape Town is large or at least the area is. The

guy who drove us to our host couple's home said that the city of Cape Town and the outlying areas have around 3 million population. So far we have only seen the area from the airport (northeast of the city) to the place where we are staying (central and a bit east, I think.) Tomorrow we will go west to Table Mountain, Robbin Island (close to the base of the mountain), and the botanical gardens (in that same area). Wednesday we will head for Wilderness.

Better head for bed. Big day planned for tomorrow, and I want to study the maps as I will probably be driving. Glad you are enjoying the tomatoes.

All my love,
Patty Ann

The use of traveling is to regulate imagination by reality, and instead of thinking how things may be, to see them as they are. ~ Samuel Johnson

The District 6 Museum housed in one of the few remaining homes in that area after the rest were demolished during the Apartheid era proved to be a less publicized but highly interesting attraction. A large canvas map covered much of the ground floor. On it, the onetime residents had marked where their houses once stood. I visited with a man who had written a book I bought about his family losing their home. The government was returning his land, but he would have to pay to rebuild the house.

The second evening in Cape Town, Tonya and I took Rhoda, Samuel, and Henry out for supper.   Right after we returned to their house, Rael called. He said he was talking to an old girlfriend who had contacted him through reunion.com. Apparently, she had decided to follow Rael's advice and make a list of what she wants in a man, just as I had done to get Rael.   Later that night, I lay in bed next to Tonya and told her about Rael talking to an old girlfriend. I asked her if she thought I had reason to worry. Tonya and I dismissed the idea. Rael and I were newly married – and in love.

The next day, my fifty-seventh birthday, Henry escorted us to the Khayelitska township community center. Then we took the scenic route to Wilderness, where we found our accommodations at the end of a winding road away from the city – a self-contained one-bedroom with a phenomenal view of the Indian Ocean. To celebrate my big day, Tonya took me to The Girls, a restaurant which turned out to be decidedly gay. Our conservative hosts, John and Anna, were surprised when we reported going to The Girls instead of the restaurant they suggested. After that, they seemed glad to hear we were married – to men.

While I had felt guilty about leaving Rael before I left Houston, my birthday was when I started missing him. He had been so thoughtful and sent me on my journey with an early birthday gift – a fully loaded iPod. I wanted to tell him about the community center in the township we had visited that day, where grandparents took care of the young ones after AIDS had killed off their parents. Images of the day danced in my head: Winnie, who had hugged me, a total stranger, as I got out of the car; the lady teaching another woman how to sew; the picket fence around two gardens; snaggletoothed smiles that lined the meeting room; the boy and then the man who said they would love to go back to America with me; the gift shop full of handmade items; and the shanties we saw as we drove away – none of them bigger than the living room in an American home. What we saw at the community center – the people's will to survive and their resourcefulness – speaks volumes about what has enabled South Africa to survive while enduring disease and political oppression.

The following day, we visited Wilderness National Park, where we took a two-mile walk through the woods, ending at a waterfall. We pulled ourselves across the river using a pontoon boat attached to a pulley system. That night we viewed an incredible sunset as we walked on the beach. I videotaped it while I said my affirmations. I wondered what Rael would think when he saw that part, if he would be impressed by the beauty of it or put off by how lame I sounded.

When I went to our hosts' house to use their Internet, John said Rael had called. I tried to call him back, but he did not answer. Then I found the following e-mail:

> *Show me a woman who doesn't feel guilty, and I'll show you a man.*
> *~Erica Jong*

To: Pat
From: Rael
Date: Thursday, May 21, 7:23 AM

Hello my South Africa love,
     Miss you and love you and wish I were next to you. It's been too long since we kissed.
     A friend from the vegetarian world who lives in Australia is in town, Dr. Fielder, and they're having a potluck for him tonight at 7:00 in Houston. I'm not sure if I can make it since I have to get the trailer ready. I say this because his longtime girlfriend is from South Africa, and he travels there often.
     Everything is going well here.

     Talk soon, love. Rael, your American Friend

Again, the briefness of his message concerned me. Plus, he did not mention my birthday in this message or in his previous one that had been e-mailed several days earlier. His closing also bothered me. I interpreted it as meaning I had relegated myself to the position of a friend rather than his wife since I had chosen to desert him while following my passion to travel.

Week 2: May 22 – 28

The important thing about travel in foreign lands is that it breaks the speech habits and makes you blab less, and breaks the habitual space-feeling because of different village plans and different landscapes. It is less important that there are different mores, for you counteract these with your own reaction-formations.
~ Paul Goodman

We took a daytrip to Outshoorn. On the way, we stopped at George, where we bought supplies, including an ice chest, torch (flashlight), and electric adapter. One of the highlights of the day was riding the ostrich at the Congo Ostrich Farm. That night I read an e-mail that sounded like the man I had married, the guy who loved me.

To: Pat
From: Rael
Date: Friday, May 22, 8:18 AM

Subject: I miss you.

Hello my love, I woke up this morning missing you badly. I rolled over and you weren't there, and I want you to be there. I wanted to talk to you. I wanted you to comfort me. I missed not talking to you yesterday. I didn't call because of what you said about the living arrangements, but I'm going to call today even if I don't get to talk to you just to make sure everything is alright. I love that you head off to Africa and experience travelling, but I miss you and that's alright. It just lets me know how much I love and need you.

We set up the trailer last night and got things ready for camping this weekend. Today is field day for Jacob at school. He rode off this morning in his bathing suit with suntan lotion all over and water-shoes on his feet. He is very excited. I love seeing him on his bike in the morning. It's so good he can do that.

I may go to Austin next weekend. I told you Dr. Fielder was in town, and I didn't go to the potluck, which I was feeling bad about. Well, last night Ricky Burke calls and tells me the LSVN is getting together next weekend in Austin to plan the chili cook-off and have fun. I tell him about Dr. Fielder being in town, and he tells me Fielder is going to be making a presentation Friday night at a vegetarian dinner and the LSVN is attending. Saturday afternoon everyone is heading to Barton Springs for a veggie picnic, going to 6th St Saturday night and having a planning meeting Sunday morning. I asked Richard, and he said it was alright for Jacob to stay there (Juanita will be in Germany) so it looks like I'll go hang out with the old crowd. Awesome!

I don't know when you'll get this e-mail, or if you can answer, but still I want to tell you how much I miss you and want to be with you when you get home.

Love, Rael

P.S. Maybe you need to go out of town to get good e-mails from me.

Life consists of what a person is thinking about all day.
~Ralph Waldo Emerson

This e-mail reassured me that my new husband had not lost interest in me after all. While I pursued my passion, he had chosen to do the same. Obviously this spoke well of our marriage and our maturity. He had not mentioned his old girlfriend since our phone conversation several days earlier, so I knew that had been an inconsequential reunion.

To: Rael
From: Pat
Date: Friday, May 22, 11:18 AM

Dearest Rael,

That was the best e-mail I have gotten from you since I don't know when. I miss you too. Today Tonya and I talked about the fact that it has been a week since we left the States. It seems longer than that. When I came down to use the Internet, John said you'd called. I asked what you said, and he said that he told you he didn't know where the hell I was. And then he laughed really big. His wife is sweet, taking care of us by fixing breakfast and giving us directions to get to this place and then that.

Today was a great day. Tonya and I rode ostrich. I have video footage to prove it. We went to the Cango Caves, which are quite large – probably comparable to Carlsbad Caverns. The second part that is accessible to the public is a crawl-through with a narrow opening and mud to contend with, so we opted to not do that. We had a leisurely drive back, stopping at a roadside stand where I bought a hand-carved ostrich egg – a pattern of the Milky Way (or that's what the artist called it). We can use it as a cover for a night-light or just set it on the bookshelf in the stand that I bought to put it on. We went to a market this evening in the town square, and I bought you some fig preserves. Then I went back to the restaurant where we went for my birthday, and I purchased a necklace I had spotted there. I am still getting used to converting USD to ZAR (rands). You have to divide by 8, which is not an easy calculation for me.

Besides the scenery and the touristy things to do and see, the aspect of Africa that strikes me most poignantly is the marked difference between the way whites and blacks live. In Cape Town we saw townships that went on for miles, where houses much smaller than a boxcar were stacked up against each other almost solid. As we have gotten away from the larger cities, we have seen less of that, but there is still a huge difference in the standard of living between the two groups of people. The whites (20% of the population) live in houses that have barbed wire on top of the brick fences, and nearly every house has a sign that reads – "Armed Response." Black men/boys stand around in the parking lots and "guard" your car and expect a tip. Rhoda in Cape Town explained that they must purchase the reflective vest that they wear, which gives them credibility. In Cape Town, I saw a young man begging at an intersection. He had only one arm and one leg on the same side of his body. He held himself upright with a crutch.

    Well, I guess I should close since I feel I am intruding on their space. Your e-mail made me want to hear your voice. I miss you and would love to wrap my arms around you. Have fun camping this weekend and next weekend when you go to Austin. Both sound like things you will enjoy. I hope Jacob had a good time at field day. Tell him I asked about him. I can just imagine him heading out slathered in suntan lotion.

All my love, Pat

Sailing round the world in a dirty gondola. Oh, to be back in the land of Coca-Cola! ~ Bob Dylan

To: Pat
From: Rael
Date: Friday, May 22, 10:03 PM

Hello my love,

> We made it to the campsite and finally got all set up just in time to go to bed. The RV park, like most of Surfside, rates like a two-star trailer park (scale of 10). We are on the main road that runs through Surfside to Galveston about 200 to 300 yards from the beach, which the kids saw while I was setting things up. The outside temperature is nice, low 70s to upper 60s so we don't need the noisy air conditioner. I'm headed to bed. I'll write more tomorrow.

Love, Rael McRael

He signed his last name, which again made me wonder what was up with that. Still, it was the second e-mail for the day, clear proof he thought of me.

Our next stops as we headed eastward were Eden Bird Sanctuary and Monkey Land, two impressive tourist attractions located right next to each other. We spent the night at Tsitsikamma National Park in a room that offered an ocean view.

The next time I checked my e-mail, I found the following note:

To: Pat
From: Rael
Date: Saturday, May 23, 10:20 AM

Hey baby,

> How's your day? I'm doing much better after a long

night's sleep. Last night while setting up the trailer I think I fixed the water leak. Today I installed the new sewer hose with the sleeve around it. It took a while getting the sleeve on. It was like sliding too small of a condom on a limp pecker. Speaking of limp peckers, mine isn't, so hurry home. I miss your kisses and hugs. I miss the passion we share as we touch and kiss and get each other aroused.

The kids went boogie boarding this morning, but wore out quickly. I'm going to wait until a little later in the afternoon and drive down the beach where it isn't as crowded. They were able to walk to the beach this morning. The temperature is still great, upper 70s, lower 80s, but we have the air conditioner on because of the humidity and all the sand in the air.

The kids are outside cleaning seashells they found, so I'm sitting all alone thinking about you and us and (Rael's sexual fantasy followed, which I have chosen to exclude due to its graphic nature). Tell Tonya to quit reading over your shoulder.

Talk soon, I hope, Rael

Traveling makes a man wiser, but less happy.
~ Thomas Jefferson

This was the type of e-mail I expected to get from my new husband – sexual innuendos, along with some that were more blatant, and he did not sign his last name. However, the opening and closing both lacked romance. Still, I wanted to believe he missed me, which fueled my growing guilt for being absent from home.

After exploring Tsitsikamma National Park, we drove on to Addo Elephant Park, another national park. Again, we had excellent accommodations. Right after Tonya and I found our cabin, we spotted a herd of kudu that we watched from our porch. We shot pictures and video of the mothers nursing their babies, the whole time marveling at the long spiral antlers on the bucks.

At 7 AM the following day, we took a safari drive with two other ladies. We saw awesome animals and scenery. In Port Elizabeth we found a B and B near the water and the airport. We walked to a mall where we mailed a package home for Tonya, and then we ate at a diner. Back at the room, we found a basket of breakfast goodies. Anticipating our flight to J'burg the next day, we repacked our suitcases. Then I walked to the B and B's office and checked my e-mail.

The traveler sees what he sees, the tourist sees what he has come to see.
~Gilbert Keith Chesterton

To: Pat
From: Rael
Date: Sunday, May 24, 6:31 PM

Hello, Patty Ann, where are you??? Call me. I'll pay the bill. Did the erotica in my last e-mail scare you away? We're still in Surfside, and it's been raining all afternoon. I left the lights on in the truck when we came back from the beach during a heavy rainstorm, so the battery is dead, and it is still raining. The local businesses are all shut because the storm knocked out their power. So we are stuck inside. Luckily we have power and the Internet and movies. The cell phone is also working.

Call me or e-mail me to let me know you weren't eaten by lions.

Love, Rael

To: Rael
From: Pat
Date: Sunday, May 24, 4:31 PM

Dear Rael,
    Sorry to worry you. We are staying in a bed-and-breakfast in Port Elizabeth. You can call me back tonight from 8:30 - 9:30 (1:30 - 2:30 your time). Here is the phone number: xxxxxxxxx, room 4. It has to go through a switchboard which is not being staffed except during office hours. I hope to hear from you then – Love you, love you, love you, Pat

> *The moment someone says to me "This is very risky," is the moment it becomes attractive to me.   ~ Kate Capshaw*

To: Pat
From: Rael
Date: Monday, May 25, 9:00 AM

    Thanks for e-mailing. I wasn't really worried. I know you and Tonya can take care of yourselves and are safe (except when driving down the wrong side of the highway). I just wanted to let you know I miss you and care about you and want to hear from you. I realize y'all are busy and have little access to phone and Internet service. I'll call you soon.

Lots of love, Rael

Again his lack of passion bothered me – six sentences, "I care about you," and "Lots of love," whoa. Don't knock me over with desire. It simply had to be his way of coping with my absence.

As we waited to get off the plane in J'berg, we chatted with the down-to-earth couple who owned the monkey and bird sanctuary we had visited several days earlier. They were on their way to negotiate a similar set-up in another country. After we secured another rental car, I asked Tonya where she had put the maps. She couldn't find them. Lost without a map, we stopped to ask a couple parked under a tree. They were too busy to tell us where we were, but luckily a farmer who came along pointed us in the right direction. When we stopped for drinks, I bought a book of maps, which for me is a real prize, due to my great need to see exactly where I am. That night I found the lost maps in my suitcase, in the pocket I had tucked them in so I would not lose them. So much for organization.

In Lynchburg, I bought a safari outfit for Jacob and a hat for Rael – similar to the one he bought himself in New Zealand. We stayed at Forever Resort, where I e-mailed Rael.

My favorite thing is to go where I have never gone.
~ Diane Arbus

To: Rael
From: Pat
Date: Thursday, May 28, 2:52 PM

Dear Rael,

We will be at Otter's Den tonight. I am not sure the number I gave you on that list of contact numbers is good, so here is a number that hopefully you can use to contact me: xxxxxxxxxx. We should be there by 6:00 our time - 8 hours ahead of you.

We have had many great adventures, which include wonderful places to stay at reasonable prices and great restaurants along the way. This morning we watched a baboon open a door and go into a nearby cabin. We had already talked to a maid who said she did not like the baboons because they are "naughty." She chased him out of that cabin, and he proceeded to break into another one. There was a notice on our door that said to keep doors and windows locked because of these little guys. Hopefully I will talk to you tonight.

Love you and miss you, Pat

To: Pat
From: Rael
Date: Thursday, May 28, 6:46 AM

Hi Pat,

Been messing with the baboons, ay? Sounds like fun. I'll call at around 7:00 your time.

I'm so anxious about you making it home. BE SAFE! I've so much to share with you. I picked a bag full of tomatoes, banana and bell peppers from the garden this morning and took them to work. I let the tomatoes turn crimson red. They looked perfect. I can't eat that many, and I've been too lazy to do anything else with them.

Jacob and I are doing fine. He got 100% right on his TAKS math test. I'll be calling soon.

Love, Rael

I feel very adventurous. There are so many doors to be opened, and I'm not afraid to look behind them. ~ Elizabeth Taylor

"Hi, Pat." What the… I knew we had been separated for nearly two weeks, but this note could have been written by his grandma, especially when he worried about me getting home safely.

To: Rael
From: Pat
Date: Thursday, May 28, 9:20 AM

Dearest husband, my one true love,

      Thanks for worrying about me. I am doing great. We are currently staying at a wonderful place – canopy mosquito netting around the bed and the cabin is perched out over a ledge with a porch that overlooks that. We watched a hippo and her baby in the river until it got too dark to see them, and they were coming in to forage for food about then too. This afternoon we took a great walk on the paths around the place, which is actually on an island. Right now Tonya is getting directions to our next stop.

      I'd best get off as you may not be able to call while I am tying up the phone with the Internet. I look forward to hearing your voice tonight. Tell Jacob I am so proud of him for making 100% on his TAKS test. He is so smart, especially with math – all those rational things that he can reason out. I miss both of you.

Love, Pat

Tonya and I were now two-thirds of the way through our trip. The recent e-mail from Rael lacked passion and our last phone conversation reflected a growing distance. While I attempted to keep him engaged, he seemed more preoccupied with "not tying up the line and interfering with what I had going there." I knew it would be our last time to talk because Tonya and I would be spending the rest of our trip in private game reserves and national parks, where I suspected there would be limited e-mail and phone service. Tonya had a cell phone, but I hated to rack up minutes on her bill.

Week 3: May 29 – June 6

We spent two days at a private animal park, Gomo Gomo. The safari trips were outstanding, and the meals were great. It was expensive compared to what we had been paying, but we did see sights there that we had not seen otherwise, for instance, we sat in the Land Rover less than 200 feet away and watched a pride of lions devouring a giraffe they had killed.

> *I have found out that there ain't no surer way to find out whether you like people or hate them than to travel with them.*
> *~ Mark Twain*

Then we drove on to Kruger National Park. The first night we stayed in Berg-en-Dahl, one of the many camps within the massive park. We spent the next five days leisurely driving from the south end to the middle of the park, seeing herds of zebra, elephants, giraffe, Cape buffalo, and a wide variety of birds along the way.

While we drove, Tonya and I talked about how we dealt with conflict, money, and relationships. I was apprehensive about what I had waiting for me when I got home. While talking in the car, I shared with Tonya my concerns about Jacob and the changes I felt were needed, which included requiring that he do something besides watch TV and play video games; playing with age-appropriate friends; and taking responsibility by accepting chores around the house. Prior to our marriage, Rael had given me lip service when we discussed these parental issues, but actual execution had never happened, so I knew I would be pursuing this quest on my own. The dread of moving back into fulltime motherhood countered my growing excitement to see Rael again. We had not been separated for that long since I'd gone to New Zealand, and then we talked every day. In South Africa, I had limited means of reaching him, and then the timing had to be right to catch him via phone – when it was available.

Before we found our last hosts' home, Tonya and I pooled our remaining money and bought a bouquet of fresh flowers to give them. Mary and Anthony had tea, cheese, and sliced apples waiting for us when we arrived at their home in Pretoria. Mary, who was anticipating retiring from teaching in July, told us about the bad conditions in the public school system. Anthony, who had retired from public relations at the embassy, still serves as a diplomat in private life as he is the epitome of hospitality.

When I checked my e-mail, I found nothing from Rael, which concerned me, but I did not want to sound like an alarmist, so I sent the following banal note:

> *Life is either always a tightrope or a feather bed. Give me the tightrope.*
>
>   *~ Edith Wharton*

To: Rael
From: Pat
Date: Thursday, June 4, 10:22 PM

Hello my love,

My good news is I figured out I will be coming home sooner than I realized. My plane gets to Houston Saturday at 12:40. I believe I told you Sunday at 2:30. I'm not sure why I thought that. Anyway, now you'll have to get all the dancing girls out a day sooner and start shoveling the beer bottles out the back door.

We are in Pretoria now, the last place on the phone list. I thought you might call, but I know you are probably busy since this is the first Thursday of the month and you have to go to your monthly meeting today. So you are probably trying to get ready for that.

We are going to Soweto tomorrow and then the Apartheid Museum – both with a tour guide who is the neighbor of the couple we are staying with. Once we fill the car with gas, I will see how many rands I have left and call you from the airport with my remaining money. Be sure to keep your cell phone with you as I do not remember your work number. It will be 7-7:30 our time that I will call. I think that is around noon your time – maybe a little earlier.

I am so looking forward to seeing you. I have a million pictures to show you and about two hours' worth of video. This morning leaving Kruger, we came upon a lion and lioness lying in the grass beside the road.

We will be back here tomorrow around 3:00 PM if you want to try to catch me here. We will leave for the airport around 5:00 to turn in the car and get squared away for the flight home. I cannot wait to see you.
All my love,
Pat

Adventure is worthwhile in itself. ~ Amelia Earhart

I woke up in the middle of the night, worrying about Rael. We had not communicated in a week. The heaviness in my chest told me something was wrong, but I reasoned that it was simply my need to see him and reconnect.

To: Pat
From: Rael
Date: Thursday, June 4, 12:40 PM

I'm just about to go to the MUD [metropolitan utilities district] meeting. I've tried calling (27 11 975-XXXX) four times and get a message, "Sorry, we cannot connect your call at this time." I miss you and have so much to share with you. Enjoy your last day and hopefully we'll talk soon. Rael

Worry is the darkroom where negatives develop.   ~ Anonymous

To: Rael
From: Pat
Date: Friday, June 5, 8:41 AM

Dearest Rael,

I just checked with Tony, my host, and he said the number is correct. Please remember you do need to add the 011 at the beginning, which is the international prefix that you put at the beginning of all calls out of the US to other countries.

From what we have learned about this country, especially from our hosts, many of the national systems are breaking down from a lack of competency that has filtered down from the top to the bottom, affecting their electrical supply, their mass transit, their school system – just about everything.

I have to tell you I woke up in the middle of the night and worried for an hour or more about your well-being. I have not heard from you, and I could imagine all sorts of bad things like car accidents, etc., so I was extremely glad to see your reply this morning. I am way past ready to hold you and talk to you and do all the wonderful things we do together.

I love you, Patty Ann

We began our last day in South Africa touring the poorest sections of Soweto. A running commentary from our guide on the atrocities that the South African natives had suffered over time added dramatically to what we were seeing. Perusing the Apartheid Museum added much factual information to what we had previously seen in person. An example of this was a large wall displaying the more than three hundred laws designed to oppress blacks that were passed during the Apartheid. The whole day felt like a crash course on how South Africa had evolved over the last fifty years.

Much of what I learned that day centered on what Nelson Mandela had done for his country. After living in prison for twenty-seven years as a political prisoner, Mandela was released in 1990 and went on to assume the presidency of his country. *Invictus*, a movie released the same year I visited South Africa does a great job of showing how Mandela used forgiveness and compassion to bring the people of his country closer. Except for our visit to the GAPA organization at the beginning of our trip, we had spent the first twenty days of our trip viewing the wildlife and the terrain. This day reminded us of the real South Africa – the one that reflects its oppression and strife. The couples we stayed with from my travel club and the people we met along the way represent the strength and the integrity that percolates to the surface of this struggling country.

I learned that courage was not the absence of fear, but the triumph over it. The brave man is not he who does not feel afraid, but he who conquers that fear.

~ Nelson Mandela

To: Pat
From: Rael
Date: Friday, June 5, 6:15 AM

I don't remember dialing the 011. That may have been the problem. Sometimes I can be so lame. I'll call about 8:15 this morning which will be 2:15 in South Africa.

I have gotten to where I love getting Jacob off to school in the morning. It is fun to watch him leave on his bicycle and then drive around the block and see him whizzing along the sidewalk to the crossing-guard corner. One morning he turned the corner onto Northfork and a pedestrian walked in the middle of the walkway. He didn't slow down. He just down-shifted, stood up on his pedals, steered the bike through the grass. Remember when he first started riding a bike?

Yesterday was the last day for bike-riding to school until next fall. Today Amber watches him. I think I may have gotten used to sleeping later though.

Talk soon. Love,
Rael

Rael's last two e-mails lacked any kind of greeting, which I attributed to his need to write them quickly. The content of the last one assured me that life would go back to normal when I got home. I did remember when Jacob began riding a bike. It happened while I still lived in the condo. Rael had called me, as excited as his six-year-old son. He had documented the accomplishment with pictures attached to the e-mail and a video that we watched the next time he came over. Yes, I had been involved in Jacob's life over the last three years, and over the course of time, I had chosen to help raise this boy into a man. I was going home to do just that.

Some people ask the secret of our long marriage. We take time to go to restaurants two times a week. A little candlelight, soft music, and dancing. She goes Tuesdays; I go Fridays.   ~ Henry "Henny" Youngman

 **Family Reflections**

The word "Africa" makes me think of safaris, which suggests the topic of guns. When I was around six or seven, which would make my brother Morgan eight or nine, he acquired a BB gun. I imagine it was for Christmas or maybe his birthday. They were close together. Of course, I thought the gun was very cool and envied it greatly. When it was still new, Morgan and I were outside playing, he with the gun and me wanting desperately to shoot it. After some time, I asked if he would share. He told me it was his, which meant, no. He laid it aside and began swinging on the A-frame swing set. Seizing the opportunity, I snatched up the gun. While I began awkwardly figuring out how to fill it with air by pulling the pump down the barrel, Morgan coolly informed me that it was out of BBs. Mad that he still controlled the situation, I aimed the gun at his face.

Unmoved by my empty threat, he stared at me while I pulled the trigger. A BB hit his forehead, just off center and about a half-inch above his eyebrow. I still remember his look of surprise and then horror. And when I recount this story, I feel the tightness that gripped my chest as I watched him run to the house, crying, while I wondered what had possessed me to do such a horrible thing. When I hear stories on the news about kids shooting one another, I can imagine the scenario. After that incident with my brother, I never wanted to shoot his or any other gun again.

We grew up with guns in our house. Dad had a thing about them. I remember as a kid watching him clean them, either while he watched television or at the kitchen table. It seemed normal. But when I had my own children, I started questioning the validity of exposing them to guns. While my first husband did own guns, he kept them unloaded, secured with a safety lock, and on the top shelf of his closet. My father did not.

> Nelson Mandela:
> "Forgiveness liberates the soul. It removes fear. That is why it is such a powerful weapon."
>   INVICTUS, 2009.

His loaded pistol sat on the bookcase at counter height, where a toddler could reach up and grab it. When we visited their home, I asked my father to move his gun, but he remained in his recliner and watched TV, so I took it upon myself to elevate the pistol to a shelf well out of the reach of my children. On subsequent visits, the gun would be back on the lower shelf, fully loaded, and without a lock. When I asked my dad why he insisted on keeping it that way, he replied that a locked gun was useless. I replied that I had yet to understand the value of guns in any condition or at any time.

During that era, Dad volunteered for the local sheriff's department. Sadly, I think he had sort of a Barney Fife reputation and no one in that organization felt comfortable working with him. Eventually, they asked him to not show up any more.

A lot of the people who keep a gun at home for safety are the same ones who refuse to wear a seat belt. ~ *George Carlin*

Nuggets of Gold

Always check out the national park system when traveling. In South Africa they were an unexpected treasure. Because advertising and travel books tend to focus on commercial tourist attractions, I tend to forget about the national park systems, but I am determined to keep them on my radar from now on.

The most gratifying travel experience comes from seeing a country from a local's point of view. Had we stayed in hotels, Tonya and I would have seen the tourist sights, but we would never have seen the inside of a township or a typical white neighborhood. Because of this aspect of our trip, we saw more of the "real" South Africa.

Though we travel the world over to find the beautiful, we must carry it with us or we find it not. ~ Ralph Waldo Emerson

Pat listens as Rael reads his pledge
to her at their wedding.

Chapter Ten
June 6 – 7: Home at Last to My Loving Husband

The heart has no secret which our conduct does not reveal.
~ French Proverb

My plane landed in Houston a little after noon. I called Rael on my cell phone while my plane taxied in from the runway. He said he would leave immediately to make the thirty- to forty-five-minute drive to the airport. In an earlier phone conversation while still in South Africa, I had understood that he would leave the house when he heard from me. At the time, I found this odd since he'd insisted on waiting for me as close as security allowed when I came home from New Zealand. But things had changed. We were now married, and although little time had passed since the wedding, I had to admit we already took each other for granted to some degree. After all, we had lived together for over a year before we made it legal. Plus, at fifty-seven years of age we were beyond acting like teenagers in love. Still, after a three-week absence, I longed to sleep in my own bed next to my loving husband.

Tonya's flight to Denver from Houston departed less than an hour after we arrived, so I helped her find her bag and hugged her good-bye before I headed for customs. I also stopped at the restroom to brush my teeth and take a birdbath in the sink. The familiarity of marriage may have diminished some of our initial passion, but I expected Rael to lavish me with kisses and hugs. Also, I thought of my carnivorous diet while away, and I wondered if he might find me offensive since he believed the smell of rotting meat emanates from the pores of carnivores.

The customs form asked about animal products, so I checked "yes" because I had a hand-carved ostrich egg in my luggage. (I'm still guilt ridden for taking tuna fish to New Zealand and not declaring it. See, that happened way back in chapter four, and I'm just now coming clean.) The guy in customs had to look up my ostrich egg to determine its texture – smooth or bumpy, which seemed to determine whether it was endangered. By this time I was so physically exhausted and ready to see my husband that I would have gladly given it to the customs officer as an I'm-glad-to-be-back gift. While I waited for the verdict, Rael phoned. He and Jacob were parked at a nearby hotel. I told him I would call as soon as I got through customs. Finally, the customs agent sent me on my way, deeming my ostrich egg merely common.

I called Rael back and still had him on the phone when he and Jacob pulled up to the area outside baggage claim. He loves hats, and I was wearing the one I had bought for him in South Africa, just like I did when I returned from New Zealand. Ready for a full embrace, I blinked in shock when he gave me a quick hug and a peck on the cheek before he loaded my luggage into the back of the car. As we got into the car, I noted that he did not open the door for me as he generally did, which also entailed giving me a kiss as I said thank you. I reasoned that he felt compelled to hurry due to the airport traffic, although few cars surrounded us.

On the way home, Jacob called my name from the backseat at least a dozen times. He wanted to tell me what Hillary, my cat, had done and all about the garden, and he wanted to know if I had brought him anything. After a brief interlude, Jacob asked if we could play a word game – one of our common car activities. Rael generally indulged him in that respect. Plus, I took it as a good sign that he was glad to have me home and wanted to settle into old behaviors. When I said sure, Rael interjected in a stern tone that we needed to find out about my trip.

Struck by his odd behavior, but appreciative of his desire to keep

The real act of marriage takes place in the heart, not in the ballroom or church or synagogue. It's a choice you make – not just on your wedding day, but over and over again – and that choice is reflected in the way you treat your husband or wife.

~ Barbara De Angelis

the attention on me, I rattled off details about the animals, the people, and the sights Tonya and I had seen. As we drove along the freeway, I noted the tension and worry that now consumed Rael, instead of the beaming face I had expected upon my return. I rubbed his shoulders as I often did when we drove, and initially he relaxed to my touch, as usual. Then he abruptly shifted away, so I stopped, again dismayed by his coldness.

Had the haggard, worried look in his eyes replaced the usual twinkle because of my absence? No matter how I justified my compulsion to travel, I had been wrong to go without him. After all, only a few short months earlier, we had exchanged wedding vows, and with that came responsibility and compromises, especially with this marriage, since Jacob needed a mom in the worst way.

When we got home, Rael helped me carry my luggage into the house. Jacob proudly showed me his surprise, a cake that said "Welcome Home." A banner made from construction paper taped together stretched across the kitchen cabinets like a huge smile repeated the sentiment. Rael bragged that Jacob had made the cake himself with only a little help from him. I noted the cut-out house that decorated the banner. This was my home, the one we had spent the last year remodeling. Rael and I had done all this work as a wedding gift to each other. It felt wonderful to be home where people loved me, and I could relax into married life.

After I took pictures of Jacob and Rael in front of the banner, I sliced the cake. Jacob wanted to know if I had brought him anything, so I started emptying my suitcase in the middle of the kitchen floor, pulling out a safari outfit, a T-shirt, a stone penguin, and a beaded lizard. He seemed pleased and immediately disappeared with his loot. Anxious to show me how much it had grown, Rael asked me to walk to the garden in the backyard. We picked as many ripe tomatoes and peppers as we could carry. I used my long dress as a sling. Then I went back with a bucket for a second load. I cut up a bowl of our bounty and ate it while I surveyed the pile of dirty clothes on the floor. Realizing it had to be done eventually, I started sorting the clothes into piles to wash. Rael watched with a pained expression as I reached under my long dress and pulled off my underwear, so I could add it to the pile. First I did a little dance, hoping

"Would you be shocked if I put on something more comfortable?"
HELL'S ANGELS, 1930.

to jar him out of his solemn mood. From the get-go Rael had made it clear he did not want Jacob exposed to anything objectionable, but Jacob was playing upstairs with his new treasures. What opposition could Rael have to my playfulness? When I came across a bunch of pamphlets, I started telling him about the bird and monkey centers. He went through the motions of acting interested, but I could tell he didn't care.

Too tired to worry about it, I announced I needed a bath. Usually I lay in the tub for an hour when given the opportunity, but excited to talk to Rael, I only soaked for twenty minutes. As I toweled off, Rael walked into the adjoining bedroom and asked if I was getting in or out. He hadn't looked at my wet hair or the towel or my naked body – or he would know. I started dressing, and wondered if I should bother. Of course, Jacob might barge in on us, so I slipped on shorts and a shirt.   Rael lay at the head of the bed, on top of the pillows, and asked me where I planned to travel next. I told him I wanted to go somewhere with him. He didn't answer. I lay on the bed perpendicular to him, our bodies forming a T. It crossed my mind that lying on the pillows like that seemed strange since it made him pointedly unavailable. We held hands.

"There's something I need to tell you," he announced.

He had said he had a lot to share during our last phone conversation and in the last two e-mails I received before I left South Africa. I imagined that he had gotten involved with another cause of some kind. When I fell from the top of his priorities list, politics had moved in to replace me. But after almost single-handedly getting Obama elected, and having tired of the homeowners' and MUD board meetings, he was overdue for a new obsession.

What are three words you never want to hear while making love? "Honey, I'm home."
~ Ken Hammond

"What is it?" I asked expectantly.

"I'm seeing someone."

"What?" Surely this was a bad joke.

"There's a woman I'm seeing, and if I don't pursue this relationship, there will always be a hole in me." He spoke rapidly, with conviction and determination – like he had practiced his lines and knew exactly what he intended to say.

I pulled my hand away from his and scooted away from

him. Stupefied by his announcement, I opened the door to a flood of information by asking how all this had come to pass. As if talking to a bosom buddy, he proceeded to tell me about SJ, the old girlfriend he had mentioned during one of our first phone conversations while I was in South Africa.

She had contacted him through reunion.com, sending a letter of inquiry the day I left. Fate had brought them back together. She had asked if he was the guy from Baytown that she had dated long ago. He had replied that yes, he was her "Rael" man. He warned me that I would hear a lot about Rael, and then he referred to a fantasyland that only they could reach. They had coined the term "Rael" when they lived together thirty-two years ago, he twenty-five years old, and she eighteen. It came from a play they had seen. The characters lived in another dimension, where time had no meaning. My husband and his new/old girlfriend now lived in Rael time while the rest of the world lived in real time. Hesitating only slightly, he said he probably shouldn't tell me all the details, but then he proceeded to do so for over an hour while I sat on the bed with my mouth agape.

> "Houston, we have a problem."
> APOLLO 13, 1995.

[Note: SJ is short for Saint Joan, because she saved Rael from this mundane life in which she found him mired. She is, at this point, living up to her name. And since Rael is intent on escaping the real world and transcending to Rael time, he is living up to his pseudonym as well.]

He described their furious e-mail exchange, numbering close to four hundred letters total in the three weeks I had been gone. He said he had seen her the previous weekend in Denver, Colorado, instead of traveling to Austin to visit his vegetarian friend. He planned to fly back to Denver the following weekend. Grasping at anything to slow him down, I asked what he planned to do with Jacob. He left the door open for me to babysit, but I slammed it shut, telling him he should take Jacob to meet this woman and her twelve-year-old daughter. Rael said he felt better about Jacob meeting SJ and her daughter, Madeline, on his own turf, so they would be coming here in two weeks, which I knew meant I needed to get my butt out of here. So Rael was essentially kicking me out of my own home – the one I had worked beside him to remodel.

He went on to tell me that the love that they shared overflowed into every area of his life. He was more loving and patient with Jacob than he had ever been. While going to work the other day, he had stopped to pick up a hitchhiker who was getting hassled by the cops, and when they asked him why he was doing that, he said there just wasn't enough love in this world. Along with this love that permeated every aspect of his life, he and she had a level of communication that was something he had never practiced with anyone else. It surpassed anything he had heard of. In fact, he doubted that anyone had ever experienced anything like it.

Desperately, I tried to reason with him, bringing up again and again the fact that we had only recently stood in the backyard, in front of my beveled window, and said our wedding vows to each other with our friends and family as witnesses. Was he lying when he said he loved me and wanted to spend the rest of his life taking care of me and Jacob? No, but he loved her more. How could he do something like this? What had I done wrong? He answered vaguely, returning again and again to his pat answer, "I love you, but I love her more."

Remembering my conversation with Dr. Humor and a concept I had clung to like a security blanket, I blurted out, "But I'm your Big Oil."

"What?" He had been ready for my objections, but not this remark.

"I'm your stable force. I'm the one who will always be here for you. In six months, you'll wake up and realize you've made a huge mistake."

"Maybe so, but I've got to do this. If I don't, there will always be this hole in my heart."

I wanted to put a hole in his heart all right, one to match the one in his head where his brains had leaked out. He was not thinking about what was good for him or for Jacob. A man I did not know had picked me up from the airport, not the man who had taken me there three weeks earlier.

What felt like hours of discussing an unthinkable topic of conversation passed before Rael left the room. I could not fall asleep even though I had not slept much in over twenty-four hours. After I'd watered the plants on the back porch, Rael walked into the kitchen where I had

Bigamy is having one wife too many. Monogamy is the same.
~ Oscar Wilde

poured myself some wine. He asked if I wanted to go out for Mexican food. A margarita sounded like a good idea. Plus, I still clung to the idea that I could turn this thing around, given the right setting and the time to do it. I poured the wine back in the bottle and walked toward the backdoor. Hesitantly, Rael said I might want to change my T-shirt since it had gotten wet while I was watering the plants. Robotically responding to his suggestion, I changed, wondering if it would have bothered him to see my nipples through the wet shirt.

While choosing chairs at the restaurant, I strategically sat facing the TV, so Rael had to sit next to me if he wanted to see it. He sat beside Jacob, granting the little boy a wish that usually went ignored. I ate little of the spinach enchiladas, my standard order since I did not eat meat around Rael. The strong margarita that usually gave me a major buzz barely fazed me.

When we walked back to the car, Rael pointedly talked with Jacob while I opened my own door – again. In later conversations, Rael shared with me that he had opened the door for SJ and kissed her, but he also gave me full credit for training him to do that. He had told her that she should be eternally grateful to me in this regard. Oddly, that tidbit of information stung when he told me, and it still hurts when I think about it. It makes all that happened in my absence much more painful and real. I had returned to someone else's life instead of my own.

At home once more, I attempted to sleep, but I found it impossible, so I wrote in my journal, my usual way of coping with stress. Looking back now at that particular entry, I am amazed by my lack of emotion. I say the obvious – that I am shocked and cannot believe what is happening, and then, practical to a fault, I go on to draw a line down the middle of the page and make a list of the pluses and minuses of the whole situation – like I had a choice about what I would do next. The pluses were that I wouldn't have to worry about raising Jacob, and I would have more time to write and travel. On the negative side, Jacob needed a mother, which I was not sure this woman would provide. The biggest drawback was losing Rael's love and affection. His devotion had drawn me to him in the first place – his frequent phone calls throughout the day, the note he slipped

M'Lynn: "Oh Ouiser, Drum would NEVER point a gun at a lady!" Ouiser Boudreaux: "Oh! He's a real gentleman! I bet he takes the dishes out of the sink before he PEES in it!"
STEEL MAGNOLIAS, 1989.

into my suitcase that told me to have a great trip, his habit of bringing fresh flowers home weekly, usually in my favorite color – purple. He now had his enthusiasm focused on someone else, some mirage from the past.

"Fasten your seatbelts. It's going to be a bumpy night."
ALL ABOUT EVE, 1950.

Clearly not welcome in my own bed, I used the downstairs bedroom, the studio/storage/guest room, adjacent to the remodeled bathroom. I tossed and turned until midnight, fighting a faceless demon who had taken over my world during my absence. Not clear exactly why I needed my computer, but determined to get it, I marched upstairs and attempted to open the door to the bedroom I had always shared with Rael. Something inside the bedroom stopped me from entering. Nearby, Jacob sat on the couch staring at the TV, his expression brimming with frustration and disappointment. "Who is it?" Rael asked impatiently. I told him I needed my computer. He removed the chair that jammed the door and let me in. I demanded to know why he had blocked the door. He said that Jacob kept bothering him – so much for being the epitome of love and affection to his son.

Later I saw on the cell phone bill that he had been talking to SJ for forty-five minutes during this time. My interruption had probably terminated the call, or perhaps he had it on speaker phone, and she listened while I lay in bed next to Rael for the last time, trying once more to reason with him. I told him his actions represented a desperate attempt to cling to his youth, and he laughingly agreed. With SJ he felt young. She had taken him back to when he was virile and sexy. Rael told me that SJ disliked AARP as much as he did, and then he ran his index finger down my nose, and said, "So there. You're on your own with that growing old gracefully crap."

Still fighting what felt impossible to accept, I climbed on top of him, pressed my chest to his, and held him. For the first time since he told me he loved someone else, I shed a single tear. He held me too. I don't know if it was out of obligation or some lingering feelings of love. He asked if I had talked with any of my friends, and I told him I had not. Saying it out loud made it real. I had not been able to admit this was happening – even to myself, much less to others, the same ones who had tried to warn me against marrying him in the first place.

Well past midnight, I returned to my bed and called my friend Lilly, who had flown to see her parents in Oregon, two time zones away. Finding her still awake, I told her what had happened, and with the telling of it, the tears flowed. She encouraged me to go to her apartment, but I told her I couldn't, that I had to talk sense into Rael. She told me not to listen to all his stories about SJ, to tell him that I did not want to hear it. Still clinging to the idea that I had not lost the battle, I told her I needed to hear it, that it helped me to understand what had happened.

Looking back on that time, I realize my behavior reflected my dependence. I could not imagine living without what I had come to rely on – Rael's attention and approval, what I had convinced myself was love. I was in intense withdrawal from an addiction I did not know I had.

My mind churned with questions as I lay in bed and willed myself to fall asleep. Stuck somewhere between the Twilight Zone and Oz, I berated myself for leaving Rael for three weeks. He wouldn't be in love with someone else if I had stayed put. How could all this happen in such a short time? What could I say or do to make him see the error in his decision? Why couldn't he take this newfound ability to communicate that he had discovered with her and apply it to our marriage? Why did he think he needed to throw out all we had built together for some transitory fling with an old girlfriend? I finally drifted to sleep around three in the morning with my brain churning, but I awoke again at 5:00, my mind still reeling with the insanity of my situation. For the last fifty-five hours I had slept less than six hours.

Political promises are much like marriage vows. They are made at the beginning of the relationship between candidate and voter, but are quickly forgotten.

~ Dick Gregory

Intent on brewing a cup of herbal tea, I walked to the kitchen and found Jacob already up. I asked him if he wanted to play a card game that Tonya had taught me on the trip. He said yes. We sat in the dining room, and I was explaining the rules when Rael walked in. Looking up at him, I wondered where my husband of three months had gone. In that moment, I saw him waver, which lit a flicker of hope within me. Rael returned to his computer upstairs, I'm sure to e-mail SJ, while Jacob and I played our card game.

Totally frustrated by my inability to reach Rael or to even find the man I had married, I decided to take a morning walk before the June temps reached an intolerable level. I hoped movement would clear my head while getting my blood flowing. Plus, exercise might relax me enough to fall asleep. I had barely gotten started when a wave of clarity flowed through me.

This is all about boundaries. Three months into our relationship, Rael had agonizingly shared with me the fact that he had sexually abused his stepdaughter by masturbating in front of her from the time she turned six until she reached twelve. His confession clearly told me he had no boundaries, but I could not hear that at the time. I wanted to believe that the counseling that he had participated in had enabled him to defy the odds and free him of the shackles of sex addiction. Since my father had been convicted of indecency with a child, I reasoned that my relationship with Rael served to heal my broken bond with my dad. I convinced myself God had sent Rael to me. I finally had someone who replicated my father in many ways, including, and most especially, the sex addict part. But Rael had been miraculously cured of this affliction, and, best of all, he loved me. Except now he didn't. He loved SJ.

> *If you've got them by the balls, their hearts and minds will follow.*
> ~ John Wayne

The fallacy of my reasoning hit me like a cosmic two-by-four. Lucidity about my illogical thoughts has come to me in stages in the months and years since I finally realized how distorted my thinking had become. Thankfully, I understood enough at that point to know I needed to confront Rael when I got home. At the house, I cut up a large bowl of fruit, sprinkled it with raw rolled oats and nuts, and doused it with yogurt and milk, my standard breakfast. Rael came downstairs, no doubt already having phoned or e-mailed SJ about how things were going on the home front. I said we needed to talk in the bedroom, away from Jacob's ears. He followed me in, and I moved my computer aside, sarcastically remarking that I didn't want anything to come between us.

Methodically, I recounted our conversation of more than two years ago, when he'd told me about sexually abusing Harmony. For communication's sake, I remained tactful while pointing out that his affair was not the act of a sex addict, but it did reflect both his and SJ's lack of boundaries. To my implication that he was a sex addict, he replied that he wouldn't talk to me if I was going to insult him. I wanted to laugh at the absurdity of his response, but I calmly stated: "What besides a lack of boundaries could this be? What other condition would prompt someone to throw away everything for something that has so little substance?" For more than an hour, we danced around the subject, jabbing and poking at the issue of not having boundaries and how it related to his and SJ's actions.

He asked me to write all this down since he didn't know if he could put it into words. I'm sure he needed to report to SJ, and he wanted it stated exactly as I had said it to him. In the past, I had written detailed e-mails concerning this exact subject – his lack of boundaries with Jacob – but he could not understand it then any more than he understood it now. Slowly rocking his torso forward and back, he held his palms against his temples and said he heard my words, but they were not making sense. He repeated this several times, continuing to rock. Looking back, I realize we were both mentally unstable – he caught in his new obsession, and I still entrenched in my own addiction. We floundered at opposite ends of a continuum of understanding, neither one of us capable of seeing or hearing the other.

> "Of all the gin joints in all the towns in all the world, she walks into mine."
> CASABLANCA, 1942.

Throughout the day Rael and I had one conversation after another, each one punctuated by his running upstairs to call or e-mail SJ. The landline was not working, so I have a record of the six cell phone calls they made that day. Apparently, he needed the immediacy of her voice to keep him going on his quest to free himself of me, so he could permanently plant her in his life.

Periodically, Rael returned to the downstairs bedroom, where he shared one story and then another about his newly reclaimed love. He seemed hungry to tell me everything – not out of guilt or malice, but rather like a friend telling another friend about his newfound love. The most preposterous story was the one involving the day he flew to Denver to consummate the love they had only experienced thus far via phone and e-mail. Smiling as he began the yarn, he related that while the bathwater ran, as he was getting ready to leave for Denver, he sat on the commode taking a crap. Seeing his wedding ring, he took it off. While contemplating what to do with it, he accidently dropped it in the toilet amid his turds. Laughing at the scenario, he said, "It was too much gold to flush, so of course, I had to dig it out." Rael assured me that it wasn't too bad since, due to his vegetarian diet, his excrement is golden brown and of course, odorless. He is the perfect example of someone who knows his shit does not stink. His story seemed too coincidental to be true, but also strangely appropriate at the same time. When I reflect on it now, I remind myself that he was sitting on the commode I had helped him install.

On a roll, he went on to describe his brilliant plan to reunite with SJ. He originally had a flight after work on Friday, but he decided to surprise SJ and arrive early. To set the stage, he ordered fourteen signs that said, "This Way to Rael." Having Googled a map of her office and a nearby lake, he placed the signs along the route to take her to the lake where he waited, sitting in a folding chair that he had bought at a nearby Target. Then he called her from his cell phone, telling her he had just boarded his plane in Houston that would take him to her in Denver. When she saw the signs, she immediately knew. At the end of a pier, they reunited and he asked her to marry him. He admitted he was quite pleased with himself. When I challenged him with the reminder that he frequently refuted the idea of building self-esteem by being proud of one's accomplishments, he said for this particular situation, he made an exception.

Upon his return from Denver to Houston, Rael found that he had left the key to his car at SJ's condo, so he had to take a taxi home. She mailed him the key, but it did not arrive until the day before I got home. He had worried that he would still have the Prius at the airport, minus the key, when I got there.

I asked what SJ looked liked, and Rael said she is nearly as tall as he, which he admitted would take some getting used to. Then he volunteered that she had a roll around her middle, which reminded me of a remark he had made one time – the only appealing fat woman is someone else's wife. He asked if I wanted to see a picture of her, but I declined, too afraid that he had chosen her over me based on beauty.

Still possessing pictures he had taken when they were together

"I'll have what she's having."
WHEN HARRY MET
SALLY, 1989.

thirty years ago, he had found them, scanned them, and e-mailed them to her. He related that she e-mailed back that she saw the love in her eyes for Rael – even then. Her response helped him to see it as well. Rael went into detail about SJ's ex being a crack addict who had multiple DUIs, one of which involved killing a mother of six. Her ex's mother had been instrumental in somehow keeping him out of jail. In fact, he had not spent one day there – even immediately after it happened.

Rael talked at great length about their incredible sex life and how they went to a place of ecstasy that he had never reached with anyone else. Three days after they found each other again (on my birthday), they began engaging in phone and e-mail sex in which they pleasured themselves and described it to each other. Of course, coming together after only two weeks into their renewed relationship had made sex even better because they got off on watching each other satisfy themselves. He called this their Rael World. Comparably, he said, I was a better lover, but SJ accepted his need to masturbate. He added that he felt sure she would eventually have other lovers than him, but he hoped he would be man enough to accept that in her and love her more because of it.

Life is a sexually transmitted disease.
~ Guy Bellamy

When I asked him if he had shared his sexual history with her, he said that he had and she assured him he was a different man now. Her response reminded me of my own when he told me the same thing. Rael also volunteered that she had been sexually abused by her uncles and a family friend. The history of sex abuse in the family also rang an eerie similarity. No wonder she found him so attractive. The more I ponder these facts, the more I understand her motivation. The same addictive instincts that had drawn me to him worked on her as well.

The topic of sex and how it had steered their whole relationship was the central theme of what made their lives together so wonderful. It sickened me to think that what Rael and I had together meant so little to him that he threw it away for an addiction. In retrospect, I now see all I had sacrificed in my own life by following my compulsive need to marry Rael. Ironically, I had done the same thing with him that I saw him doing with SJ. Addiction has driven both of us.

All this talk about sex prompted me to ask if he had been unfaithful to his previous wives. He answered that he had, but as those were one-night stands, he never told Jill or Sandra about them. Besides, his other two wives had rejected him. Wow, I got to be the one who left fingernail marks on his back. SJ was different. He loved her; they had already discussed their wedding and set a date for one month after we divorced, the minimum legal time to wait.

Still thinking I needed to look out for Jacob's best interests, I harped on the idea that Rael needed to discuss the situation with Jacob. Apparently tired of me bringing it up, he said that Jacob knew about SJ. I asked him how, and he said that the day before I came home, he was talking to her, and Jacob said something about him talking to me. Rael told him it was not me because I was on the other side of the world, and I was asleep right now. Jacob's behavior in the car on the way home from the airport, upstairs the night before at midnight when he wanted to enter his father's room, his restlessness at 5:00 AM, and his eagerness to spend time with me now made sense. Like me, the world he knew was falling apart.

I criticized the way Rael related with Jacob, saying he treated him like a buddy or a friend. At the best of times, they interacted as grandparent and grandson. He countered with the fact that I also treated Jacob like a grandchild. I replied that while I had been assertive on some counts, like teaching him to say "please" and "thank you," I wasn't going to be the wicked stepmother who parented while Rael copped out with unlimited gifts and a ridiculous allowance. His response was that he had rarely given him $20 a week as promised. I said that was worse – he promised the kid one thing and then gave him less or nothing.

Once more, I told Rael he would wake up in six months and regret what he had done. He admitted that could happen, but he had to stay with his plan, he had to see this through, otherwise there would be a huge hole in him. Along with that, he said that he and SJ filled the void in each other, that they matched each other's needs. I told him that was a classic description of co-dependency, and it was a relationship that would not last; they were joined at the hip and when one of them went the other direction, they would both fall down. Gleefully, he responded that I might be right,

God gave men both a penis and a brain, but unfortunately not enough blood supply to run both at the same time.
~ Robin Williams

but he had to follow his dream.

Toward the end of our marathon talk, we improvised our own undoing of our wedding vows. He took off my wedding rings, the one he had given me when he proposed and the one I had moved from my right hand to my left during our wedding ceremony. Neither of the rings had been off my left ring finger since March 7. In turn, I took off his wedding ring. His had been other places than on his hand, but we did not acknowledge that within the context of our ceremony. He shed a few tears, and I did as well. With those simple acts, the bones sanctifying our union had been uncrossed. We were no longer husband and wife. Legally we were still married, but we no longer had a commitment to each other – not that he had been slowed by that concept, but I had finally given in verbally, if not emotionally.

When a woman steals your husband, there is no better revenge than to let her keep him.

~ Anonymous

When Rael returned to the downstairs bedroom, after once more communicating with SJ, we stepped into the bathroom and reminisced about the time we had worked on it together. He speculated that I would miss my claw-foot tub most since I had dreamed of it before it existed in its current surroundings and had basked in it once we completed the project. Apparently relieved to discover a way to compensate me, he committed to pay for remodeling my upstairs bathroom at the condo. As we brainstormed the idea, I quickly understood he planned to do much of the work himself to cut costs. I didn't say so at the time, but hell would freeze over before he stepped foot in my condo again.

Around 5:00 PM Rael asked if I wanted to help him make spaghetti sauce, saying we could use the vegetables out of the garden. He had already cooked a big pot of tomatoes. I told him I felt like I had the flu because I was feeling achy and feverish. My hands shook and chills washed over me, but I was programmed to do whatever Rael asked, so I walked to the kitchen and began chopping up zucchini, squash, and peppers. For a brief interlude, I slipped into a delusional state in which I believed I had come home from South Africa to my normal life, that all this silly business about an affair had been a dream, a strange form of jet lag.

Another wave of chills washed over me. Once more, I told Rael I felt bad, and I still had not gotten any sleep. He commented that I should take sleeping pills; he knew I didn't like to do that, but this was certainly a time that called for such things. I told him I had taken two Tylenol PMs the night before, and they had done little to help me sleep.

While I stood there talking, Rael volunteered that he had told SJ about my accusation that neither one of them had boundaries. He then added that after several phone calls and e-mails she was still hurt that I would say such a thing, but she had also admitted that I had a point. He went on to explain that SJ had had affairs with married men, and she admitted that she was starting to not care that Rael was married. But he explained this time she felt it would be different. Why? Because they had so much in common – they both liked sex, they were passionate, and they had their Rael World. He admitted that they had differences, like his vegetarianism versus her carnivorous diet, and he liked camping while she did not. When Rael commented that everyone had to make up their own mind, I said I had been coerced into eating vegetarian along with embracing camping trips – against my stated desires. He gave me a blank look that said he did not understand what I meant. I started to cite examples, but then I reminded myself of the two-day conversation we had already endured and knew it would be futile.

Thankfully, Jacob slipped into the kitchen and asked if I would play a game with him after supper. Glad to end the conversation, I told Jacob I needed to spend time with him right then because, once we had eaten, I planned to take a bath and immediately go to bed. He and I played our new card game, and then the three of us sat down at the table. While I picked at my food, we talked about the fact that I planned to drive to my mother's house ten hours away the following day. I agreed to take Jacob to Y Camp, but I wanted to sleep as long as I could, so I said I would take him when I got up. Having eaten little, I put a lid on my bowl and stuck it in the refrigerator. After a bath, I took a sleeping pill and lay down about 8:00 PM.

Four hours later, I woke up with my heart racing, and I literally could not focus my eyes. Everything appeared blurry. After putting on my

"Dave, this conversation can serve no purpose anymore. Goodbye."
2001: A SPACE ODYSSEY, 1968.

glasses, I pulled out my journal and began writing even though I could not see the lines on the page. Worse than that, bizarre, unrelated ideas ricocheted in my mind. I could not form a cohesive thought. Terrified by the nightmare state I could not seem to awaken from, I began scribbling in my journal. Apologizing to Patty Ann, my inner child, I told her I knew that I had neglected her. I had heard her screaming, but I could not stop what I was doing. In fact, the louder she had screamed, the more I held my hands over my ears. I told her I wanted to hear her now, and I begged her to wake up and help me. Again, I apologized for ignoring her and listening to Rael instead of her. I promised I would listen if she would just wake up and tell me what to do.

Switching to my nondominant hand so that I might tap into that part of my brain that still thought with clarity and reason, I wrote in a childlike scrawl, "We are strong. We can do this. Call on the people who love us." Then I made a list of the people I thought would be there for me if they could, both alive and dead. My daughter Ashley was at the top of the list. She had been working all weekend, pulling two sixteen-hour shifts as an X-ray tech, and I was sure she was asleep. I hesitated to wake her, but I also knew I would not be able to get up and take Jacob to Y Camp in the morning, so I walked to the kitchen and left Rael a note telling him to take Jacob in the morning, as I was not well.

Reasoning that I would call Ashley and ask her to commit to collecting me in the morning after she had a chance to sleep, I called her cell phone. She answered right before I thought it would go to voice mail.

"You'll help me. You can help me; I know you can help me." As I stammered this insane statement, I knew I sounded deeply disturbed, but I also knew I urgently needed her.

"What is it? What do you need?" she asked, sleep slurring her words.

"I need you to come and get me in the morning. After you've had a chance to get some sleep, you come and get me."

"Okay, I'll come, but why? What's going on?"

"He has a girlfriend. Rael's going to marry his girlfriend."

"What? He has a girlfriend at the house?"

> *Ninny Threadgoode: "A heart can be broken, but it will keep beating just the same."*
>
> FRIED GREEN TOMATOES, 1991.

"No, she's in Denver, but as soon as he gets me out of the house, he's going to marry her. You go back to sleep, but you come get me in the morning. Okay?"

"I'm coming over right now. You grab your things, and I'll be there as quick as I can."

"Okay, that's good. I've already got a bag packed. I washed my clothes from the trip, and I put them back in my bag. I have my computer in its bag, too." I sounded like a teenager preparing to spend the night with a friend rather than a woman preparing to leave her husband of three months.

Still worried that Rael would dash off to work and leave Jacob alone, I added to the note I wrote earlier, telling him in large printed letters that Ashley had agreed to help me. I put the time, 1:15 AM, and signed the note. For good measure, I left my bedroom door open so he would see that I was not there.

Ashley arrived in thirty minutes. She helped me to the car, and we left. As we drove to her house, I apologized for marrying Rael. I blurted out that he was a pedophile – that I had known it all along, but had thought it would heal my relationship with my dad.

She held my hand and said, "It's okay. You're back, and that's all that matters." This was exactly what I needed to hear and to believe.

I rattled on and on, realizing that I sounded crazy, but ecstatic to finally be in the company of someone who sincerely loved me. She told me that as she drove to my house she checked her phone to make sure I had actually called, and she had not dreamed this insane scenario. Then, needing someone with whom to share what was happening, and to make sure she had not gotten caught in a dream that would not end, she called my son Drew. She also shared that part of her had hoped I might answer the door with a bloody knife in my hand.

At her house, she directed me to her spare bed, where she lay beside me and held me until we fell asleep.

The quickest way to a man's heart is through his chest.

~ Roseann Barr

 **Family Reflections**

Still in shock, after the following incident, Mother told me the story not too long after it happened. One day after we kids had grown up and moved out of the house, Dad sat in the dining room cleaning his pistol. Mother sat at the breakfast bar close by. They talked while he worked.

When Dad finished, he playfully pointed the gun at Mother. She responded by saying that he had better not shoot her. He said not to worry that it was empty. Dad pulled the trigger, the gun fired, and Mother heard and felt a bullet whiz past her face before it lodged in the wall behind her. It had missed her by less than an inch. Stupefied by what had happened, she said she could not believe he had done that. He responded that he obviously wasn't aiming at her or she'd be dead right now. So he wasn't at fault.

Sitting nearby when she told me the story, Dad acted a bit sheepish and sort of chuckled like a misbehaving child who had been caught in the act but had, as usual, wormed his way out of facing any real consequences. Mother had every right to tell the story with outrage, anger, and resentment, but, of course, she did not. It was another one of those incidents that she related with minimal emotion and certainly no judgment toward my dad.

All marriages are happy. It's the living together afterward that causes all the trouble. ~Raymond Hull

Nuggets of Gold

I don't want to replicate my mom's behavior in marriage, although I find it all too easy to do so. In both of my marriages, I unwittingly acted like my mother. I did not want to be a selfless doormat, but I felt destined to do just that, no matter how much rhetoric or energy I gave the opposite point of view. It almost felt like my DNA dictated my behavior. I will take full responsibility for assuming a mousy role as a wife. As much as I fought the idea, I found myself slipping into that stereotype of the sycophant who could not think for herself.

"Love means never having to say you're sorry."
~ LOVE STORY, 1970.

The saying, "Something good will come out of this," truly applies to me. For example, at forty-five, I had an accident involving a horse and a trailer that shattered the left side of my pelvis. The doctors said I would probably walk again, but they predicted a limp. In the hospital, my long-time walking buddy stared at the twenty-five-pound weight attached to my leg and asked me what good could come out of all this. At the time, I had no idea, but somehow I found the drive to recover from two surgeries, rehabilitate my atrophied muscles, and learn to walk again. As anyone who knows me can attest, I do not have a limp. That accident caused me to reassess many aspects of my life, move forward on most of them, and leave behind some limiting beliefs I had about myself. So good came from it, even if it wasn't instantly apparent.

What I want and what is best for me often are two different things. I did not want to walk away from my marriage. We had just tied the knot. At the time, I felt like my world had imploded on itself. But as I look back years later, I realize what a blessing has come from something I did not want to give up and would have fought to save had I had the opportunity. Good things truly do come out of the worst situations.

I do not need to marry someone just because I am attracted

to them. In my case, it is a strong indicator that I should run the other direction. As Dr. Humor once told me, after a party, don't go home with the one you are attracted to. Accept a date from the guy who wasn't particularly exciting. The boring guys are the ones who are the best fit in a long-term relationship. And once I find someone I feel okay about, I don't need to live with them. For that matter, I don't need to sleep with them. And it is perfectly okay, if not preferable, to just be friends, and if they want more than that, it's not my problem.

I'd rather set my hair on fire and put it out with an ice pick than relive the two days after I returned from South Africa.   ~ Pat Grissom

I am the flow of change, and I am grateful for the gifts
that shifting brings.
                                              ~Pat Grissom

Chapter Eleven
June 8: One Flew Out of the Cuckoo's Nest

It does not make sense to say something does not make sense to someone who does not make sense, but sometimes, what else can you say? ~ *Esmé Raji Codell author of* Educating Esmé

Monday morning I woke up alone in the guest room at my daughter's house. I had slept restlessly for four hours, but I had slept, which was a significant improvement over the last four days. Ashley lay on the couch, exhausted from a weekend of working two sixteen-hour shifts and going home in between the two to a toddler – and rescuing me in the middle of the night. We recounted the bizarre incidents of the previous night: my calling her, starting off the conversation with the statement, "You'll help me," and then proceeding to tell her that I needed her to come get me in the morning, after she had a chance to rest. She repeated her wish that I would answer the door holding a knife dripping with Rael's blood.

After all, wasn't what I had just been through justification for killing a spouse? Ashley and I recalled widely publicized cases where anger superseded reason and the wife toppled over the brink – for instance, the detached and then reattached penis in the Lorena Gallo Bobbitt case. We recounted the Sarah Harris story. Sarah lived near my condo before checking into prison for accidentally running over her husband a couple of times in the parking lot of the hotel where he had bedded his mistress. Yes, passion and rage against a husband doing something

*Three rings of marriage
are the engagement ring,
the wedding ring, and
the suffering.*

          ~Anonymous

unacceptable is publicized although not condoned – legally. And I am thankful my emotions did not take me there. While I am aware that losing touch with my emotions has caused me to shut down in certain areas of my life, on this occasion it served me well. At least I am not doing jail time or struggling with the guilt of injuring or killing someone – not that the concept hadn't occurred to me. As I began coming out of the fog induced by a lack of sleep and shock due to the circumstances and the inappropriate information Rael had shared with me over the previous two days, I started forming terribly malicious ideas about him. I wanted to kill him.

At the same time, I could not get my mind around what had happened. None of it made sense. The terror of not being able to focus or see enough to read my journal the previous night lingered with me like a bad movie, except it had been real; I was living it and struggling to swim to the surface of what felt like a sea of confusion. Rael had actually done and said all those things – my new husband was in love with someone else, and I could not figure out where that left me. I had e-mailed Dr. Humor the previous day, thinking he would get my message on Monday and respond, but I was too disoriented to check my e-mail. Since my shoulders and neck were tied in knots, I phoned several massage salons but found none open on Monday morning. Instead, Ashley and I decided to get pedicures at a place where we knew they would massage our legs and shoulders – not the same but a good second. Ashley had taken me to get a pedicure the day before my wedding, so we returned for another round of pampering.

While we sat in the massaging chairs at the nail salon, the events of the previous two days kept playing through my head like a song that I could not turn off. Here I sat, doing something that seemed so normal while my world as I knew it had turned upside down.

After the pedicures, I stopped at the bank and took Rael's name off my account. The week before I left for South Africa, I had made a special trip to the bank to put his name on my account and to order new checks with my married name. They sat on top of my pile of mail when I returned from South Africa. We stopped at Chick-fil-A, where I ate my first real meat meal in several days. It satisfied a hunger I did not know I had because, when we returned to Ashley's house, I slept for several hours, which felt heavenly.

Monday night I checked my e-mail, hoping, even though I knew it was sick of me to do so, that Rael had decided he had made a huge mistake, and he wanted me back. Hadn't we done that twice before? No, actually there was no "we." There was only "me" when I decided to break it off, and he convinced me he could not live without me, that he would love me forever. Nothing could ever change that. Nothing.

Further devastated by finding nothing in my e-mail account from Rael, I admitted to myself that he really did not love me, that he had lied to me for the last two and a half years. Departing the house at 1:00AM and leaving a note that said I was too ill to take Jacob to Y camp had elicited not an ounce of concern on his part. He did not care if I lived or died. In fact, his life would be greatly simplified if I did expire. Intent on hurting him with the same callous response, I sent the following detached e-mail:

> *Optimist: someone who figures that taking a step backward after taking a step forward is not a disaster, it's a cha-cha.*
>
> *~Robert Brault*

To: Rael
From: Pat Grissom
Date: Monday, June 8, 11:37 PM
Subject: logistics

I plan on taking you off my cell phone plan tomorrow.
I expect you to:

- Initiate and pay for all expenses related to our divorce.

- Pay for a contractor to remodel my upstairs bathroom at the condo...I will provide an estimate. I want this put in the divorce decree.

- Pay for packing and moving all of my furniture and personal items back to my condo.

Pat

To accomplish great things, we must dream as well as act.

~ Anatole France

Life is what happens while you're busy making other plans.

~ John Lennon

Again that night, I slept fitfully, still reeling from my lack of sleep and the abrupt shift in my life from thinking I would come home to someone who loved me to gradually accepting the idea that I had been replaced in my absence. The next morning, Ashley lay sleeping on the couch, still trying to catch up on her sleep while I fretted about what to do next. I had already decided to go to my mother's house in Lubbock, six hundred miles away, but I couldn't stay there indefinitely, and at some point I had to have a place to live. I thought of the condo, and then I thought of the family that now lived in it. In my over-stressed mind, I toyed with the idea of calling Candy and asking her to move. It had been over eight months since the hurricane. Surely they could live in their house by now.

When I woke Ashley and told her my thoughts, she responded, "Just call Candy and tell her what's going on. I'm sure she'll volunteer to find another place." It sounded too simple. But as soon as I shared what had happened, Candy assured me she would figure out some place else to go. Their house was not yet livable, but she was well connected and would devise a plan. That little bit of good news made me feel somewhat better. It couldn't change what had happened, but at least with time I would have a place to live, and lick my wounds.

To: Pat
From: Rael
Date: Tuesday, June 9, 5:55 AM
Subject: Re: logistics plus early morning fears

Hello Pat,
Business:

- I have an appointment with Colin Spacey this afternoon to discuss our divorce, and I will cover all expenses.
- I have already gotten a new mobile phone account, and it uses the same phone number I had under T-Mobile. I assume that took me off your account, but you may want to verify.
- I will handle all expenses of moving your items back to the condo.
- I prefer knowing the cost of the remodeling job before agreeing to pay for it, but I may be able to accommodate you on this request. My initial thought is handling this outside the divorce.

Personal:

I hope you are starting to recover from the shock of this dark moment in your life. Once you have had time to process what has happened and hopefully feel like it, I would like the opportunity to talk to you again. You may have things you need to say to me, and I to you. I will gladly make the time to do this.

I told Jacob, as much as he is able to listen to in one sitting, about what is happening to us. I asked him how this made him feel, and he answered, "I don't like

"Mama always said life was like a box of chocolates. You never know what you're gonna get."
    FORREST GUMP, 1994.

going to the psychologist." It was difficult to not chuckle at this. I think he has picked up my dark wit.

It is the early morning that I face the most fear of this path I have chosen. Before the exhilaration of the dream has taken over, I ask myself, "Oh my God, what have I done?" There are so many blind unknowns ahead. My life was so content and mostly happy. But I have taken a bite of the apple and cannot return to Eden. I have seen a truth I did not know existed, and I am drawn to it like a mosquito to blood. There is a happiness and joy out there that can permeate every aspect of life. Does it hold just as much sorrow? Is it a temporary illusion? Or will cynicism and fear make it fade? I do not know. I would have to ask Anatole France, "If I have a dream of great things, must I act as well?"

Rael

P.S. I BCC'ed SJ this e-mail as well.

Life is a rollercoaster. Try to eat a light lunch.
~ David A. Schmaltz

When I read the flowery part about him biting the apple and being drawn to blood like a mosquito, I recognized the charm creeping into his e-mail. It did not surprise me to see that he had blind-copied SJ. Jacob's response about not wanting to go to a psychologist referred to the time over a year earlier when he had accompanied me to my therapy appointment. I find it interesting that he linked that time with the current upheaval in all of our lives. Please note, while I had all kinds of emotional responses to his references to talking to Jacob and his early morning conundrums, I do not address those in my response.

To: Rael
From: Pat Grissom
Date: Tuesday, June 9, 12:53 PM

Rael,

I spoke with Candy today and told her my situation. She has agreed to make every effort to vacate the condo by the 21st of June. I would like to have the divorce papers finalized and signed by both of us that day.

I must insist on putting the remodeling job in the divorce decree to guarantee that it happens. I can put together a rough estimate, which I will adhere to once it is established, whether it goes over that amount or not. I would rather not deal with you on this matter outside the divorce. And I expect to receive a money order for the agreed-upon amount for the remodeling when I sign the divorce papers.

I would like to see a copy of the divorce decree as soon as possible. Also, please include the clause concerning your financial responsibility for having my furniture and personal possessions moved from your address to my condo address by a professional mover.

Will you hire a moving company or do you want me to select one? I expect them to pack all of the nonfurniture items, wrap the furniture for moving, transport all of this to my condo, and move my furniture in and your furniture out of there.

Pat

When you come to the end of your rope, tie a knot and hang on.
~ Franklin D. Roosevelt

Ashley drove me back to the house I most recently called home, so I could get my car and drive to Mother's house. Lubbock offered a refuge in which I hoped to escape or at least temporarily hide out from my current insane situation. My life felt out of control – like I had taken a hallucinogenic drug, the effects of which would not leave me.

It was nearly 5:00 PM when we arrived at Rael's house. As I was antsy to get away from there lest we encounter him, Ashley and I agreed to take both cars to a nearby fast-food place and decide what to do next. Over supper, we discussed the absurdity of me making such a long trip on so little sleep, especially since most of it would be done at night, if I adhered to my original intention. We agreed to meet back at Ashley's house, and I planned to drive to Lubbock the next day.

> *When you get into a tight place and everything goes against you, till it seems as though you could not hang on a minute longer, never give up then, for that is just the place and time that the tide will turn.*
> *~ Harriet Beecher Stowe*

From the time Ashley picked me up early Monday morning until Tuesday night, I had fed her bits and pieces of what happened after I returned from South Africa. Around 7:00 that evening, Ashley and I sat down and I gave her a chronological recount of everything that had happened, starting from when I landed in Houston until she arrived at my doorstep to take me home with her. I told her about the speed at which Rael and SJ moved from old friends finding each other after thirty-two years to virtual sex partners via phone and the Internet and then physically meeting up less than two weeks after their correspondence began. Even before they reunited physically, they were talking marriage and living together for the rest of their lives, one big happy family with Jacob and Madeline, with all this information being provided by Rael in the two days after I arrived home. While recounting all of this, I finally began to understand what a creep I had married. Telling the story to Ashley brought the truth into focus. My realization made me wonder how I could have been so far off when I thought he was the man who would love me for the rest of my life.

When Ashley and I made ourselves stop talking around midnight, I had a new vision of what I needed to do, which was certainly not to be the complacent little wife who continues to support Rael's every whim. If I signed a divorce agreement in two weeks, I would be giving him exactly what he wanted. No, I had taken my time getting into this marriage, and I would take my time getting out.

Having finally stepped out of the fog to some degree, I sent a detailed e-mail describing the events that had transpired to the lawyer who had handled my first divorce and had remained a friend.

All night long the details of Rael's affair continued to churn in my head. Recounting them to Ashley had only fueled my anguish. Wednesday morning I got up after little sleep, determined to escape Houston and put at least a small part of this behind me. I could not erase the memories of my weekend from hell, and I could not stop thinking about Rael and what I once thought we shared – a committed future together.

> *Birth and death were easy. It was life that was hard.*
> *~ Tom Robbins from Jitterbug Perfume*

When my daughter walked me to my car that morning, she hugged me, and I told her I planned to write a book about what I had been through. The name De-raeled struck me as a great title. The world needed to know about my husband, the world's biggest jerk. An account of his shenanigans felt like the perfect way to derail him.

Having had too little sleep in the last six days, I began the drive to Mother's house. I knew I needed to stop and rest along the way, but I also knew that when I closed my eyes to sleep, Rael's face haunted me and his assertion that he loved someone else kept ringing in my ears. At one point, I became so disoriented that I pulled up to an intersection where I needed to turn and sat there totally confused, not knowing which lane I should turn into. While driving in South Africa, Tonya and I had developed the habit of following someone to stay on the correct side of the road since they drive on the left side rather than the right. But now, I was out in the country and I had no other cars to follow. Broken and lost, I waited for another car to come by to indicate where I should drive. It finally did, and I proceeded, still feeling like I had returned to a world I did not know. My lack of orientation while driving exacerbated the situation.

Several hours later, I had to stop to use the restroom. When I stepped into the convenience store, I saw the sign for the restrooms on the opposite side of the large, open room. By then I was so zoned out, I stood there and reasoned how to get from one side of the building to the other. I saw other people walking past me, and I decided if they could get there, I could too. Slowly, I walked down an aisle, and miraculously, I found myself where I needed to be. This may sound ridiculous, but I was truly that disoriented. And I was driving – subjecting other people to my delirium.

I'm not sure how, but I made it to Lubbock. Several times along the way, Mother called my cell phone to check on me, but she could not begin to imagine how deranged I had become. When she opened her garage door, I saw that several cardboard boxes blocked me from parking my car in the garage. By then real paranoia had set in. I refused to leave my car outside where anyone could see it, so I hauled the heavy boxes to the storage shed in her backyard. Again, I acted out of compulsion, driven by the same irresistible urge that had taken me to Lubbock. After I parked my car in the garage, I opened a bottle of the wine I had brought with me – one left over from the wedding. I had collected it from the house when Ashley and I retrieved my car. Then I sat down to eat the meal Mother had prepared, but I couldn't swallow more than a few bites. I excused myself, drew a hot bath in her whirlpool tub, and drank my wine while the water churned around me. That night I slept more than I had in the seventy-two hours since this ordeal began.

Fortunately, Mother had scheduled an appointment with her therapist, whom I had talked with on previous occasions when I accompanied Mom to a session. I thought of Dr. Vine as our family therapist, for nearly everyone in the family had at one time or another escorted Mother when she went to see him. He had seen us through Dad's arrest, Mother and Dad's divorce, and my brother's death. Dr. Vine asked me several times at that first visit and at a subsequent visit later that same week how I felt about Rael. I needed to hate him

"Gimme a whiskey, ginger ale on the side. And don't be stingy, baby."
ANNA CHRISTI, 1930.

in order to get over this, but I didn't. I still wanted him to love me, and I could not get my mind around the concept that he did not. I fell in that commode along with his ring.

We are not necessarily doubting that God will do the best for us;
we are wondering how painful the best will turn out to be.   ~ *C. S. Lewis*

 **Family Reflections**

While growing up, the concept of boundaries meant nothing to me. In fact, I have a good friend who reacts to the statement, "Boundaries? What's that?" the same way I do – it either strikes us as incredibly funny or excruciatingly sad, depending on our mood.

Twenty years ago, Mother and Dad were attending a church where the minister who had been there quite a while had the opportunity to move to a new church. Mother wanted to give him and his wife a going-away gift, so she sent Dad to their house with a crocheted angel she had made. The minister was not there, so Dad gave the angel to the minister's wife. As he left, he gave her a hug. While pulling away, he tweaked her breasts. Like a naughty school boy sharing his exploits with a friend, he drove home and told my mom about what he had done. When she related the story to me, I asked her how she had responded. She shrugged her shoulders, and I knew she had done and said nothing. She never questioned anything Dad did, so it stood to reason that this was one more incident she accepted as "just the way he is."

Ten years later Dad was asked, on two separate occasions and at two different locations, not to volunteer – first, at the church, as the bus driver for a field trip of some kind. It seems he got a little too familiar when he hugged the teacher in charge of the event, perhaps repeating what he had done to the minister's wife. Next, a female employee at the hospital where he volunteered in the library said he had acted inappropriately toward her. My mom never questioned his explanations that these incidents resulted from misunderstandings. In fact, it took her several years after they divorced to see how terribly inappropriate his behavior had been. She grew up in an era,

Once we accept responsibility for choosing our lives, everything is different. We have the power. We decide. We are in control.   ~Will Schutz

a time, a family, and a location where a woman did not doubt her husband's behavior. And while I do not hold my mother accountable for the blinders I wore while married to Rael, I do acknowledge that I patterned myself after her.

A year or so before my parents separated, they visited me in Houston and helped me sell crafts at a Christmas bazaar. Myra, a friend of mine, was selling her artwork in the show as well, and she sat at my table with Dad while I worked at the checkout stand. When I returned to the table, I saw Myra's look of dismay. After my dad left the area, she whispered to me, "I can't believe your father is so rude. He told me I was fat." Reverting to the way we – my entire family – had always excused and ignored Dad's behavior, I said, "That's just my dad. You have to learn to ignore him." Now I shake my head and wonder how I could have been so insensitive to my friend. She had expressed her pain caused by my father, and I had cruelly ignored her.

I believe it is prompt accountability for one's choices, a willing acceptance of responsibility for one's thoughts, behavior, and actions that make [the soul] powerful.   *~Alice Walker*

Nuggets of Gold

Sometimes it takes something cataclysmic to awaken me from the trance I have created. By ignoring my own feelings so long, I built up a numb wall of oblivion to the fact that I was not present in my relationship with Rael. None of the events that happened before we married woke me to the truth of what I was getting into – not the lack of compassion when my father or brother died, not his inability to offer caring when I had my second oral surgery or when I ended up in the ER. It took realizing that my husband loved someone else to finally understand what I had done to myself, and even that didn't prompt me to leave my self-made prison. I would still be there trying to make it work if Saint Joan had not come to my rescue and liberated me by essentially helping to boot me out the door. Watch out for those cosmic two-by-fours. They will get you every time. Thankfully this one hit me square in the head and eventually knocked me back to my senses.

> *It is not what happens,*
> *but how we react to it.*
> *We are 100% responsible*
> *for all our experiences.*
> *~Louise Hays*

     Boundaries are something I have to set for myself. I can think of one example after another that gives proof of the fact that I was raised without good models for setting boundaries or expecting them from others, but what good does that do for me in the long run? It keeps me stuck in victim mode. I have to set my own boundaries and realize that no one is going to do that for me. It has been a difficult and painful learning experience, but I fully understand that it's not about what my dad or my mom did or didn't do. It's all about what I do from now on. I can't change what I did in the past, but I can change what happens in the future.

     I am in charge of teaching the people in my life how to treat me. I have never been more devastated than when Rael told me he loved someone else. Looking back at our relationship prior to that, I realize that I had communicated to him that it was okay for him to treat me any way he wanted to, that I would put up with just about anything he did – because I did. None of what transpires in this book would have happened had I left the first time he treated me badly. So if I want someone to treat me with respect and compassion, I have to communicate to them that I think I am worthy of that, and that I will accept nothing less. Most important, I have to honestly believe that I am worthy of love in order to convey that to someone else.

Personal responsibility is the brick and mortar of power.
~Shelby Steele

Pat Grissom, *Self-portrait*,
colored pencils

Pat Grissom, *Self-portrait*,
watercolor

Chapter Twelve
June 11 – 24: I'm Out of Here

"I'm so miserable without you, it's almost like you're here."
Song by Billy Ray Cyrus

After Mother and I left Dr. Vine's office, we drove to Mother's church, where we helped make heart-shaped pillows for the patients in the hospital who have had heart surgery. Since respiratory issues are common after heart surgery, patients are encouraged to keep their air passages clear. Hospital personnel teach patients to hold a pillow against their chests while they force themselves to cough. The church group makes these heart-shaped pillows to use for this purpose and the unspoken message is that they care, which is healing in itself. Candy called on my cell while I cut out felt hearts. She had found a house. A huge sense of worry immediately lifted from my shoulders. Hallelujah.

Back at Mother's house, I started researching moving companies. Number one, I wanted to have some control over who handled my things, and number two, I didn't want Rael to end up being the one who tossed my things into a rental truck and called it good. He was not concerned about me in any form or fashion. His feelings on that matter translated clearly in the many stories he had told me about his new love without regard for the impact of that information. Plus, I had heard little from him since I left in the middle of the night, after telling him in person and in a note that I felt sick. Obviously, Rael had little time for anything other than his obsession with SJ and moving her to Texas. Getting rid of my stuff by the quickest means possible helped him to achieve that goal.

To: Rael
From: Pat
Date: Thursday, June 11, 3:20 PM
Subject: moving details

Rael, I spoke with Candy this morning. They have found another place to stay and feel they will be out of the condo by June 22nd, so I can move back in. I do not want you to pack any of my things as you will already have quite a bit to do by sorting out my things from yours. Plus, I know your weekends are tied up between now and the 22nd. So when you hire the moving company, tell them they will be packing household items as well as wrapping the furniture prior to loading and moving all of it. Let me know how early they can start on the 22nd, and I will be there to let them in. Hopefully, they can get it packed and loaded in one day.

Having had a few days to think about what is going on, I have decided that I unfairly pushed you to get the divorce papers ready much quicker than was realistic or practical for either one of us. Once I have gotten my things back to my condo, I will be ready to start working out the details of our divorce.

Please note I left the decision about hiring the movers up to Rael, knowing that once he felt in control, he would pass the responsibility to me. Am I a well-trained Southern woman, or what?

Pat To: Pat
From: Rael
Date: Thursday, June 11, 3:33 PM
Subject: Re: moving details

Hi Pat,

      It sounds like you have a much better handle on the move. Would you mind arranging the moving company? I will work at completing as many of the items as you mentioned. Do you want me to disassemble the big worktable for the move? Do you want me to disassemble the stained glass shelves in the garage? My goal is to segregate as much of your stuff as possible to make the move easier. I'll let you know how I arrange things. Rael

P.S. I was wearing the yellow shirt you sewed for me, and I went to clean my glasses when my nosepiece caught at the spot you sewed. I think I tore the shirt by cleaning my glasses.

      I did not respond to his comment about his shirt as he said it to hook me, which it did.

      Still fully addicted to Rael, I continued obsessing over him, which did nothing to relieve my insomnia. I averaged four hours of sleep each night, although recalling all he had told me about his affair added to my conviction that I had to do something to stand up for myself. I knew I wanted to write a book about this experience. That was clear to me after laying it out in detail for Ashley. But my emotions focused on loss and resentment, which was not where I wanted to stay. I had been at Mother's house several days when I decided to write an e-mail to my friends, asking for their love and support.

> *Truly, it is in the darkness that one finds the light, so when we are in sorrow, then this light is nearest to us.*
> *~ Johannes Eckart*

From: Pat
Date: Monday, June 15, 10:33 PM
Subject: request for prayers and support for me

Dear Friends and Loved Ones,

  I apologize for sending a group e-mail, but I feel compelled to inform you on what's happening in my life, and at the same time ask for your prayers and support.

  If you had asked me a month ago about married life, I would have told you things were great. You would probably have received the same answer from my beloved husband. But a little over a week ago, when I got back from my three-week trip to South Africa with my friend Tonya, I came home to a man who is having an affair with his first love. He intends to move me out and her in during the process of the next month. She contacted him via Reunion.com the day I left Houston. By the fourth day of my absence, they were engaged in heavy-duty phone and e-mail sex. By the second week, he had flown to Denver to spend the weekend with her. I know all this because he told me – and I sat there for two days and listened – dumbfounded, stupefied, and shocked, but I listened.

  After two days of this, I had a nervous breakdown, and terrified my daughter when I called her in the middle of the night, begging her to come get me. Prior to my call, she had no idea this was going on, and I had been too shocked and ashamed to tell her. Last Wednesday, the 10th, still disoriented from a lack of sleep, I drove ten hours to Mother's house. At one point, I had to figure out which side of the road I should drive on since I was so sleep deprived, and I had focused for the previous three weeks on driving on the left side of the road. I arrived in Lubbock truly a basket case.

I am scheduled to get my stuff moved back to the condo on the 22nd of June. Once I get settled into the condo again, we will get together and celebrate my emancipation. While this has been the most shocking experience I have ever been through, it is also a great opportunity to reclaim my individuality and revel in the fact that his timing is wonderful. He could have waited several years, when I would have been totally immersed in the marriage.

I have the rest of the summer to recuperate and put things back together before I start teaching again. I will get through this, and I will be stronger, having survived. In fact, I have decided to write a book using this story to warn other women about the seductive charm of men who operate strictly from their own desires and needs without regard for who is hurt in their quest to "fulfill their dreams" (Rael's phraseology when he told me that he had to pursue this relationship, lest he have an emptiness for the rest of his life).

Right now, I'm playing the part of "Accommodating Pat," who just wants him to do what is best for him as long as he pays for the move and gives me some money to remodel my condo bathroom. I do not want to tip my hand to him at this point, but there will be restitution. Please stay in touch. I am accepting all the emotional support I can get right now.
Love,
Pat

> How we spend our days
> is, of course, how we
> spend our lives.
> ~ Annie Dillard, Pulitzer
> Prize-winning author

Admitting I had made such an error in judgment was mortifying. I was comforted to get a number of loving and supportive replies, including the following in response to the letter I had sent to my lawyer the week before.

We can be cured of depression in only fourteen days if every day we will try to think of how we can be helpful to others. ~ Alfred Adler

To: Pat
From: Lonnie
Date: Monday, June 15

Pat,

I am so very sorry to hear that your promising marriage has fallen apart. I know you are in shock right now and doubting your abilities to choose men. I encourage you to have legal representation, and you know I am available for you. You are a very special person to me. So as your friend and legal advisor, please do not provide him with any information and do not sign any legal papers. In theory, a divorce should be quick, but there is severe emotional damage to be addressed. Embarrassment is not an issue. Your true friends understand and the rest don't matter. Take your time recovering at your mom's. Indulge yourself in all the caring and love you can. He cannot get a divorce legally for 60 days from day of filing so there is time to come to an agreement. Usually I suggest counseling but I do not think it would work here as the trust bond is shattered.

At the very least he should pay all your moving and resettling expenses. Yes to him remodeling your bath in the condo. He should pay any debts you incurred during the marriage and since separation if they were made necessary due to his acts (hotels, etc).

Please do not let him tell you more about his affair. It is his guilty mind trying to convince you it wasn't his fault. You do not want or need to know the sordid facts and you surely do not want to let him feel less guilty.

Hold your head up high, my friend. Know that I am here for you.

Lonnie

An Idea Is Born

Frantic for something to occupy my mind, I started reading a true story Mother gave me entitled *Same Kind of Different As Me* by Ron Hall and Denver Moore. It is a remarkable book about a friendship that forms and thrives between two unlikely men – the husband of a woman who volunteers in the kitchen of a homeless shelter and one of the men who frequents the shelter. When the woman develops cancer, the two men work together, supporting her emotionally throughout the trials of her illness. The illiterate homeless man who asked for nothing from the wealthy volunteers becomes a genuine friend to the couple as the husband struggles to deal with his wife's illness and death. Together the two men orchestrate the building of a chapel as a memorial to her at the center where she volunteered. This true story prompted me to think beyond the rage and hurt that I was experiencing and to ask myself what good could come of my experience. Also, I wanted something beneficial for others to come out of the madness my life had become – but what?

Then I thought of the countless women who found themselves in my situation – married to a self-centered jerk who only cared about himself. I had been smart enough to get an education. I was financially stable, but the vast majority of the women who end up in a shelter have no means of supporting themselves. They don't have a therapist they can call when things get rough. I had no real knowledge of the background of these individuals, but I suspected they also came from dysfunctional families of origin, some of them much worse than mine. Several years earlier, I had volunteered at a resale shop that benefited a women's shelter, where one of the requirements was to watch a film about the typical woman who ends up in a shelter. The film stressed the likelihood of women leaving a shelter going back into an abusive situation – either the relationship they left or another one with the same emotional makeup and brokenness.

I decided I had to do something to make this experience mean something besides just a dark period of my past. What I had experienced was the result of making bad choices. Others who ended up in similar

> *The greatest use of life is to spend it for something that will outlast it.*
> ~ *William James*

situations had probably done the same. As an educator I had seen countless young people start college determined to create a better life than they had experienced so far. Some were fresh out of high school, often with young children already; some were older and had children who were nearly grown, but all of them were clear that a better education would enable them to create a better life for them and their kids.

I was well educated, and I saw a therapist regularly, but I had still made choices that landed me in an unhealthy situation. What was the missing piece? Self-worth. I got what I believed I was worthy of receiving. I knew going in who Rael was, but my core values told me that he was as good as I deserved. He fit the profile of the person whom I felt destined to seek as a husband based on what I had learned about relationships and marriage from my parents.

This was my target. These were the women I would help. Somehow I would do something to help women who found themselves floundering in unhealthy relationships and who were financially unable to help themselves. Within an hour, I thought of a name, and actually the acronym came to me before the individual words that it stood for: OACES. I loved the sound of that, a life-giving place in the middle of a desert, an organization that could make the difference between life and death. Yes, I know it isn't "spelled correctly," but that in itself is part of the charm of it. Somehow having the word "ace" in the name added to the beauty of it, an ace being the high card in a suit of cards. Working out what the letters stood for also came to me fairly quickly. Initially OACES stood for Overcoming Abuse through Counseling, Education, and Self-Worth. "Counseling" and "education" came to me immediately, and then I bounced between "self-esteem" versus "self-worth" until the latter won out.

It was nearly two years after this original idea that I realized the C stood for "Change" instead of "Counseling." On a plane bound for California to present at a national conference, I struck up a conversation with the lady next to me. Before the plane took off, I had reaffirmed my conviction that there are no coincidences. She had grown up in a dysfunctional home in Honduras. She told me about her and her mother's plight as they entered the United States illegally, and then the injustices that they had endured when they

> *He who does not live in some degree for others, hardly lives for himself.*
> ~ *Michel de Montaigne*

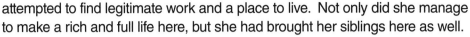

attempted to find legitimate work and a place to live. Not only did she manage to make a rich and full life here, but she had brought her siblings here as well.

She too was driven to help women who were disadvantaged. As I began telling her my story and relating the name of the organization that I planned to start, I had not gotten the entire name out when it struck me that the C stood for "Change." In my description of what I hoped to accomplish, I said that my ultimate goal was to help women understand that if they can change how they see the situation, they can make different choices, which will immediately enable them to redirect their entire lives. Counseling is invaluable in helping an individual see their part in the process, and it is part of considering options, which can be combined with education. No, "Change" had to stand alone; it is the key ingredient, the necessary element if someone is going to get out of the cycle of abuse. If we keep doing what we've always done, we keep getting what we've always gotten. Another reason the concept of change is so pivotal in this process is that as humans we tend to resist change – back to the dilemma of initiating a "new swing." If I'm trying something that feels uncomfortable for me, I tend to go right back to doing what feels normal – like falling in love with someone who could be my father, except twenty years younger; someone that I should know better than to love, but I did it anyway because it felt normal; it was what I had grown up with; it felt coded in my DNA, etched in my brain.

In some way, suffering ceases to be suffering at the moment it finds meaning.
~ Viktor Frankl from Man's Search for Meaning

Initially, I felt committed to the name OACES because it came to me so quickly and had so much significance. A couple of years down the road, however, when I officially started the business, I realized it would be a stumbling block since the spelling was odd and the words it represents created a need for explanation. Plus, I had real reservations about including the word "Abuse" in my business name. I wanted my company name to generate positive energy, not weigh it down with the issues that triggered an individual to seek refuge in a shelter.

While wrestling with the dilemma of what name to use, I talked with a friend, and after I sent her an e-mail with a list of potential options, she replied with a great idea – Devoted to Empowering Women. The acronym spells DEW, which suggests moisture, a healing element. Then I met with Pam, my publishing consultant, and told her my proposed business name. The next day, she called me to say she had a suggestion – Dedicated to Empowering Women. "Dedicated" sounded more positive, so I agreed. She had already told me I needed to get my name as a domain name, so I got that, along with this book's title. Thus Dedicated to Empowering Women or DEW, finally emerged.

Backtracking in time to my recovery period at Mother's, I explored every option to find emotional peace, including attending a group at Mother's church that offered healing prayers. I don't typically gravitate to old-time religion, but because my mental state still felt like watery Jell-O, I was willing to try anything. In the prayer circle, two women sat with me, and asked why I needed their prayers. I gave them the condensed version of what had happened. Then they stood and laid hands on me while I remained in my chair, with one behind and one in front of me. They prayed, and I honestly felt some relief. Afterward, the one who faced me said she saw angels behind the lady who had her hands on my head. She reported that she had never seen that before. They agreed that my mission was officially sanctioned. This experience added to my conviction that I had turned a positive corner.

While at Mother's I compiled the e-mails I had gotten from Rael during my trip. I compared these with my journal entries to see if I should have known what waited for me in Houston. The following are the indicators I found:

Men should be like Kleenex – soft, strong, and disposable.   ~ Cher

May 21 – Four days after I left, Rael signed his e-mail "Your American Friend." He had begun distancing himself. This was the day after their first "incredible night of virtual lovemaking."

May 22 – He sent me an e-mail in which he wrote his sexual fantasy. It was not me he was thinking about when he wrote this. He said in a different e-mail that same day that he missed me badly. He may have had an ounce of conscience about what he had started with SJ, or he was simply horny.

May 28 – Rael was eager to end our phone conversation, saying he wanted to let me get back to what I was doing. In fact, he needed to get ready for his trip to Denver the next day. Later that day in an e-mail he told me he had so much to share with me.

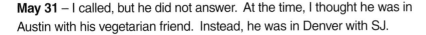

May 31 – I called, but he did not answer. At the time, I thought he was in Austin with his vegetarian friend. Instead, he was in Denver with SJ.

June 3 – I woke up in the middle of the night, worried because I had not talked to him and he had not sent an e-mail in over a week.

June 4 – In an e-mail he repeated that he had so much to share. When he tried to call, he left off the international prefix. Since he had called me numerous times before that, I suspect he was subconsciously sabotaging his effort to reach me.

Once I received my cell phone bill for the time I was gone, I found numerous calls to and from Denver. Of course, by the time I found these, it simply verified what I already knew.

While I could not see it then, it is easy to see in hindsight the stages of grief that I went through during this ordeal while I was still talking to Rael and immediately afterward. As soon as he told me, I shifted into denial. It could not be happening. The fact that I stayed there and tried to "talk sense into him" validates my need to bargain. The anger and subsequent depression phase came later – after I had gotten moved and time had convinced me it was not just a bad dream. Acceptance was the last stage, of course, but that took quite a while.

On the way back to Houston, I stopped in Austin and spent the night with a friend who had once been my neighbor. When we lived next door to each other, we got up before dawn and discussed the world's problems while we covered a four-mile walking route. She and I took a long hike the morning after I got there, and we discussed the merits of marrying at our age. We decided there weren't enough payoff to endure the aggravation involved.

The next night, I stayed with Ashley, who said she would go with me to Rael's house the following day and stay with me while the movers finished packing my things. When we got there, we found a letter that Rael had written detailing what he had done so far and what still needed doing. He had made several copies of it and distributed them around the house; he had also e-mailed it to me. Upstairs I found SJ's suitcase and Madeline's backpack, complete with an R-rated movie, *What Happens in Las Vegas Stays in Las*

> *See, the human mind is kind of like...a piñata. When it breaks open, there are a lot of surprises inside. Once you get the piñata perspective, you see that losing your mind can be a peak experience.*
> *~ Jane Wagner*

Vegas. Just what you'd expect a twelve-year-old to watch, especially if she is privileged to every detail of her mother's affair with a married man – according to Rael. While Ashley took care of her infant daughter, I sorted through the Christmas decorations, separating mine from Rael's.

Right after I began packing the pantry, Rael called on my cell phone. He wanted to know if everything was going okay. *Yes, yes. We're moving right along.* He asked if I had seen his note. *Yes, and I understand everything.* Then he asked, "So are you going to be ready to sign the paperwork later on today?" He went on to say that he felt sure he would get back most of the $2500 retainer since this was going to be quick and easy – like I'd be relieved to hear that.

I responded, "You know, I don't think hurrying through this divorce is fair to you or to me. I mean, it took me a while to decide to get married, so it is going to take a while to get out of it as well." I figured he was already committed to paying for the movers, so I had nothing to lose at that point. Once I signed the divorce papers, I would lose my negotiating power, and I would never see the money he said he would give me to remodel my bathroom at the condo. What advantage was there to agreeing to something that I knew would never happen? Besides, by that point, I had already started thinking about getting a lot more than five or six thousand dollars out of him. He had well over half a million in his retirement fund, and I figured he needed to give me some of that for compensation. Furthermore, I rationalized that any judge would think I should have a lot more since I planned to use it to fund my project to help women's shelters. Obviously, I needed a reality check about what would likely happen in a divorce court, but those were my naïve thoughts at that point.

Rael cleared his throat and asked how much longer I thought the movers would take as he only had a certain amount of cash. I assured him that they would take a credit card and verified it with the foreman of the team. After we hung up, my daughter fussed at me for talking to Rael, but I told her I wanted to keep it amicable until I had my stuff out of there. As the three movers worked in individual rooms, I drifted around the house, looking for items that Rael had missed when he divided our things. I had lived there for a year and a half and our recently remodeled home contained all my worldly goods.

> *No one is in control of your happiness but you; therefore, you have the power to change anything about yourself or your life that you want to change.*
>
> ~ Barbara De Angelis

When Rael and Jacob got there at 5:00, the movers were preparing to drive the truck to my condo. Not everything would fit in one load, and they needed to bring Rael's furniture at the condo back over to his house, so I followed them to the condo and directed them as they unloaded the truck. It was after 11:00 PM before they returned to the condo with the second load. All totaled, it cost a lot more than Rael had anticipated, which did not bother me in the least. If he could jet back and forth from Denver to Houston and bring his girlfriend and her daughter down here, then he had plenty of money to move his wife's things back to her house. With my condo a sea of boxes, I spent the night with Ashley again.

The next day when I started unpacking, I immediately thought of things I had forgotten – the shelves in the storage unit where Rael parked the camper, a few of my potted plants, wind chimes. And I needed to go back to get Hillary, my cat.

Thursday, two days after I moved, I went back and looked around Rael's house. It is hard for me to write that the house belonged to him since I had invested so much emotional and physical energy in it. Those were the issues I wrestled with as I opened the double doors to the master suite, the bedroom Rael and I had planned to move into after I got back from South Africa. He had already moved the bed from upstairs and had it made, complete with two pillows. I don't know if he put my old pillow on SJ's side of the bed, but I took it nonetheless. I also checked out my former clothes closet. Now her clothes hung there, all evenly spaced. They were the ones in the suitcase in his upstairs bedroom that I'd seen the day I moved my things out. I admired my claw-foot tub and the beveled glass window – the perfect bathroom, the one I had worked so hard to create. My wedding gift to Rael. I had considered asking the movers to take the window out and move it along with everything else, but I reasoned that it would only get broken, and that eventually I would use it as part of the negotiations, once we got down to talking money. He could pay me for it, or he could cover the cost of moving it.

Hillary did not go willingly. In fact, I had to chase her all over the damned house. Her world was changing, and she wasn't sure she wanted to go along with it. I didn't blame her. If I could have found a way to avoid that whole mess, I would have opted out myself.

The healthy and strong individual is the one who asks for help when he needs it – whether he's got an abscess on his knee or in his soul.
~ Rona Barrett

 **Family Reflections**

> *The hearts of small children are delicate organs. A cruel beginning in this world can twist them into curious shapes. The heart of a hurt child can shrink so that forever afterward it is hard and pitted as the seed of a peach.*
>
> *~Carson McCullers*

When I was three, I remember my mother driving me to the doctor while she held my infant sister in her arms. My older brother must have been with my dad or grandmother. I felt weak and needed Mother's comfort, so I tried to lay my head in her lap, but I couldn't because she was driving and holding Ruth at the same time. I remember how the expression on her face said that she couldn't deal with all this, and she wished I wasn't asking so much of her. I remember thinking I should get a turn too. Somewhere along the line, I should get a turn.

A few days later, when I was getting out of the hospital, Mother stayed in the car with Ruth and my brother while Dad went in to get me. The doctor gave me one more shot of penicillin, but first he had to find a bruise-free spot on my tiny butt. I went into shock. The way my dad told the story, I died, but the doctor managed to bring me back to life. Dad used to embellish stories, so I don't know what actually happened. The fact that Dad told the story, and that it seemed important to him that I had lived, was a big thing for me. It meant he cared. See how desperate I was for an indication of his love.

As I grew older, my health improved, but I still got sick periodically until I reached the ripe old age of eighteen. I was engaged, and the second time my fiancé visited me in the hospital in a two-month period, he told me that he could not marry me because I was too sickly. If I had not been lying down already, I would have fallen to the floor. Something inside me shifted, something powerful and strong. Desperate to maintain the relationship, I promised him I would not get sick again. I have been amazingly healthy ever since then.

It took me years of living my promise to my future husband to realize the connection between my conviction and how that affected my life, particularly my health. It has taken even longer for me to connect my fragile health with the misinterpretation I made as a child: Daddy will give me the attention I need if I am sick. As a young engaged woman, I had subconsciously tried that ploy to keep my fiancé, but it had backfired on me, so I quickly did the opposite. Ultimately, I am the one who benefitted from my change in strategy for I have enjoyed good health since then, with the exception of an occasional cold or a bout of the flu. Still, I wonder how much I internalized other detrimental messages from my childhood and used them in destructive ways. My inability to remain true to myself within the context of my relationship with Rael certainly indicates dysfunctional core beliefs at work.

Parents, deliberately or unaware, teach their children from birth how to behave, think, feel, and perceive. Liberation from these influences is no easy matter. ~Eric Berne

Nuggets of Gold

> *Self-esteem is the*
> *capacity to experience*
> *maximal self-love and*
> *joy whether or not you*
> *are successful at any*
> *point in your life.*
> *~Dr. David Burns*

The people who love me will be there for me, but only if they know I need them. Just as Ashley showed up as soon as I told her I needed her, others who love me were immediately there for me, but I had to let them know. When I have been in the depths of despair, it has been hard for me to see that I have resources. Having come out on the other end of this experience, I realize that I have as many options and opportunities as I am willing to allow myself. My willingness to avail myself of help is an area in which I struggle, but I am also blessed when I finally do call and see that others do love me and care about what happens to me.

What I require/tolerate in a relationship is a good measure of my self-esteem. Rael treated me well until he started realizing that he didn't have to in order to keep me. My reaction to his actions told him that it was okay to take me for granted, to ignore my needs, and to generally fail to respect me. That all happened early in our relationship, beginning soon after I moved in with him, but I didn't get the full impact of it until I learned that he had fallen in love with someone else. Obviously, I had put up with too much. My actions and tolerance had given him permission to do anything he wished to me. Because I had put up with so much, he expected me to embrace whatever he did, which I did – until I finally didn't. Had I held on to and insisted on self-respect I would have received it; I would have obtained it, or I would have left long before I was replaced. That's part of having good self-esteem, a willingness to take up for myself and to treat myself well, so that others realize what is acceptable to me.

I am only responsible for my own happiness. I thought I had found love when I married Rael, but I had not. My grandmother used to tell a great story about a guy who wanted his date to hold his hand. His come-on line went like this: "Nobody loves me, and my hands are cold." The target of his affections responded, "Your mama loves you, and you can sit on your hands." This woman knew herself and her responsibility to herself and others. Some day I want to be able to respond in kind, but more than that, I want to make sure I love myself first and come from a place of knowing that self-love is the source of true love; that it is not how someone else responds to me, but how I treat myself.

Self-esteem is the reputation we have with ourselves.
~Nathaniel Brandon

Pat Grissom, *Family of Origin*,
watercolor

Chapter Thirteen
Summer – Fitting the Pieces
Back Together

Some luck lies in not getting what you thought you wanted but getting what you have, which once you have got it you may be smart enough to see is what you would have wanted had you known. ~Garrison Keillor

The reality of what had happened began to sink in as I emptied my clothes from the boxes that filled my bedroom. I saw evidence of SJ packing my things – jewelry wrapped in tissue; Rael would never have taken the time to do something like that. As I hung up my clothes, I saw that she had taken the trouble to fold each item. To rid myself of the image of her hands on my things, I called friends and talked. Everyone wanted to know the details of this bizarre tale. I laughed and shared the account Rael told me the last two days we were together and how sorry he would be when we finally went to divorce court. Ellie, one of the friends who had tried to dissuade me from dating Rael in the first place, confronted me – I was far too glib to be operating in reality. I told her I was thrilled to be home and to once more have an ounce of sanity in my life. My life felt anything but sane, but at least I had my condo back, and I could start reassembling my life. She was right; I wasn't dealing with what had happened. While grateful for a place to live and time in which to start healing, I also felt numb and shell-shocked. Fortunately, I had most of the summer to begin the recuperation process.

When I related my experience, most people, including my

therapist, responded, "I never liked him." I could not see that while in the relationship, and now that I was physically out of it, I still had a hard time accepting that people felt that way – not that I lacked clear evidence of what a despicable person Rael had been. I had numerous personal experiences to reflect upon as well as countless stories of his love for another woman – told to me by the jerk himself. Still, I struggled with my conflicted feelings, finding it impossible to shift from loving him one minute to seeing him as pond scum the next.

Before sitting down with Lonnie to discuss divorce negotiations, I began fantasizing about blackmailing Rael out of a large sum of money. Besides wanting to retaliate, I justified my daydream through my altruistic intentions of starting a business to help women's shelters. When I mentioned my devious plan to a longtime friend, she reminded me that acting on my vision would not bode well with the Universe – what goes around comes around. She also reminded me that what Rael had done would catch up with him in time – I didn't need to play God in this situation, and whatever means I needed to start my organization would come to me. I heard what she said, although I resisted her suggestion to let "the Universe" take charge.

In a session with Dr. Humor, I shared with him my fantasy about blackmailing Rael. In my mind, it would be simple to contact Rael and let him know I expected him to give me a large sum of money, say $100,000. Otherwise, I would be happy to share my tale of woe with Big Oil who would, of course, be outraged that their employee acted so immorally, getting paid, as he often told me, way too much to do his "cush" job. In response, Dr. Humor shared a situation in which someone attempted to extort money from him, and he had been wise enough to involve the police. He said he would much rather see me in his office than visit me in prison. His message hit home, and I quickly gave up my daydreams of going to the dark side, but I did not give up the idea of getting something out of the divorce. If I couldn't have the relationship, I figured Rael owed me for what he had put me through.

My friend Ellie called again, and we had a lengthy discussion about whether or not Dr. Humor had erred by "letting" me marry Rael in

> *The man who opts for revenge should dig two graves.*
>
> *~ Chinese proverb*

the first place. She argued that he should have stopped me. I told her that I didn't hold Dr. Humor responsible for my actions, but it did make me question what I was getting from therapy. Thinking back to when I first started seeing Dr. Humor, I realized it had been five years since I started showing up at his office every other Friday morning. Considering my choices over the last couple of years and what I was currently experiencing, I wondered how much real progress I had made.

After my conversation with Ellie, I decided to pursue these issues with Dr. Humor at my next visit. I opened the discussion by raising my concerns: could he have predicted Rael would do this, and if so, why had I not seen this coming? Dr. Humor said that, based on what he knew of Rael, having met him when he accompanied me to my sessions and from what I had told him about Rael, he figured the marriage held little chance for success, although he did not think it would fold this quickly. He added that he had debated with himself about confronting me on this issue, but decided I had to go through this in order to get the lesson I needed from it. As consolation, he pointed out that I probably would learn much more this way than if we had ended up being married ten years and then split, which he originally considered a much more likely scenario.

For those of us who have had to endure incredible losses and sorrows, life demands an awakening of a much more profound nature than those who have not.
~ Katherine Woodward Thomas from Calling in *"The One"*

Looking for help in every conceivable format, I attended a local CODA (Co-Dependent Anonymous) meeting. Afterward, I spoke to the group leader, who recommended a therapist, Glenda. She specializes in codependency, and she had trained at The Meadows in Arizona with Pia Melody, a recognized expert in the field of codependent and addictive relationships. While Glenda practiced in the Houston area and specialized in what I urgently needed, she was in the process of phasing out her practice here and relocating to another town. She had lost her home in Ike and had decided to use the opportunity to escape the threat of future hurricanes.

When I called Glenda, she said that she did not make appointments with new clients until they have stopped seeing their current therapist. She encouraged me to be a big girl, face Dr. Humor, let him know that I intended to switch to someone else, and then call her back.

Propelled by her edict and motivated to move on, I saw Dr. Humor at his next available time slot, which happened to be an evening appointment that had canceled. Once I told him I thought I had learned all I could from seeing him, he spent the rest of our session trying to talk me out of shifting to a new counselor, which reinforced my conviction to do the opposite of what he advised. He argued that many female therapists don't like men, and are therefore incapable of effectively counseling on relationships. Then he went on to say that he had clients attend the Meadows, which was quite pricey, but that it had done little to no good as far as changing their behavior. As I stood up to leave, I said that I had seen him for five years, and I thought I should move on. Plus, the therapist I wanted to see would not be here much longer, so I needed to take advantage of her remaining time here. Because I hate confrontation, I implied that I would return to his practice once Glenda had left the area.

God gives every bird his worm, but he does not throw it into the nest.
~ Swedish Proverb

Shortly after I arrived home, Dr. Humor telephoned to say he had checked his records and surprisingly saw that five years had indeed passed since we started working together. He wished me well and said that our time together had been a pleasure. I suspected he mostly wanted to optimize the chance I would return as a client. Still, I appreciated him calling.

Having the summer off from teaching to spend time and energy on myself was a true blessing. For the past several years, I had participated in the wellness yoga classes at the college, so I began attending yoga practice regularly at the YMCA, where Rael had a family membership. Since he was paying for it, I figured I might as well use it. Plus, I delighted in the idea of taking advantage of him, although it made no difference to him moneywise as long as Jacob attended Y camp, which I had signed him up to do. The stretching and strength- building yoga poses gave me something to focus on while I lost myself in the moment, and the calming and relaxing movements worked wonders for my knotted shoulders and neck muscles.

While holding a pose during practice one day at the end of the summer, I daydreamed about teaching yoga. That afternoon I opened an e-mail from a yoga studio I had never attended, telling me about a teacher training program scheduled to start in January. It was expensive, but I decided finding it on the same day I mused about teaching yoga was an omen.

Besides doing yoga and seeing a therapist, I continued walking, which involved saying my affirmations. Recent experiences made me look at my affirmations differently. I had said these same statements of my core beliefs for years, fully believing that each time I repeated them I became more of what I wanted to be. Now I questioned whether I understood what I had repeated countless times. Maybe I needed to change the wording or even the order in which I said them.

> *My barn having burned to the ground, I can now see the moon.*
> *~ Chinese Proverb*

A few weeks after I moved back to my condo, my cousin LaVern, who had married Rael and me, called to say her sister had died. When she told me she was going to Lubbock by herself to start cleaning out Teresa's house, I volunteered to go with her. We discussed the affirmations as we drove. LaVern had done the workshop series with me the year before, so she knew about my affirmations. We talked about the wording, the length of each one, trying to shorten each to its key elements, and we deliberated the order in which I said them. When I used them as part of the workshop series, I had arranged them in the order that seemed to correlate to the chakras of the body, the seven energy centers that are located along the spine, starting at the coccyx or tailbone and moving up to the crown of the head. Each one has a special purpose, e.g., the first one at the base of the pelvic floor is the foundation chakra.

Around midsummer I had the epiphany about what I should title this book. Knowing it was Rael who had actually given it to me with his story about dropping his wedding ring in the commode made *Too Much Gold to Flush* the perfect title. Before I had the ability to comprehend the depth of what I would learn, I knew it offered great potential for what I would glean from this experience and what I wanted to offer the rest of the world.

I filled many journal pages, both electronic and handwritten, trying to sort out my feelings and trying desperately to get some perspective while understanding what had happened. I read numerous self-help books that seemed to relate to my situation. I got regular massages. Chris, my colorful tattoo-covered masseur, was properly shocked at my telling of what I had experienced. We commiserated about the trials of love and lovers while he kneaded my shoulders and back.

Not long after moving back into my condo, on one of my morning walks, I spotted an interesting find atop a pile of trash – a purple gift box the size of a hatbox, complete with a wide satin ribbon tied around it. I decided that the Universe had drawn my attention to it as another resource for healing. Each night I wrote a love letter to myself, slipped off the bow, and put it in the box. Initially, I wrote them to me from me. Then I started writing them from different key people in my life – my dad, my brother, my uncles, my aunts, anyone I could think of who I would like to believe cared enough to say something comforting.

> *Character cannot be developed in ease and quiet. Only through experience of trial and suffering can the soul be strengthened, vision cleared, ambition inspired, and success achieved. ~ Helen Keller*

After I had settled into my condo again, I made an appointment with Lonnie to start the legal aspect of the divorce process. She had recently closed her office of many years and was in the process of moving everything to her home, which quickly turned into a maze of paths created by countless cardboard boxes full of files from previous cases. Because she had cut back on her workload and now faced major health issues, I wondered if she wanted to take my case, but she assured me that she would do it. Having reviewed the correspondence I had gotten from Rael and his lawyer, she immediately deemed Colin Spacey, Rael's lawyer, an incompetent. He had not done the paperwork correctly. She advocated waiting in order to rack up some time in the marriage. She told me that half the money Rael spent on SJ and her daughter belonged to me since it was part of community property. I agreed to sit tight. The idea of hurting him financially sounded good to me.

Added to that, I thought about the date Rael had shared with me that he intended to marry SJ, which was to be one month after I signed the divorce papers. I'd love to be able to truthfully say that I no longer wanted to be married to him, but I can't. If he had shown up at my door that summer and told me this had been a big mistake, and he wanted to take me back, I fear I would have succumbed to his charm. It would have taken little from him to win me back – I was that addicted. Now I realize how truly fortunate I am to have this in my past, but at that point I remained deeply mired in my own dysfunction.

To nourish me socially that summer, I organized a game night with friends. We started meeting once a month in each other's homes. Everyone brought something healthy to eat, and after we ate, we played games. I also continued to call friends, especially people I had known for years but had not spoken to since I had been preoccupied with my relationship with Rael. Judy, a friend I had known since art school in my early twenties, began calling me on a regular basis – just to offer the love and support she knew I needed.

> *We have to believe that even the briefest of human connections can heal. Otherwise, life is unbearable.*
>
> *~ Agate Nesaule*

I began attending the Cenacle Retreat Center again. Initially the sisters asked me where I had been. I met privately with Sister Mary and told her what had happened – the exact thing she had warned me about; the narcissistic pedophile still had no boundaries. I told her of my idea to create a support organization for women in shelters. She gave me information about groups in Houston that would benefit from my support. I volunteered to help with several retreats, and I attended a couple of retreats as a participant. During one Cenacle retreat, I studied the few pictures I have of myself as a child. Using colored pencils, I drew a self-portrait on black paper. In it, I am around six. Then I watercolored another self-portrait at age seven. In both of these, I look like I am supposed to be happy because I am wearing a forced smile, but a pained expression in my eyes conveys a deeper truth.

At home I went through all my old photographs and developed a design for a watercolor collage. This design ended up being a combination of two photographs: a group shot of the family when I was three, with another, larger picture of me at age eight superimposed over the images of my mother and dad in the group pose. My mother's and father's heads blend into the older version of me in the center of the painting. Mother's eyes are vague and indistinct. The painting represents the enmeshment of our family, my parents' influence on my thinking, my distorted vision, and my mother's inability to see what is happening around her. The scared and emotionally beaten expression on the eight-year-old version of myself is painful for me to look at, although I totally identify her image with those formative years.

During this phase of my recovery, I started realizing all the emotional suppressing I had done throughout my life. It had begun at an age before I had the concept of denying my feelings. By the time I met Rael, I had become an expert at tuning out the numbness that accompanied my ability to lose myself in a relationship. Refuting my feelings became second nature. I honestly could not feel – or perhaps I had convinced myself it was easier and less painful that way.

It takes courage to grow up and become who you really are.

~e.e. cummings

Fall – Back to Work, Back to Reality

Returning to school in the fall added to my misery. Rael's and Jacob's pictures hung on my office walls. Returning from one meeting after another – the substance of the first week of the semester called "in-service" – I caught myself checking for the familiar blinking light on the phone that had once told me I had a message, nearly always from Rael. Again and again, I found myself thrown back to that painful realization – Rael no longer loved me; in fact, he never had. I had simply wanted to believe he did while ultimately his actions spoke louder than his words.

Although I plunged into the new semester, eager to find something to occupy my mind, I also resisted teaching reading again as I had not taught that since I accepted the department chair position two years earlier. Plus, I passionately loved teaching study skills, where I was more likely to impact my students' behavior. Having a routine and schedule felt good. Over the summer I had lost weight because I no longer ate out with Rael or made a diet of starchy vegetables such as corn and mashed potatoes – his idea of a great meal. Beginning a new

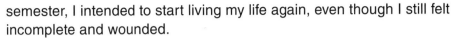

semester, I intended to start living my life again, even though I still felt incomplete and wounded.

Because I had had my name changed to my new married name, everything, including the class schedule, had McRael all over it. Friends I had not seen since before I got married embraced me and congratulated me on my new marriage, and I had to tell them what had happened. Of course, they expressed shock and outrage. When my colleague next door asked me about my summer, I gave him a synopsis of my experience. He could not believe that someone had been so callous – such an indisputable jerk. While it felt good to hear people champion my side, it also reminded me of what a schmuck I had been to get into this situation in the first place.

After a few days of this, I went home and cried my way through a chick flick. Then I called my sister, and while I sobbed and told her how crappy I felt, I painted the background of the Father's Day present I had started for Rael over a year earlier – a collage of pictures of Jacob, Rael, and me. On the background, I used a salt technique that had enthralled Jacob when he watched me work on my kids' paintings. I wanted this painting to turn out great, so that when Rael eventually saw it, he would see how much he had lost by abandoning the marriage. I thought about attaching a sticky note to it that said he could cut out my face and insert his current wife's photograph – whoever that was at the time. Once the painting dried, I added it to the pile of things that were his and had gotten mixed with mine when I moved. In my imagination, I saw him find it among his things, see our smiling faces, and feel regret for what he had done.

I stalled on making another appointment with Lonnie, not wanting to face the inevitable divorce. Reconciliation could not happen, but I had neither the strength nor the heart to walk away from the dream I once banked on to make me happy.

I talked to LaVern and said that I was having a hard time feeling angry at Rael because he hadn't done anything bad to me except fall in love with someone else. She tactfully reminded me of his complete lack of consideration concerning how he told me about his new love, his

> *You don't develop courage by being happy in your relationships every day. You develop it by surviving difficult times and challenging adversity.*
>
> *~ Barbara De Angelis*

ongoing lack of concern for me since I had returned from South Africa, and the damning fact that he would even do all this in the first place. It helped to talk to someone not mired in my distorted thinking. Rael and I never went through the falling-out-of-love phase, so I could not wrap my mind around how I was supposed to hate him, much less muster the emotional energy to get angry at him. Besides, I had grown up believing anger was unacceptable, so I honestly did not do it well – if at all.

When I had mentioned this to Dr. Humor right after my blindsiding experience of returning home, he reminded me that I wasn't completely happy before or after the marriage – there had always been things that weren't right. At the time, I figured that marriage was like that; after all, I couldn't expect to stay on an emotional high the rest of my life. Now, I see that I had blocked my growing dissatisfaction to keep the addictive relationship intact even before we tied the knot.

Also in my conversation with LaVern, we explored what I missed about Rael. As I answered her questions, she pointed out that it wasn't Rael that I missed, but his attention – calling me on the phone, bringing home flowers, and telling me he loved me.

While walking a labyrinth, I had an epiphany: just because a guy says he loves me does not mean that I must love him in return. That may strike the average person as rather obvious, but for me it was a new concept. I grew up with such a deep craving for acceptance that if someone said they loved me, then surely I loved them back. The first time I told Rael I loved him is still a vivid memory because I was so hesitant to make that commitment. Once I did, though, I was totally hooked. Saying I loved him sealed the deal.

When I talked to my friend Ellie while Rael and I were dating, she asked me several times if I loved Rael. I remember thinking, *Of course I love him – he loves me, so I love him*. It never dawned on me that I could not love him when he acted like he was crazy about me. Now, I realize that Rael does not have the capacity to love; but while we were together, he said he loved me, and since he seemed emotionally identical to my father, I was staunchly convinced he did.

There came a time when the risk to remain tight in the bud was more painful than the risk it took to blossom.   ~ Anais Nin

Journal Entry   September 7

It has only been in the last month that I have been able to fully see what a total jerk Rael was. Upon returning to teaching after being out for the summer, I found myself telling friends what had happened and seeing their reaction of shock and outrage that someone who supposedly loved me would treat me like that. That helped me to finally get to the point of anger and loathing. Then a few days ago, I toyed with the idea of playing the part of the little girl I thought my dad and then Rael wanted me to be. As I wrote in my journal that morning, it occurred to me that I am the same person in a grown-up body. I am that little girl who has learned a lot about taking care of herself, and I no longer live in survival mode, changing my behavior in order to be what I think will make me more lovable. It sounds so simple, but the results have been monumental.

The addictive feeling that I had for Rael is now gone. I can truly say that I no longer yearn to hear from him or see him. I no longer doubt my ability to reject him should he come slithering back to me. The first day walking with my new mind-set, it occurred to me that fear is my trigger point. When I fear rejection, I automatically shift into whom I think someone will accept or desire. So when I feel fear, I need to ask myself what is happening, whose love am I afraid of losing? Is it worth me losing me again to risk going back into survival mode? Never. People like my dad and Rael can never truly love me. They were in my life to teach me to love myself, to be true to myself.

Pain is inevitable.
Suffering is optional.
~ M. Kathleen Casey

Journal Entry   September 12

Not long after Rael and I separated, he sent me an e-mail saying that in time he thought we should sit down and talk to each other. I might have things I would like to tell him, and he might have the same. That will probably never happen. When he sent that, he was still working under the assumption that he and I would remain friends after all this was said and done. How idiotic. For my part, I am finally mad. What I was not able to feel initially, I finally have reached – full-blown anger. I may not be able to tell him in person, but I'd like to imagine facing him over a huge platter of fried fish and tell him the following:

1. I think you're despicable. I never imagined you dumping me three months into our marriage. Of course, if I did, I wouldn't have married you. Your actions prove that you have no regard for anyone except yourself. You don't care about me, Jacob, or even the new girlfriend.

2. You are clueless about hurting people along the way – Harmony, me, Jacob, Richard, Jill – just about anyone who has attempted to be part of your life. Narcissistic people like you and my dad don't have a clue about other people's feelings.

3. You will never know what it feels like to have an enduring, loving relationship. All of your relationships are shallow and sick. I imagine whatever you have with SJ will be short-lived. If it hasn't ended yet, it will when one of you

finds another focus.

4. Jacob wants desperately to please you and have a relationship. He knows he can get any toy or trinket that he wants from you, but that's a poor substitute for a loving father. What you did with SJ and the way you treated me says volumes to him about how you treat the people you supposedly love. If you did that to me – someone you supposedly loved, according to your wedding vows – what will you do to him when you tire of the relationship?

5. I look like the victim in our little melodrama, but I am actually the winner because I am walking away with a load of gold in the lessons I learned from this experience. You, on the other hand, are stuck in a cycle of addiction that will keep on repeating itself unless you decide to do the work it will take to stop it.

6. Remaining true to me is the only real gift I have to offer anyone, and I was not able to do that with you, and I am sorry. When we met, I doubt I possessed the ability to remain true to myself. If I had, I would not have married you, so it's a moot point, but a valuable lesson to me.

7. Knowing you has given me a totally new perspective on myself and my relationships with men. While ours was the epitome of a bad relationship, I did not know that until it ended. This life-altering crash course was as effective

> *Life is not what it's supposed to be. It's what it is. The way you cope with it is what makes the difference.*
> *~Virginia Satir (1916-1988), American Psychologist*

and as painless as possible. Initially, I loathed myself for choosing this situation. Then I came to realize that it was one of those life lessons that I had to experience, rather than hear about secondhand from someone else. I had to live it.

So that's what I would tell you if we sat down and talked today. It's been good having this time to tell you what's on my mind.

Thanks,
Pat

> We all wear masks, and the time comes when we cannot remove them without removing some of our own skin.
> ~ André Berthiaume
> from Contretemps

Journal Entry   September 16

While I have of late found it impossible to write about the story of our courting, marriage, breakup, and the aftermath, I am noticing a gradual shifting of how I see Rael. I went from total disbelief and shock to excuse-making (like my mom used to do) to a growing and building anger to relief and appreciation (that he did for me what I could not do for myself), and now I am somewhere in the middle of all that. I still feel shocked and keep telling myself he will one day wake up and realize what a prize he has thrown away – me. Then I worry that he actually will, and I wonder what I would do if he showed up on my doorstep. Mostly, I tell myself that he is still very much enamored with SJ and will not quickly desert what he so recently gave up everything to get. Either way, I am lucky beyond words to be through with him.

The other day in an e-mail response, LaVern mentioned the betrayal issue and how that would enter into my struggle to deal with all this. She's right. It's a big piece. Rael telling me he loved me for two years and then abruptly turning his back on me for another woman feels pretty damned crappy. I can tell myself how lucky I am to be shed of someone like that, but when it comes down to the final analysis – I got dumped on, so I do struggle with rejection.

This morning while I walked, I thought about the difference between Rael and my dad. Rael was complimentary and positive, which is the opposite of Dad. They were both sex addicts, without boundaries, control freaks, egotistical and narcissistic, and manipulative. So bottom line, how do I feel?

- Thankful that I got out of the situation as quickly and as painlessly as I did.

- Sad that I am going through all the grieving and dealing with rejection and betrayal.

- Ready to move on and eager to get past the divorce.

- Anxious about what will result from the divorce monetarily.

- Curious what's going on in the McRael household with Rael, SJ, Jacob, and Madeline.

- Confident that I will choose more wisely next

> *People are like stained glass windows: they sparkle and shine when the sun is out, but when the darkness sets in their true beauty is revealed only if there is a light within.*
>
> *~Elisabeth Kubler-Ross, M.D.*

time, if there is a next. (At first, I was most fearful about this – that I would get back into another bad relationship.)

- Thankful to have more time to do as I please. Glad to have my freedom back.

- Content to be without a partner, but also occasionally thinking about what it would be like to be back in a relationship – what the trade-offs would be.

- Hurt that Rael thinks I would lie down and let him walk on me, which I temporarily did.

- Tired of the whole process.

Like the sky opens after a rainy day we must open to ourselves.... Learn to love yourself for who you are and open so the world can see you shine.

~ James Poland

Journal Entry   October 3

At my last counseling session, Glenda asked me what I would say to Rael if he was sitting there with us. While it is still difficult to get as mad as I want to be, I was able to muster quite a bit of anger, what she referred to as self-righteous indignation, and while I do not want to stay in this place, I am glad that I can finally see him for the creep he is. How can anyone who supposedly loves someone treat them the way he treated me? It takes a real lowlife to coerce me into marriage as he did, and then turn around a little over two months later and throw himself at another woman. He didn't just flirt with her for a while; he blatantly threw himself at her and he had the gall to tell me about it in detail. He is a despicable, lying cheat who has no morals, no conscience, and no regard for anyone but himself and his sexual needs. He did not care what happened to me or to his son. He only cared about what he got – nothing more significant or meaningful than satisfying his immature, animal need for sexual gratification.

    I could also be justifiably angry at SJ, but honestly I feel sorry for her. "Desperate" does not begin to describe her – living with a married man, after having had numerous affairs with other married men, according to Rael. Lucky for me neither one of them hesitated, that they saw this as their golden chance to reclaim their youth and the love of their lives. It may take time or it might happen before Rael and I are officially divorced, but eventually she will realize – as I have – that there was a reason why two ex-wives willingly gave him up. He is a selfish, narcissistic psychopath (without the ability to feel emotional attachment to anyone) who will do anything to satisfy his own needs. He has no real friends because he cannot build relationships. He does not care about or for other people. His wants and needs dictate his thoughts and actions.

    Do I hate him? Yes, but I do not want to maintain that negative energy because he does not deserve any part of me, not even my anger. Continuing to fuel hate takes energy and drains productivity. I need to hate him now, but I look forward to the day that he means no more to me than a bad memory, a mistake from which I have learned hugely, and a bump in the road – preferably in the form of roadkill.

> *The world is full of suffering; it is also full of overcoming it.*
> *~ Helen Keller*

The forgiving state of mind is a magnetic power for attracting good. No good thing can be withheld from the forgiving state of mind.
~ Catherine Ponder

Journal Entry   October 12

I have struggled with a paradoxical emptiness/fullness feeling about my life in general. I feel incredibly lucky to be out of my relationship with Rael, but I also feel lost as to what I want to do now that I have all of this freedom. I don't want to fill it for the sake of filling it, but I also fear falling into a state of loneliness. Still, being alone should not mean that I feel lonely. I want to find peace and contentment in my own good company. While dating, I seem to lose myself. I would like to have a relationship without losing integrity, especially sexually, and especially with a man. Why can't I be happy just enjoying my own company?

I'm doing better all the time. I keep saying that, hoping it is true and telling myself that if I say it enough, I will eventually brainwash myself into believing it.

Journal Entry   October 20

I am through parenting – everybody. I will spend time with my friends, my children, my grandchild, my mother, and the people I work with, both fellow teachers and students, but I am through parenting them. The only person I am going to parent is me. The last few nights I have been writing letters to myself from people in my past who I know loved me – last night it was Mardee and Aunt Lillian. I don't know who will write to me tonight, but it will be someone from my past who I know loves me, and I will write what I know is in their heart. Their souls will tell me what to write. When I do this, the letters just write themselves. And then I put them in my purple box.

Journal Entry   October 22

Today Glenda and I did an exercise in which I found my adaptive child (that part of me who coped with my childhood) at age nine. I talked to her. That was hard for me. I struggled with whether I was doing it right. I feared that there was not enough left of her to find. I got in touch with emotions that I was not aware of, and I understood that the forlorn-looking little girl is not who I am or was. She is not the lost child. She is the child who took over when I couldn't cope, a substitute for the real me. By nine, according to Glenda, she may have been the second or third replacement. I had to adapt young, and I had to do a total revision. That's why I fear I won't find the real me among the memories. I fear that I have lost that individual – that she gave up and left long ago.

My greatest fear is that all that is left is the robotic, emotionless, need-less person who has nothing of my original self left to share. I want to reclaim the freedom, spontaneity, and joy that must have been there at birth. I want to find that part of me that is pure and whole. I want to find my soul. I want to unearth it from the false beliefs, illusions, lies, and adaptations that I have manufactured over my lifetime. She is the child I will be writing to; she is the part of me that I want to find amidst the empty shells that look like me.

He that cannot forgive others breaks the bridge over which he must pass himself; for every man has need to be forgiven.
~ Thomas Fuller

The reason to forgive is for your own sake. For our own health. Because beyond that point needed for healing, if we hold on to our anger, we stop growing and our souls begin to shrivel.
~ M. Scott Peck

Journal Entry   October 31

I see clearly for the first time in my life that my relationships with men have always been based on what Glenda calls love addiction. When I was in the relationship with Rael, I displayed addictive behavior. I could not step outside of what I was doing long enough to see myself. Instead, I spiraled deeper and deeper into the addiction. When I first entered the relationship with Rael, I didn't act addicted, but I quickly tuned in to what he wanted and became that – like eating vegetarian. On our honeymoon, I relaxed and ate what I wanted, thinking I had him. Wrong. I find some comfort in looking back and seeing that I had started being true to myself once more. Sadly, that's when I lost him. It makes me wonder if my renewed independence encouraged him to jump ship.

I feel a little guilty about being so happy to be alone – only a little – but mostly I'm focused on making my life a good place to live. As Glenda would say, I am busy being me, and I am intent on getting past the idea that I need someone else to make my life complete. It's all about self-esteem and self-worth. That's hard to develop, but I can't think of a better gift to give myself. Liking me has been one of my hardest undertakings, mostly because I've always judged my own self-worth by what I perceived others thought of me. If I don't use other people as my gauge, then maybe I can bypass the dead ends like Rael, and this time, do it right.

The real paradox of this scenario is that giving up my self guarantees my unhappiness, when someone asks me, either overtly or covertly, to do so. In the past, I did this because I thought I needed to in order to get his love. I did it with Rael, and I did it with every guy I dated. I quit being me and started being who I thought they wanted me to be.

Journal Entry   **December 23**

It is close to Christmas, which makes me think of the last three Christmases and how each of them involved Rael in varying degrees. Lately, I wonder if Rael has any regrets, if he has come to his senses, or if he is still blindly in love with his new/old love. I wonder what their life is like. I think about how immature he is and always has been. Of course, I never wanted to see that when I was with him, but now I can, clearly – too late, but lucky for me the Universe took over and took care of me. I would still be stuck in my addiction if SJ had not shown up.

I saw Glenda today. She described my addiction as needing attention from men. That's what I miss from Rael – the attention. Otherwise, I am glad to be able to come and go as I please, eat what I want, and generally live my life independent of anyone else. We did an exercise in which I spoke to my teenage self as an adult and eventually took her into my heart, so that I could teach her she is precious and special and does not need the attention of men. She is unique and independent and

> *One forgives as much as one loves.*
>
> *~ Duc de la Rochefoucauld*

worthy without anyone else validating her worth. I never got that as a child and the idea feels wonderful. I want to focus on that – being the parent that I have always needed and wanted.

I need to go to bed. I have much to do to get ready for Christmas Eve tomorrow.

Forgiveness is not an occasional act; it is a permanent attitude.
~ Martin Luther King

 **Family Reflections**

When I think of childhood memories of Christmas, I think of presents and how they measured up compared with what my classmates received. One year, before I had formed the concept of measuring my success of Christmas against my peers, I received a gift that had no real monetary value. And the idea of it stays with me to this day. I had reached the ripe old age of three or four. My dad's cotton crop had not yielded enough to pay the note at the bank, much less have money left for Christmas gifts. My resourceful mom made child-size kitchen appliances and furniture from orange crates – thin-walled wooden packing boxes. I remember her painting them, knowing they were more special than something she could buy at the store. Her resourcefulness throughout the years has been one of her greatest gifts to me.

> One way to make children miserable is to give them everything they want.
>
> ~ Anonymous

The Christmas of my thirteenth year a large box appeared under the tree several days before Christmas. It was store wrapped, but it did not have a name on it. We speculated on what Dad had bought for Mother since it was a sure bet Mother hadn't spent the money on something that would merit professional wrapping. Was I ever shocked and surprised when it turned out to be mine – a very cool stereo on which to play my coveted Beatles records.

Another special Christmas was the year I got a Chihuahua puppy, which I named Toby. I had wanted a dog like that for what felt like forever. Several years earlier, my family had spent the night at a cousin's house. When my mom and I took a walk in the neighborhood, we saw a Chihuahua dog, and I immediately fell in love. After that, I never tired of begging my mom for a little dog like the one we had seen. Unfortunately, two months after I got him, Toby found the unlucky half of a wishbone, swallowed it, and died. I was heartsick and eventually saved my money and bought another Chihuahua, determined to take matters into my own hands rather than wait until I got another one after interminable begging. Peppy, my second Chihuahua, lived into her teens.   Sadly, she met her demise under a tractor wheel when the hired hand did not see her. By then she had become so crippled she could not move fast enough to get out of the way.

I wonder why it is a dog doesn't get to live that long, but he still has to die old.   *~ Anonymous*

Nuggets of Gold

I must give myself time to heal, so I can accept and realize the lessons in a life-altering situation. Time is my friend, even though it felt like I would never get over Rael. Immediately after I had been blindsided by his change in course, *I wanted* to get the message and move on. Mostly, I did not want to go through the pain and anguish that I knew processing this experience would entail. Time is a major healer, though, and while it is not the easiest truth to embrace, it is the most dependable.

My instinct supplied a number of successful strategies for mending a broken heart. I already consistently journaled, so giving myself permission to spill out my thoughts on paper came naturally. Some of my greatest insights came when I allowed myself to write whatever popped into my head. Drawing and painting were other creative expressions that had comforted me in the past, so turning to visual images enabled me to express a level of feelings that went beyond words or explanation. Without consciously realizing my motivation, I found myself drawn to dramatic movies – the bigger the tearjerker the better. Watching others go through trials and tribulations flipped a switch on my own suppressed emotions, and I would cry for hours, fully satisfying my need to express my sadness. I had used affirmations prior to this major upheaval in my life, but during this healing process, they became even more important to me.

Believe that life is worth living, and your belief will help create the fact.
~ William James

Pat Grissom, *Affirmations*
watercolor

Chapter Fourteen
Spring – Hell Hath No Fury Like a Woman Scorned

When life gives you a hundred reasons to cry, show life that you have a thousand reasons to smile.   *~ Anonymous*

After Christmas and before the semester started the second week in January, I spent innumerable hours going through the paperwork my lawyer had received from Rael's lawyer in response to our requests for discovery. What Rael had sent was sketchy, but it still indicated how he spent his money, which gave me the information I needed to start building a spreadsheet, justifying why he owed me $100,000. From the bank and credit card statements that he sent, I created a long tally of the charges from restaurants, plane tickets, gifts, anything that indicated he had spent money on SJ and/or Madeline. Along with that, I created a list of his monthly expenses, including mortgage, groceries, utilities, maid service, all the outlays that contributed to their mutual support since she now lived with him, and he was paying for everything. With the slow real estate market, I doubted SJ's ability to get a job decorating model homes, as she had done in Colorado, so I figured she was financially dependent on him.

I secured estimates from several builders on remodeling my upstairs bathroom. I got quotes on moving the stained glass window I had constructed, and I did a price breakdown on recreating the window to determine its value. The week before Rael and I married, the stock market had dipped significantly, causing both of our retirement accounts to drop in value. As the market had since bounced back, my investments recovered at the same rate as his, so I had no basis for adding any of his retirement to what I felt he owed me. My strongest argument was that we were legally married, yet he was supporting another woman and her child.

> *Turn your wounds into wisdom. ~Oprah Winfrey*

Once I completed my spreadsheet and sent it to Lonnie, I focused on the spring semester. My classes included three different preps, two different study skills classes, and a reading class. All three used new texts. Right before Christmas, I opted to pilot a different textbook, *On Course* by Skip Downing, for one of my study skills classes. Since *On Course* has such a fresh and motivating methodology, I found myself restrategizing my overall approach in all of my classes. Too many students worked full-time and the messages they received on their cell phones held more interest for them than what I had to say. Throughout my years of teaching, I had seen countless students make irresponsible decisions, never realizing their failures were a reflection of these choices. I hoped that this text might help them see their part in creating their lives and bring them back "on course."

Along with struggling to stay two steps ahead of my students concerning the texts, I also decided that semester to introduce a new project I called a Five-Year Plan and Vision Board. Over the years I had made vision boards as a means of defining my goals, but they often found their way to the back of my closet, largely forgotten until I found myself compelled to create another one. I displayed my old boards and told my students to start collecting pictures that would depict their dreams in seven areas –career/education, charitable giving, family, relationships, health, recreation/adventure/travel, and financial. These categories came from a book I had picked up at Starbucks entitled *Five* by Dan Zadra. I used the quotes, stories, and interesting facts within the book to inspire the students as we progressed through the semester.

The second part of the project included writing a five-year plan that included long-range goals from each of the seven categories. I asked my students to envision where they wanted to be in five years in each of these areas. Then they broke these goals into smaller steps – one or two for each year. The last class session, I showed my new vision board first and modeled telling the group the highlights of my goals in each area. Along with a plan for each of the next five years, I asked them to give me self-addressed envelopes with Forever stamps. Over the following five years, I am committed to mailing their plans to them along with an update on how I am progressing on my dreams. So far, I have mailed back three semesters' worth of goals and have received positive responses from former students.

The new semester also began my yoga teacher training that had started the last weekend in January. From the first day of the first weekend, I knew I had jumped into something over my head, and I'm not talking about kicking into a headstand. I had ten to thirty years on most of my classmates, which gave them a decided physical advantage. I was thankful two of the other sixteen trainees were in their mid-to-late fifties, like me. The program consisted of six marathon weekends in which we attended class for twenty-four to thirty-six hours over the two to three days of each weekend. A long list of books occupied our "free time."

In our life there is a single color, as on an artist's palette, which provides the meaning of life and art. It is the color of love.   ~ Marc Chagall

One of the key things that I learned early on is that yoga is not simply a physical practice. In fact, it began as a spiritual practice and the yoga poses developed later in its evolution. Yoga has its earliest roots in India and the poses all have Sanskrit names, which added to the voluminous information that I attempted to absorb as part of this training. I started this training with a naïve point of view conceived from taking yoga at the college's wellness classes and the YMCA. Between keeping up with teaching and my yoga training, I had little time to think about Rael or what he was doing or not doing about our divorce.

In February Lonnie and I completed and returned the questionnaires Rael and his lawyer had requested for discovery. Following that, Lonnie received several requests from Rael's lawyer to move forward on the divorce. We countered with requests for more detailed responses to our discovery. In April Lonnie related that Rael had a new lawyer. I figured he had depleted his retainer and wanted to get someone who would more effectively bring our marriage to a close. Later I would learn that he had other legal issues besides the divorce.

When Lonnie pressed to set a date for mediation, Rael refused, saying he owed me nothing – his retirement had not gone up any more than mine and our marriage was too short to amass anything together. His response upset, but did not surprise, me. I knew he would resist giving me money, but the reality of his lack of caring added salt to my still open wound. When I e-mailed Lonnie requesting input on how we should proceed, I got minimal responses. I was too busy with work and yoga training to give my divorce the energy it needed to find its completion, so I set it aside until I had finished both – the semester and then the yoga training.

Being myself includes taking risks with myself, taking risks on new behavior, trying new ways of 'being myself', so that I can see who it is I want to be. ~ Hugh Prather

My obsession with yoga teacher training oscillated between commitment to finish what I had started and a dread of having jumped into something beyond my capabilities. My friend Lilly listened to my constant whining and self-doubt, always countering with reassurance that she knew I could do whatever I set my mind to, but she also assured me that I had the right to give up if I decided to. After filling one journal page after another with what felt like an avalanche of doubts and fears, I finally came to the conclusion that I did not have to complete the training. I had started it purely for my self-gratification, and if it became too much for me, I could quit. Rarely had I granted myself approval to give up, but this felt like a good place to start. Allowing myself permission to toy with the idea of walking away from this venture offered a level of self-parenting and nurturing that I had never before embraced.

Looming at the end of the teacher training program stood the practice teaching, when each student submitted three lesson plans and taught one of them. Always the overachiever, I started thinking in terms of a whole series of lesson plans that correlated to my affirmations and the chakras. This seemed like the perfect way to tie together everything I was learning. Once the semester ended in May, I spent my time working on seven yoga/chakra/affirmation lesson plans.

In June, with great trepidation, I taught my lesson to satisfy the requirements for the class. I lacked fluidity on cuing the poses, but I felt totally satisfied with the content of the lessons and the fact that I had completed the program. To this day I have never taught a class beyond that one training session. I don't have to, and I don't want to – and no one can make me. I actually learned a great deal, but I still don't feel qualified to lead others through a yoga practice. Every time I go to a class, I learn something because the training made me a better student. It made me aware of my body and the difference between putting myself into a practice and just simply getting through a practice. It truly is a union of body, mind, and spirit, which defines the word "yoga."

One of the key things that came out of creating these yoga lesson plans was an even deeper and more thorough analysis of my affirmations and how I had used them. Immediately after I separated from Rael, I saw both the underlying effects on me as well as the areas where I said one thing and did something else – like being present. I was anything but present in my relationship with Rael. Still, I believe the affirmations had overall long-term positive effects. Since I began saying them over ten years ago, I have felt their gradual and steady influence on my life, and the act of correlating them to the practice of yoga offered yet another step toward reaping the maximum benefits from thinking, saying, and living their truth.

These are the affirmations I say daily and strive to live by. The bullet points under each affirmation explain what it says to me.

> *One has just to be oneself. That's my basic message. The moment you accept yourself as you are, all burdens, all mountainous burdens, simply disappear. Then life is a sheer joy, a festival of lights.*
> *~ Bhagwan Shree Rajneesh*

Affirmations

I am present, emotionally, mentally, physically.

- Spirit created me, and I have not left my source.

- My soul – not my body – is made of a divine substance.

I am the flow of change, and I am grateful for the gifts that shifting brings.

- My world is an ever-moving progression of experiences.

- Each one offers me the opportunity to see my life with fresh eyes.

- Each movement or shift offers a gift, even if I do not immediately see it.

I am unique, precious, and authentic.

- I am the only one who can be me.
- I offer myself unconditional love.
- I am genuine and real.

I am one with all souls, earthly and eternal.

- All souls, those who occupy a body and those who do not, create one being.
- That being is Spirit.
- My soul is part of this collective energy.

I am the creator of my life. I mold and make my world.

- Each encounter with myself and others offers opportunities to express Spirit through me.
- Every choice I make forms my life and how I experience it.

I am my vision, how I see myself and others.

- How I interpret relationships with myself and others defines who I think I am.
- All of my thoughts determine my vision – where my thoughts take me.

I am entitled to miracles. Through forgiveness, I know I am love.

- A miracle is a shift in perspective.
- Forgiveness is the act of releasing old or false ideas.
- Love is my source, and I have not left my source.
- Seeing my world with new eyes is a miracle.
- Seeing/accepting this truth is a miracle.

> *You must understand the whole of life, not just one little part of it. That is why you must read, that is why you must look at the skies, that is why you must sing and dance, and write poems, and suffer; and understand, for all that is life.*
> *~ Jiddu Krishnamurti*

Journal Entry   June 20

It has taken me the better part of a year working with Glenda to finally get my head around who is in charge in my life. When I first went through this whole experience with Rael, I thought I needed to let my little girl take charge and operate from what she wanted to do since I had never allowed her to express herself. By working with Glenda, I have come to realize that it was through my child's adapted behaviors that I got to the state that I was in when this whole thing with Rael came to a head. I was seeking value in the relationship by what I could do for him. Basically, I lost myself. I fit the mold of what I thought he wanted from me. I was his Stepford wife, and he was my daddy, the narcissistic male who raised me, but could never express love for me. The key difference with Rael was that he said he loved me. By his actions, I can see that he obviously did not, but I wanted to believe it when he said he did. In fact, that was the payoff for me. I could put up with a great deal to get what I had always wanted – someone who looked identical to my dad telling me he loved me. Ironically, that person could not genuinely love someone; otherwise, he would not resemble my father.

I know this sounds insane, and it is, on many levels, but it is where I was when I found myself attracted to and totally sucked into the relationship with Rael. Now I dread ever having another relationship for fear that history will repeat itself. It is hard for me to even think about being attracted to someone else, but if I were, panic fills me at the idea of him being just like Rael and Dad in spite of my commitment to never repeat this behavior again. Hopefully, having seen it played out so clearly and in such an intense and concentrated way, I understand the message and have

> *The happiest people seem to be those who are producing something; the bored people are those who are consuming and producing nothing.*
> *~ William Inge*

finally internalized it.

This has been the biggest lesson for me – to hold on to me, to value who I am, to honor the fact that I survived, and to give myself permission to be me, to apologize to no one for who I am, to be totally, unequivocally me.

Summer – My New Lawyer Makes a Surprising Discovery

The truth is that our finest moments are most likely to occur when we are feeling deeply uncomfortable, unhappy, or unfulfilled. For it is only in such moments, propelled by our discomfort, that we are likely to step out of our ruts and start searching for different ways or truer answers.

~ M. Scott Peck

Once I had completed the yoga teacher training, I turned my attention to my pending divorce. I had not heard from Lonnie since April, when she told me Rael had refused to participate in mediation. Fear took over, and I wrestled with the idea that his rebuttal negated my right to get anything monetarily out of the divorce. My reasonable mind knew better, but I started feeling panicky when I e-mailed and did not hear back from Lonnie.

I talked to Monica, a friend, and told her about my inability to contact my lawyer and the litigation process that had lasted over a year, without an end in sight. She said her sister April was a mediator and was well connected in the legal system. Monica said April would help me if I called April and told her I was Monica's friend, so I did. April and I met a few days after I contacted her. I told her about my short marriage, Rael's sexual abuse of Harmony, and my frustration about not receiving a response from Lonnie. We talked for a couple of hours, and April vowed to help me.

The next day Lonnie finally returned my call to let me know that she had health issues and had to give up my case due to doctor's orders. She recommended me to someone else. Before I made an appointment with Rachel, the new lawyer, I spoke with April, who told me that she knew of that particular law office, and it was the preferred firm in the county in which my divorce had been filed.

I continued to walk, and during the summer, I got up early, so I could finish before it got too hot. A tall, friendly man who ran opposite the counterclockwise movement of the pack began making flattering remarks as we passed each other on the loop at the park. His comments about how good I looked and my beautiful smile made me anticipate seeing him again. We began slapping hands as we passed. One day I was ready to head for the house when I saw him cooling down on a park bench. I headed in his direction, intent on striking up a conversation, but when I walked over, he no longer seemed excited to see me. Rather than face possible rejection, I turned and walked away. He seemed preoccupied; and what did I think I was doing, approaching a man – to do what? Flirt? Didn't I have enough on my plate? Legally, I was still married. And what the heck did I need with a man? For all I knew, he was ten years younger than I and would find it humorous that I found him attractive.

The same day I made my aborted approach on the tall, hunky stranger in the park, I met Rachel, my new lawyer. She and I discussed the pros and cons of continuing with what Lonnie had scheduled so far, which was a trial date the first week of the fall semester. I hated the idea of getting a sub for that particular time, but I also did not want to drag this thing out any longer. Rachel felt that a judge would be sympathetic, especially since the case had been mishandled by the opposing lawyer, who had not given complete discovery, and refused to go to mediation. Rael's actions that led to the divorce would also add sympathy to my side, although from her reaction to my story, I sensed she doubted a girlfriend or an affair elicited much compassion in this day and time. The other option was trial by jury, which would drag out the process and also require an additional $1500 retainer. Although Rachel had not received my files from Lonnie, she felt that it would be wise to go with what we had thus

I believe that we are solely responsible for our choices, and we have to accept the consequences of every deed, word, and thought throughout our lifetime.
~Elisabeth Kubler-Ross, M.D.

far, rather than insist on a jury trial. I wrote a check to her office for $3500 – more than I had in the bank, so I transferred money out of my savings.

The next day I left for a trip to Oregon, where Lilly and I would visit her parents. When I changed planes in Denver, I checked my phone messages and found a message from my new lawyer. She had spoken with Lonnie, and together they had decided that we should go with a jury trial, for which she was filing the required paperwork, since this was the last day to do so. While I felt somewhat dismayed to realize the decision had been made without my input, I also trusted Lonnie to steer my divorce correctly.

Several days later, Lilly, her parents, and I were sightseeing when Rachel called my cell phone. She had spoken with Rael's new lawyer, who shared that he was representing Rael on a criminal case as well. Curious, Rachel did some research and found that Rael had been arrested April 7 on four counts of possession of child pornography. He was arrested again the following week for tampering with evidence. She surmised that he had been caught via a sting operation over the Internet, and that his second arrest resulted from attempting to go back to the site to erase the transaction. I called Ashley, who looked it up on the Internet and sent the information to me via an e-mail. SJ had signed the bail, which amounted to $90,000. The cost on that would be 10% or $9,000.

In reaction to Rachel's news, Lilly commented, "A leopard does not change his spots." Her words rang with clarity and truth. I thought about the time Rael had sat down with me three months into our relationship and told me about his incestuous relationship with Harmony. That incident correlated with my father's history, and it made me think of the man I had been engaged to marry in high school, who later served time in prison for sexually molesting his stepdaughters. What attracted me to these men? Why did they keep coming back into my life? What was I doing to repeat the pattern? Rael's lack of boundaries was evident throughout our relationship, especially at the end, when he hooked up with SJ. If I had been the one he called to

> *They say you learn the most from your most difficult experience. What a stupid system.*
>
> *~ Anonymous*

bail him out of jail, would I have done that? I fear I would have. My mother would have. I was my mother when I was with him – anything he did was okay. I totally understood what drove SJ and why she did what she did. I had, and have, complete sympathy.

When I arrived home from Oregon, I forwarded the information to Richard (Jill's husband whom she married shortly before she died) and Sarah, Jacob's aunt – Jill's sister. They informed me that Rael "and family" were on their way to Florida to take a Disney cruise destined for the Bahamas. Jacob had bragged about having a passport and his eagerness to use it when they saw him a few months earlier to celebrate the Fourth of July. Sarah said she would speak to an attorney about Rael leaving the country while on bail. The next day, I received a phone call from Sarah saying she had talked to Wade, her husband, and they'd decided to avoid traumatizing Jacob by not informing the authorities of Rael's whereabouts. She reasoned that it would be too upsetting for Jacob to see his father arrested should that happen when they were checking in or getting off the cruise. After mulling over what I should do, I e-mailed my attorney, who gave me the phone numbers I could call to report the situation. I did.

That night I spoke with April, the gal who had vowed to help me with my slow-moving divorce case. She spent the next day trying to find someone who could stop a man out on bail for possession of child pornography from taking a Disney cruise. I spoke with her via phone the following evening. She was in the middle of telling me about her fruitless, frustrating day, when she received a call back from the head detective handling Rael's case. He wanted any information I had to give him. I compiled a list of names, addresses, and phone numbers of people who knew Rael (including Harmony's, whose information I had acquired when we addressed our wedding invitations).

I did not speak with April after I handed off the contact information, although I did get a phone message saying the detective was appreciative of what I had given him through her. In her phone messages, April said that the detective had had Rael on his radar for some time. I don't know if that meant since he was arrested in April

> *Winning does not always mean coming in first... real victory is in arriving at the finish line with no regrets because you know you've gone all out.*
> *~ Apolo Anton Ohno, Olympic champion speed skater*

or if they were on to him before that. Also, April said that if Rael was convicted of two separate crimes having to do with sex abuse he would automatically get a life sentence. In a phone conversation with Sarah, Jill's sister, she had alluded to the possibility that Rael had done things to Harmony that were far worse than what he confessed to me. What had he done to others that he never told me about, little girls who would never tell for one reason or another? He never got caught, so why mention it? And how would I ever know about them, so why tell me?

When I met with Glenda and told her about the situation, she asked what had happened with Jacob and Madeline. I told her I did not know. She said I was obligated to contact Child Protective Services (CPS) or she would be required to do so. That afternoon I went home and called the number she had given me. While waiting for an agent to come on the line, I began filling out a report via the CPS website. When a woman finally came on the line, she talked me through the lengthy questionnaire. A few days later I received a letter saying that a file had been opened for both Jacob and Madeline.

The longer I knew about the charges against Rael the more it brought up my repressed anger toward him. I wanted to grab him by the shirt collar and shake him and scream in his face and tell him what a hideous person he had been to me and to every other woman he had ever been around. I totally understood why Jill had left him, why Jacob had never spent a night with Rael after they divorced, and why she married on her deathbed to keep Rael from getting Christopher, Jacob's half brother, when she died. Christopher's biological father was out of the picture, so logically Rael would take him, along with Jacob. Early in our relationship, Rael and I discussed the circumstances of him taking custody of Jacob. He told me then that he had consulted a lawyer to make sure he would get Jacob upon Jill's death. I now understand their motivation – hers to marry and his to see a lawyer. I seriously doubted anything would happen to Rael due to the possession of child pornography. He had that uncanny ability to stroll away unscathed, no matter what he had done.

Do something for somebody every day for which you do not get paid. ~ Albert Schweitzer

Fall – "My D-I-V-O-R-C-E Becomes Final Today."
~Tammy Wynette

When school started, I varied my walking routine, but that did not keep me from watching for the guy who had flirted with me. After weeks of not seeing him, I decided his efforts to get in shape had been short-lived. After all, most people can only take so much of the Houston heat. Every time I walked in the park, I watched for him, optimistic our paths would once more cross, he would grace me with his flattering remarks, and we would once more slap hands as we passed each other.

A dear friend, Colleen, developed lung cancer, so I began driving to her home near Austin once a month to visit her. She and I talked about the chakras and the importance of keeping a positive attitude about healing physically and emotionally. Based on my desire to help her, I decided to get private tutoring from Holly, my yoga instructor, on how to clear the chakras using aromatherapy. The tutoring session included checking my own chakras, where Holly determined I had a block in my heart chakra. While I silently pooh-poohed the power of her incantations, I did follow through with her prescription to open my heart chakra. Every three days for a month, I infused the oil she gave me while saying an affirmation she wrote on a card. The next time I visited Colleen, I used what Holly had taught me to check my friend's chakras and found them open and spinning. I didn't have the courage to check my own heart chakra again since I doubted the prescription Holly gave me had the power to change what had been permanently blocked by my dysfunctional childhood.

Doing nothing for others is the undoing of one's self. We must be purposeful, kind, and generous, or we miss the best part of life's existence. The heart that goes out of itself gets large and full of joy. We do ourselves most good by doing something for others.   ~ Horace Mann

---

Journal Entry   October 3

We are going through the final steps, the drafting and redrafting of the documents to dissolve the marriage.

> *Your pain is the breaking of the shell that encloses your understanding.*
> *~ Kahlil Gibran*

It has been a long-drawn-out, painful experience, and it has been exactly what I needed to get the lesson I came here to get. I was reading Marianne Williamson's book *The Gift of Change*. On page 97 she says, "Sometimes He uses our suffering to hone us, as it makes us more humble, more contrite, and more open to guidance we'd rejected before." Wow, is that ever true. I never understood the connection between how I saw myself and my relationship with my dad before I went through this. I never understood that my self-image was based on how others reacted to me and what I saw of myself through others. Of course, I saw little of the real me when trying to look through others' eyes.

Marianne Williamson goes on to say on the same page, "Sometimes difficult experiences have the effect of a storm. Afterwards we see a beauty in the sky and a cleanness in the air that were not there before." How true. Knowing that I am an expression of Spirit who is love gives me the perspective that allows me to see the truth of judgments and disrespectful treatment by others. What Rael did was not fair, but I have no control over what others do or say, especially about me or in relation to me. All I can do is live my life the best way I know how and not allow myself to get caught up in judgment and defense. I am not a victim. I am a creator.

I can adhere to the truth of who I am, or I can revert to my childhood strategy of molding myself into a form that I think will garner me love and acceptance. How could Rael or anyone else have truly loved me? I never risked being me. I operated under this belief that I could never be authentic and acceptable.

My father could not love himself. On some level he

knew that he was hurting others, but he chose to live the victim's life. He chose to be controlled by his addiction. He had no regard for others. He lived out of fear rather than love.

I am my perspective, how I see myself and others (my sixth affirmation). I am not responsible for how others see me, but I am responsible for how I see myself and others. When I look at myself through my God-eyes, I see myself as a manifestation of Spirit. I see myself as love. When I look at myself through others' eyes, I see myself with fear and doubt, and I am a victim. The only way I can live authentically is to live my life grounded in my truth, adhering to what my heart tells me, listening to Spirit, seeing with my God-eyes, thinking with my God-mind. Help me, Spirit, to think, speak, and act from a place of love and authenticity.

In mid-October, when Rachel and I finally prepared to make an offer for what I wanted out of the divorce, she and I differed on the amount. I argued we should ask for more than we would ultimately accept, but she countered that we needed to be "reasonable." Plus, she pointed out that her strategy would save money since it would cut out the back-and-forth negotiations. In theory, her argument worked, but when we made an offer, Rael shot back a ridiculously low counter. That was Rael's game; it gave him room to go up. We had already established our high point, and we had nowhere to go but down.

After several iteration, we settled for exactly half of what we initially proposed. I should have followed my instincts and asked for twice as much as I wanted, but hindsight is twenty-twenty. One stipulation of the divorce was that Rael deliver to me the items of mine in his possession, and I would return his property to him. A date and time had been designated in the final draft of the divorce decree.

> *Compromise used to mean that half a loaf was better than no bread. Among modern statesmen it really seems to mean that half a loaf is better than a whole loaf.* ~G. K. Chesterton

Journal Entry   November 20

The divorce was final 11/9 – eleven days ago.
Yesterday I went down to the social security office and
got my name changed back to Grissom. Today Rael was
supposed to bring my stuff to me. Of course he did not,
which was what I feared would happen. Lilly and I sat at
the table and played cards to pass the time. The whole
time I eyeballed every car that drove past. Well past the
appointed time for him to show, we went for the pedicures
we had already promised ourselves, and then we went
out to eat. I felt/feel like a total idiot. As we were drafting
the divorce decree, I mentioned to Rachel that I thought it
would be better for Rael to bring the stuff to me before we
signed the paperwork, but she assured me I would have
legal recourse if he didn't do it. Well, he didn't, so now I
can try to get it out of him myself, or I can forget it, or I can
go through the expense of recontacting her and letting her
contact his lawyer. Or I can commit a total faux pas and
contact his lawyer myself.

The stuff I want from him is more about principle
than "things." I would like to have the large roll of art
paper, and I would like to have my silverware that I got with
cigar bands that my granddad saved for me, but the real
issue is that he agreed to do it, but then he didn't. What
a jerk. I wouldn't be going through this if he weren't. He's
the one who has missed the boat. He was married to a
beautiful woman who was willing to give up everything to
raise his kid. And I would have, too, but SJ circumvented
me from doing that. I couldn't do it for myself. She caused
something to happen that would never have happened
otherwise – or it would have taken a long time for me to

finally wake up.

The last couple of years have been hard – incredibly hard. God, I am so thankful that I got out of there with my sanity. I do think You meant for me to get out and You intend for me to write a book that I can share with others. Thank you, Spirit, for creating this experience that I have learned so much from, and help me to live the truth of the lessons from now on out. Help me to know, Spirit, that you express through me. Help me to remember this experience every minute for the rest of my life and to live from it – to believe in myself and to believe in the fact that you will always be with me – to write the book, to get it published in the best way possible, to get it out there for others to read, to create my dreams of building an organization to help abused women, to build a scholarship fund, to support women to believe in themselves. If it was hard for me, and I am supposedly an educated woman, how much harder is it for women who are raised in abusive situations who never have the opportunities I had?

The purpose of life is to matter – to count, to stand for something, to have it make some difference that we lived at all.   ~ Leo Rosten

To: Rael
From: Pat
Date: Saturday, November 20, 6:23 PM
Subject: exchange of stuff

Because you did not come today at 2:00 p.m., I will assume there was some confusion about the date since it was changed several times over the process of getting our divorce decree finalized. Please let me know when you can bring my things as I would like to give you back the items I have of yours. If I do not hear from you in the next few days, I will contact my attorney and see what legal recourse I have.

Pat

To: Pat
From: Rael
Date: Sunday, November 21, 4:19 PM
Subject: Re: exchange of stuff

Sorry I missed delivering the stuff yesterday. I will be on that side of town tomorrow (Monday) evening. May I please drop the stuff off at 6:00 PM?

To: Rael
From: Pat
Date: Sunday, November 21, 8:36 PM
Subject: Re: exchange of stuff

I won't be here. You can leave my things on the front porch, and I will put your things out there as well.

Monday morning I piled his things on my front porch. Among them was one item that I left there with some apprehension – the Father's Day painting that I had finished for him a few weeks after I moved back to the condo. It was his and I certainly did not want it, but I also did not want to send a message that suggested I yearned to have him back. In all honesty, I must admit I fantasized about Rael seeing that painting of him, Jacob, and me, and thinking about all he had given up. Not that I regretted how things had turned out; I just wanted him to feel a tug of remorse or loss. I wanted him to realize what an idiot he had been.

Mid-December I looked on Facebook at SJ's page and saw she had changed her last name to his. She had posted a picture of them sitting on a couch, looking over their shoulders at the camera. His face was clean shaven, and he wore a hat even though they were indoors, probably to cover his bald head. She had on a lacy top, perhaps her wedding dress. The picture and the idea of them being married upset me more than I thought it would. I had a hard time sleeping that night, seeing that picture in my mind and thinking about all that had led up to it.

A woman has got to love a bad man once or twice in her life to be thankful for a good one.   *~Marjorie Kinnan Rawlings*

 **Family Reflections**

Each player must accept the cards life deals him. But once they are in hand, he alone must decide how to play the cards in order to win the game.   ~ Voltaire

Much of my relationship with my dad was about negotiating, and I never felt like I came out ahead. Growing up on a cotton farm, I started hoeing as soon as I could tell the difference between a weed and a cotton plant. Around age ten, I asked Dad to pay me ten cents for every half-mile row of cotton I hoed. He agreed, and I kept a daily tally on the calendar. When I had accumulated several dollars' worth, I told him how much he owed me, to which he denied setting up any kind of agreement. He said my pay was a bed to sleep in and food to eat.

The year before I went to high school, a discussion about who would be valedictorian of my junior high class spurred me to strike another bargain. Since he thought Diane, who also had good grades, would get the honor, I asked him if he would buy me a horse if I managed to get the highest grade point average. Once more he readily agreed, saying Diane's dad, as a member of the school board, wouldn't let me beat out his daughter no matter what grades I made. Long story short, I proved him wrong. After a year or more of reminding Dad of his promise, which he repeatedly denied, he told me he had bought a Shetland pony from our neighbors a mile away. Realizing that Dad had ignored my suggestion to buy another neighbor's horse that I openly yearned for, I walked a mile to retrieve the Shetland. The "not-actually-a-horse" pulled me off innumerable times by grabbing my sock with his teeth and pulling like hell. The reward for my achievement felt more like a penalty, so I asked Dad to get his money back. I doubt he paid anything for the pony. The neighbors looked completely disappointed when I walked the Shetland back to their house.

Nuggets of Gold

Although I never intend to be in the position of getting another divorce, I will always spend whatever it takes to have good legal counsel. Dragging out the divorce did end up costing me in time, heartache, and money, but I had the satisfaction of knowing it cost Rael in like manner, and that I did it on my own terms. While standing up for myself, I stopped Rael and SJ from marrying a month after they got me out the door. I have pride in myself instead of membership in the I-should-have club, where I would sit and whine with the other wish-I-had affiliates.

Doing the "right thing" is scary, and it is hard to know what the final impact may be, but it is the correct choice to make. I felt I was butting in when I gave the contact information to April to give to the detective on Rael's case, but I also felt optimistic that justice might be served by my actions. Harmony's life had been irreparably damaged, but others could be saved exposure to him. I later found out that because he was not convicted, the authorities were unable to stop him. I wish they could have. A pedophile on a Disney cruise is not a good mix, and he needed to know that there was a limit to what he could do.

It is one of the most beautiful compensations of this life that no man can sincerely try to help another without helping himself.
~ Ralph Waldo Emerson

Chapter Fifteen
Spring After DIVORCE – Endings and Moving On with My Life

How much longer will you go on letting your energy sleep? How much longer are you going to stay oblivious of the immensity of yourself?
~ Bhagwan Shree Rajneesh

The beginning of a new year felt especially monumental. My divorce had finalized, and I started working with a new therapist because Glenda had finished transferring her practice to another city. For years I had studied *A Course in Miracles*, but beginning a new year felt like the right time to make a commitment to doing the daily lessons, so I made that part of my morning quiet time.

January marked the beginning of another monumental milestone – my last semester to work as a college professor. Starting with the week of in-service, I began a countdown of the Mondays that remained before I no longer needed to show up ready to impart knowledge to hungry minds and apprehend cell phones from unsuspecting victims.   I had looked forward to retirement for years, but seeing it on the horizon terrified me.   What would my life look like when I didn't have to show up on a Monday morning with a dazzling lesson plan? Change – the big blessing and the big obstacle. What gifts would come with all this shifting?

For Christmas, LaVern gave me a book, *Calling in "The One"* by Katherine Woodward Thomas. Initially, I rejected the idea of reading it because the cover touts its ability to help the reader find the perfect mate. I had gone on enough manhunts, thank you. LaVern quickly explained that a friend of hers had read the book and found it a great way to find and claim herself. Theoretically, holding onto that discovery makes for a better connection with an intimate partner. That was the part I still doubted – my ability to be authentic in an intimate relationship. I still felt captive by those negative core beliefs. Should I ever muster the courage to date again, I feared migrating to someone like Rael and re-creating the whole scenario once more. I started reading the book and realized LaVern's wisdom in giving it to me. *Calling in "The One"* focuses on finding me in a relationship, whether it's with someone else or the most important relationship I have – the one with myself. I joined the online class and started working through the chapters. I asked Lilly if she wanted to go through the book with me, and she agreed to do so once we had finished going through the journal exercises in the *On Course* book. Fair enough – one self-help program at a time. We decided to do it over the summer.

Where your pleasure is, there is your treasure. Where your treasure is, there is your heart. Where your heart is, there is your happiness.

~ St. Augustine

Rather than teach three different courses as I had done in the fall semester, I elected not to teach the study skills class that used the *On Course* text. While I loved the content of the course, the reading and the advanced studies skills classes offered enough of a challenge for my last semester. Before Christmas, my proposal to present my Five-Year Plan and Vision Board Project at the On Course National Conference in May had been accepted. Between preparing for the presentation and doing the *On Course* journals with Lilly, I figured I would stay involved with the *On Course* mind-set, which advocates assuming responsibility, i.e., being a creator rather than a victim.

Right after the semester started I got the following e-mail from a member of my travel club:

To: Pat
From: Thelma
Date: Thursday, January 20, 8:24 PM
Subject: Affordable Travel Club

     We live in the NW corner of Washington State
and will need a house/cat sitter from May 31st until July
12th. Our sweet cat needs extra-special care, as he is
diabetic and requires shots two times a day. We know
that this request may be hard to fill, but perhaps there is
some ATC member who would be interested. If you've
not given injections before, it is easy to learn and Paddy
cat is most accommodating. There is also a kennel
nearby that you can use for a night or so if you wish.

Hoping to hear from you.
Thelma and Ben

*They are able who think
they are able.*
    ~ Virgil, Roman poet

     I responded the same day, so no one else would seize the
opportunity before I did.

To: Thelma
From: Pat
Date: Thursday, January 20, 9:40 PM
Subject: Re: Affordable Travel Club

Yes, I am interested. I am retiring from teaching in mid-
May and am currently writing a book that I hope to finish

by the end of the year. House-sitting for you sounds like a good fit for a writing retreat in a nice area of the country while it is hot here in Houston.

I have not given shots to animals, but 25-27 years ago I gave my son allergy shots when he was 3-5 years old, so I figure I could certainly handle giving shots to Paddy cat.

If you are willing, I would like to talk on the phone and get to know you a little better before I commit to anything. Is there a good time I could call you in the next week or so?

Looking forward to talking to you soon,

Pat

> *It isn't until you come to a spiritual understanding of who you are – not necessarily a religious feeling, but deep down, the spirit within – that you can begin to take control.*
> *~ Oprah Winfrey*

These e-mails began a series of conversations to finalize the plan for me to travel to Ferndale and house-sit while Ben and Thelma explored Europe. The timing and the location felt like the Universe offering up the perfect place and environment for working on this book. Plus, house-sitting would give me time and a lack of distractions, so I could write. I wanted to finish the book in order to convey to the world what I had so painfully learned – that nothing and no one outside myself can make me happy. I create my own happiness by being authentically me. While I pumped myself up with thoughts of independence, I also continued to look for my tall, handsome stranger at the park. I had felt such an adrenaline charge when he commented on my smile and called me beautiful.

Throughout the spring, I collected notes to write this book. The whole time, I fought a growing sense of panic. The more I thought about the actual writing process, the more I wrestled with deciding on the proper organization and format. Having the perfect place to work on *Too Much Gold to Flush* reinforced the idea that the Universe supported my intention to make this book a reality.

Mandy, my new therapist, and I immediately clicked. From the first time I saw her, I felt totally at ease. Seeing a new therapist meant retelling my story, but because Glenda had sent her a summary of my history, it took little time to encapsulate what Glenda and I had spent months processing. While Glenda relies heavily on Pia Melody's work, Mandy has her own style. I can't say I like one over the other. They both offer compassion and encouragement, which are the two ingredients I require in therapy.

Although I was not using *On Course* as a text, I still used the key concepts in all my classes, as the message translates to any subject. Besides the victim-versus-creator spiel, I lectured my classes on the difference between inner defender, inner critic, and inner guide. The inner defender blames others when problems arise. It's not their fault because everyone and everything else is against them. The inner critic beats him or herself up, thus believing that he or she is incapable of dealing with the situation. The inner guide is that voice of wisdom that knows they are capable and looks at options to develop a plan of action. And as the strategies are implemented, the inner guide monitors for ongoing problems and offers viable options in order to eventually reach success.

The sermons I imparted to my students along with the journal exercises I was doing with Lilly began to percolate in my subconscious. One afternoon on Mandy's couch, I heard myself say in reference to how I saw myself in intimate relationships with men, "I don't want to describe myself as a victim but. . . . " All at once, it hit me. If I didn't want to be a victim, then why did I hang on to those negative core beliefs that I learned as a child? The truth seemed so simple, but the ability to move from where I was to where I wanted to be felt monumental. Still, I had the awareness of what was blocking me.

Later that night, after supper with Lilly, I wrote the following journal entry:

> *Resolve to be thyself;*
> *and know that he who*
> *finds himself, loses*
> *his misery.*
>   *~ Matthew Arnold*

The world is a looking-glass, and gives back to every man the reflection of his own face.
~ William Makepeace Thackeray

Journal Entry   February 4

While I talked to Mandy yesterday and told her about the *Calling in "The One"* lessons, I discussed how powerless I felt in intimate relationships. I described my addictive behavior – aware that my behavior collided with my well-being, but powerless to do anything different. I said, "I do not want to describe myself as a victim but. . . ." When I said it, something clicked. I knew these words held significance, especially the "victim" part.

Then later, when I ate supper with Lilly at The Fish Place, I realized as we talked that I had adapted my parents' role models – especially Mother's, of playing the victim. I had accepted the idea that I was powerless to change how I dealt with my childhood. I could not change the events, but I did have the ability to see things differently, and so far, I had chosen to see my limitation rather than the possibilities.

With this new insight, I saw that I have options. This shift in thinking allowed me to open up to a new perspective. Furthermore, and with great excitement about the possibilities, I accept and acknowledge and celebrate the fact that I am no longer a victim. I get to choose how I live my life, and I do not choose to be a victim.

By choosing to create my life. . .

1. I am no longer concerned with meeting others' expectations. I only need to meet my own.

2. I am in control of my life, and it feels great.

I am free, I am unlimited. Right now.

3. I am unencumbered by the past.

4. I am free to move forward.

5. I forgive and let go of old ideas that do not serve me.

6. I give myself permission to see things differently.

7. I open myself to unlimited options.

8. I operate from an excited, limitless perspective.

9. I feel thrilled by the possibilities, joyful to finally make that shift, and proud of myself for finally breaking through.

10. I deny the power my past once held over me.

11. I acknowledge the truth that happiness, peace, joy, contentment, self-love is a state of mind.

12. I chose to love and protect myself.

> The universe is transformation. Our life is what our thoughts make it.
>
> ~ Marcus Aurelius

To get ready for the national *On Course* conference the first weekend in April, I began working with Priscilla, the audiovisual specialist at school. Synchronicity had brought us together at the end of the fall semester, over cookies at a holiday get-together. At that time, I told her about what I wanted to do, and she immediately began brainstorming ideas for making a video to use as part of the presentation. In the spring, once I had written the script, we scheduled a time for Priscilla to come into the classroom and film a series of activities we did as one aspect of their vision board and plan. This particular class dealt with charitable giving. Priscilla used material from this to put together a fifteen-minute video, which brilliantly featured how my students spoke from their hearts about the work they and their families already did in service to others. For the conference presentation, rather than haul examples of display boards, I carried a DVD and a laptop. Seeing the process my class went through to create their vision boards and five-year plan would effortlessly convey the key ideas of the project at the conference.

Halfway through the semester, I found out about a writer's conference that fit my style of writing. Another appealing aspect of the conference was the promise that someone who attended would receive a contract and a $10,000 advance from Hay House, the company sponsoring the workshop. I reasoned that my book had just as good a chance as any to win the contest. The event was offered in two locations – New York City at the end of May; and San Diego, just down the road from the On Course National Conference at Long Beach, where I was presenting the same weekend. Why, I don't know, but I debated whether or not to go to New York (a place I had never been) the weekend before I left for Washington to house-sit, or to San Diego, where I would already be presenting at the conference. In the end, I decided to go to the workshop in California – arrive Thursday, present Friday, and drive from Long Beach to San Diego Saturday morning to attend the writer's workshop that day and the next.

The On Course National Conference went well. I presented to a full house at my break-out session, and I received positive feedback on the evaluations. As usual I found the conference inspiring. At the Friday night session, I had the opportunity to get up and speak to the other presenters. Terrified at the prospect, I forced myself to take my place on stage, since I needed to get used to the idea of talking in front of strangers. When I opened my mouth, an abbreviated version of this book tumbled out, along with a commitment to take what I had learned from this experience and use it to benefit women who were or had been in abusive relationships and were ready to make the necessary changes to move forward in their lives – to move from victimhood to creatorhood.

The mind of man is capable of anything – because everything is in it, all the past as well as the future.

~ Joseph Conrad

Afterward, several people said they admired my determination and decision to use my experience in such a positive way.

After going to the writer's conference that same weekend, I decided against entering the contest. I did not want a publisher because I wanted to control every aspect of its production. Plus, if I eliminated a publisher, I had more profit to give to the shelter. Then it hit me – the shelters could use it as a fund-raiser. If sales directly affect them, they would have a vested interest in its success.

The last weekend in April, my colleagues from school gave me a surprise retirement party at one of their houses. I received many gifts, most of them purple, along with gift cards for a massage and a bookstore. My office walls at school were covered with Beatles posters, so my colleagues also gave me a set of Beatles DVDs. When I worked in my office at school, I sometimes glanced up and saw students admiring my pictures of the Fab Four. A typical comment at that time went something like, "We're just digging your walls."

In May, before the semester ended, I received a subpoena to appear as a witness for the state at Rael's court case for possession of child pornography – I guess in reference to the information I had given the detective by way of April, the mediator. I had already scheduled to house-sit in Washington on the court date, June 20th, so I contacted the district attorney's office and told them I would not be able to appear. The first person I talked to said that they try to work with people in my situation. My son Drew talked to a lawyer friend who advised me to request a letter from the district attorney's office acknowledging my inability to appear in court. I called back and this time the district attorney's assistant told me that I would not be released, but she thought the case would settle as a plea bargain. Otherwise, I would be in trouble if they went to court. The consequences did not sound appealing, but I refused to bail on my commitment to house-sit because of the subpoena. Besides, it sounded like Rael would end up with probation or community service.

Graduation felt weird because it would be the last one I attended

> *Don't simply retire from something; have something to retire to.*
> *~Harry Emerson Fosdick*

as a faculty member. My colleagues asked me why I even showed up, and they didn't seem to understand when I said it gave me a chance to say good-bye. It offered closure. I don't remember anything the speaker said. What I do remember is looking around at my fellow teachers and thinking about the twenty years I had taught at San Jacinto College. Many of my colleagues had been there longer than I. Some of them were also retiring. There is no harder or more important job than teaching, unless it is parenting, and often the roles are interchangeable.

The day after retirement, Lilly took me on a great adventure in which we spent the entire day practicing retirement. First, I attended a yoga practice on my own. Then she picked me up at the condo and took me to breakfast, followed by a trip to a bookstore where I used my gift card from the retirement party, and then to a resale shop where I bought a cool purple-and-white striped scarf. We toured houses in a subdivision where I would like to live, and then we went out to dinner where we ordered onion rings, of course, before we took in a movie. What a perfect day full of all my favorite things.

I took a week off before spending the last week of May cleaning out my office. What I thought I could do in two days took five. All semester, I had assured myself I would clean out little by little, but that did not happen, so I brought more home with me than I originally intended, but I got it done.

Those that say you can't take it with you never saw a car packed for a vacation trip.

~ Anonymous

The last Saturday of May, after checking two fifty-pound bags, I boarded a plane bound for Seattle. In the overhead bin, I stored a twenty-five-pound suitcase filled with my computer and resource books. From Seattle I rode the bus to Ferndale. As Ben crammed my huge suitcases in the back of their Volkswagen Jetta, he commented on the amount and weight with which I had traveled. The next day, he and Thelma showed me around their one-acre homestead, which included a barn and a number of flower beds and gardens. We did a driving tour of the area, stopping first at the nearby farm that provides produce for a food bank where Ben and Thelma volunteer on Thursdays. Then we drove to Bellingham, the closest town of any size, where they pointed out areas of interest indicated on a map Ben had clearly marked. Thelma shared phone numbers and e-mail addresses for a walking group, Women Expanding Boundaries (WEB). On Monday, Ben and Thelma left with a carry-on bag each. Their total luggage weighed less than one of my bags, and they would be gone for six weeks.

The cool temperatures of the Northwest offered a huge reprieve from the extreme summer heat of Texas, where record-breaking temperatures fueled numerous wildfires. Throughout my stay, I marveled at the joy of wearing a sweater in June and July. The locals could not begin to appreciate how much I enjoyed what seemed to them a great inconvenience. Daily, I soaked in the 60-degree temps and cherished the cool environment in which to walk. The first afternoon by myself, I walked a four-mile square, which became my regular walking route when I was "at home."

The mind is an iceberg – it floats with only one-seventh of its bulk above water.

~ Sigmund Freud

That evening, Tonya called to say that she would like to visit. To verify their approval of me entertaining guests, I called Ben and Thelma, who were spending the night in Seattle before they left early the next morning. They said yes, so Tonya's visit the first of July gave me a weekend to look forward to. Food is one of my top priorities, and my first venture off the premises landed me in a grocery store, driving Ben and Thelma's car, which they had graciously offered to let me use.

The next day, I found one of the many parks in the area, a wetlands area close to Ferndale. As I started up the stairs of an observation tower, I tripped on a shallow step and fell forward, whacking my head on the wall in front of me. Dazed, I rubbed my forehead and wondered what would have happened if I had suffered a concussion. I was alone in a part of the world where no one knew me. I thought of a similar time when I had gone to New Zealand. It had not taken me long to make friends, and I hoped for the same outcome here.

After I left the wetlands park, I drove to an artsy theater in Bellingham, the Pickwick, where I watched an interesting documentary entitled, *I Am*. It was written and produced by Tom Shadyac, who also brought us *Bruce Almighty, Ace Ventura*, and *The Nutty Professor* before he had a concussion that threw him into a deep depression. Ready to commit suicide and figuring he had nothing to lose, he began exploring the teachings of great spiritual leaders. After extensive study, his diagnosis was that America is mentally ill. We live our lives amassing wealth and measure our self-worth in dollars and cents. While applauding his conclusions, I had to smile when Shadyac showed at the end of the film that he sold his Beverly Hills mansion, moved to a mobile home park, and accepted a job teaching at a community college – a profession from which I'd recently retired. What a great postscript for a film with a powerful message.

Let go of the past and go for the future. Go confidently in the direction of your dreams. Live the life you imagined.
~ Henry David Thoreau

Alone and without a schedule, I began wondering how I would fill the void. Besides writing, what else did I want to do? I experimented with various places in the house to write and finally ended up at the dining room table. After perusing the bookshelves, I found several novels that piqued my interest. Still concerned about the subpoena, I called the district attorney's office once more to see if I could find out more about the case. The person I spoke with repeated that I would not receive a release from my obligation to appear in court, but she also said that she thought it would settle before it went to court. She told me to call back on the day of the trial.

My first Thursday in Ferndale, I went to the farm to volunteer and immediately gained the title of the quintessential house-sitter who even does the hosts' volunteer work while they are gone. Matia, the leader of the group, put me to work transplanting cucumbers from the greenhouse. During a break, I had a chance to visit with the other volunteers while I consumed a peanut-butter sandwich I had brought from home. When I mentioned I had gone to the Pickwick the day before, Dorothy offered two passes for the next time I went. Barbara, who is also a member of the walking group, told me more about how the group carpools to the location where they will walk, and she gave me directions on how to find the parking lot where the group meets. When I got home that afternoon, I was exhausted from laboring on the farm, but it felt good to connect with other people, to know I had a place to go where I could ask questions, and to know that I was doing something that would in the long run benefit others.

My first Sunday in Washington, I found the parking lot Barbara had described to me and joined the WEB group as we carpooled to Washington Park via Chuckanaut Drive, a scenic and curving road that runs from the historic Fairhaven District of Bellingham to the Skagit Valley farmlands. Our walk explored the coastline, a wall of stone carved by a glacier, and a number of sightings of wildflowers and wildlife, including a giant slug. Joining the WEB group gave me the opportunity to see sights I would have missed on my own and to meet people with common interests – walking and sharing.

The next day, Monday, I joined a yoga class I had discovered when I explored the websites of various churches in the area. The group was in the middle of an eight-week session, and Lauren, the instructor, graciously allowed me to attend the second half.

In the evenings, I watched a series of videos of Marci Shimoff interviewing self-help celebrities. She posted them in a daily e-mail over the course of ten days. One of the first interviews was with Lisa Nichols, who shared a practice of looking in the mirror every morning and telling the person she saw seven reasons why she was proud of her, why she forgives her, and what she is committed to doing for her. I left my notes from that interview on the counter in the bathroom as a reminder to do this practice daily, which I did. A few weeks later I bought Marci Shimoff's book, *Love for No Reason*, a guide to loving oneself. I was amazed to find that the helpful information is organized around the seven chakra centers of the body – of course. All the necessary pieces kept falling into place.

Every moment of your life is infinitely creative and the universe is endlessly bountiful. Just put forth a clear enough request, and everything your heart desires must come to you.

~ Shakti Gawain

With so many wonderful opportunities, it became a challenge to do what I wanted to do and still find time to write. Plus, I did have responsibilities around Ben and Thelma's farm – watering the plants on the patio and weeding the raised garden bed. Daily, I collected the mail and the newspaper, and twice a day I gave Paddy cat an insulin shot. As long as he had food to munch on during the process, he took the shots well. In the morning, after I cleaned out his litter boxes, he purred through a ten-minute grooming session of combing his thick orange-and-white fur. When he found me working at the computer, he sat in my lap, so I could stroke him while I worked. At fifteen years of age and weighing in at twenty pounds, he was quite the charmer.

During my second hike with the WEB group, I began visiting with a woman who had a similar background to mine. She had retired from teaching study skills at a local community college and had divorced after spending "forty years in the wilderness." After putting up with her husband's unfaithfulness during all of their marriage, she had reached a point when she finally stood up for herself. As she put it, "I finally passed my own course," meaning she accepted responsibility for her choices – the same thing she expected from her students. While my recent marriage had been short compared to hers, I certainly identified with other aspects of her experience.

Monday morning, June 20, I called the phone number on the subpoena and inquired about the status of Rael's trial. The person I spoke to asked if I was the victim in this case. I told her I had been subpoenaed by the state as a witness against him. She told me he had gotten a five-year sentence, which he had started serving June 16th. In shock, I hung up and immediately called Ashley. Neither one of us could believe it. Staying connected via our cell phones, we each looked up the details of his case on the county website.

Rael's mug shot, staring at a point in front of him, made me think of a time that a policeman stopped him after he ran a red light. It happened immediately after midnight, when we had just left home and were driving to the Texas Hill Country, four hours away. We chose that time to travel, so Jacob, who lay in the backseat not buckled up and covered with a blanket, could sleep. The policeman glanced toward the backseat and asked if anyone was in the car besides us. Rael continued staring straight ahead, and said there was no else in the car. The policeman asked why we ran the red light and Rael told him he'd stopped but he didn't think it was going to change because we'd sat there for a while, which was true. After the policeman left, Rael told me that was the secret to dealing with that kind of situation – don't make eye contact. I wondered now if he was going to spend the next five years not making

Our lives improve only when we take chances – and the first and most difficult risk we can take is to be honest with ourselves.

~Walter Anderson

eye contact.

After I found out that Rael actually got jail time rather than a slap on the wrist, I struggled with my conflicted feelings. He deserved what he received, although it seemed severe given it was a first offense. I wondered if the information I had submitted to the detective's office had made any difference. Was he serving a longer sentence because I had made sure that the bail bond company knew that Rael, a man charged with possession of child porn, had gone to Florida and was on his way to a Disney cruise that would take him out of the country in the company of a shipload of kids? Should I put this in the book or would he someday read it and call on the friends he made in prison to settle the score? Rael is not a vindictive person, but if he thought I had played a part in his conviction, how would he feel? And what did I care what he thought? Was I still operating on what mattered to him? He was guilty of the charges, and much more. Even if what I did helped prosecute his case, I had nothing to do with why he had been arrested and sentenced in the first place.

What were his thoughts at this moment? Had he possessed child pornography when we were together, or was his and SJ's relationship so sexually based that moving on to child pornography was simply the next step? From what Rael had told me, I knew how sexually oriented their relationship had been from the beginning. Perhaps the child porn fueled Rael's need to get more and more excited sexually. I recalled a session I had with Dr. Humor when we discussed my apprehension about certain sexual acts that Rael preferred. Dr. Humor had advised me that men tend to push the limit and want more and more sexual stimulation. He advised me that the woman must set limits on what she can accept. After that session, I went home determined to set boundaries, but my limits were promptly ignored, and rather than stand up for myself, I did what I typically did – I went along to get along.

Rael had admitted having an incestuous relationship with Harmony from the time she was six until she turned twelve, so it seemed logical that he would find child pornography most stimulating. But I had never seen it in the house. The idea that he had been arrested for having

Part of being sane is being a little bit crazy.
~Janet Long

it came as a total surprise. I knew he was a pedophile, but I wanted to believe he was smart enough and disciplined enough to not act on his impulses. He is an addict, though. I understand that from my experience of doing things that are self-destructive in the face of knowing better.

All of this hit me in stages over the course of the next week. I oscillated between thinking he had reaped exactly what he deserved and wondering how he would cope with the isolation and what I and others predicted would be a rough time, given his conviction. From what I have gleaned on the topic, a pedophile ends up at the bottom of the pecking order in prison. A prison term must be miserable, but inhabiting the bottom rung of a well-defined caste system must make it worse. Knowing Rael, I could see him maneuvering his way through his jail time, befriending this person or that, playing up to the guards and getting on the inside track, so he would not have to deal with common thieves and murderers.

> We must embrace pain and burn it as fuel for our journey.
> ~ Kenji Miyazawa

Maybe I gave him too much credit. Prison won't be like being married to a codependent woman who slinks off in the night when she comes home to find her bed has been filled by another woman. Rael will do his time. He will probably get a pardon for good behavior after serving half of his sentence, but he will be in there long enough to impact his life. Hopefully, he will let this punishment do for him what our separation has done for me. I'd like to think that given enough time, he might realize that he actually did hurt countless women. I pray that he might come to some realization about how much his behavior impacted Harmony's life. His attitude when I knew him was that she needed to get over it – sort of the equivalent of my dad's favorite phrase, "suck it up."

So, Rael, now you have a chance to finally get in touch with your feelings. When my brother died, you said that you had dealt with death because you had lost so many people. I don't think you ever actually dealt with death. You treated it like any other deeply emotional issue; you swept it under the carpet of life and charged ahead, looking for the next obsession. Well, here's your new obsession – getting through this prison term, and hopefully learning something along the way.

For me, the most troubling aspect of Rael's conviction was its correlation to Wayne and my father. All three of them had been found guilty and were publicly known as sex offenders, pedophiles. All three of them were part of a web I had woven in my desperate need to find love. On some level, all three of them had rejected me, which was their greatest gift to me because at the peak of our relationships, I doubt I would ever have mustered the strength to walk away from Wayne or Rael.

To escape what I processed during the day as I slogged my way through old e-mails from Rael and copious notes about what he had told me during our last weekend together, I read novels. The first one, *Blessings* by Anna Quindlen, reminded me of how much I loved her writing. The day I started *The Help* by Kathryn Stockett, I got an e-mail from Lilly telling me she was also reading it. Neither one of us knew the other one had any intention of doing so. Then it became a race to keep up with each other. Initially, I found the book hard to get into, but once I got into the flow of the main characters' thoughts, I could not wait to read the next chapter and the next. I identified with the setting and the era, the south in the '60s. *The Help* deals with issues about race, particularly what the maids of that era were forced to endure. Somehow all of that fit with my own emotional struggles. While I have never had to fight racial battles, I have waged a lifelong struggle against feeling inferior largely because of my gender.

Tonya arrived as planned for the Fourth of July weekend, and every day we found a different place to hike. While she was there, I gave myself a reprieve from writing. By then, I had quite a bit done, and I needed to get away from it for a while, so we had fun hiking, eating organic veggies out of the garden, and talking and talking and talking. The afternoon after I drove Tonya to the Seattle airport, I returned to writing. There was much to do, and I felt an urgency to get it done before I returned to Texas and the lovely distractions that awaited me – friends and family.

Thursday at the farm became my regular "play day," when I worked my butt off and thoroughly enjoyed my coworkers. One day Barbara and I ruthlessly trimmed the tomato plants of blight and ended up getting a little

> *There are no mistakes, no coincidences; all events are blessings given to us to learn from.*
> *~Elisabeth Kubler-Ross, M.D.*

carried away, to the point of scalping a few innocent tomato vines. Andrea and Jerry often joked about getting stuck on a weeding detail, particularly baby carrots, which were the proverbial needles in the weed-infested haystack. Their foster-child Cameron usually fell under Nicole's expert tutelage. Dorothy and Jo Marie both had a professional background in organic foods, so they offered insight into that sort of business as we did things like build a bed of straw around squash or gather chards. Pat M., who lives in co-op housing and often cooks huge group meals, organized a couple of get-togethers where those who attended chopped, sautéed, grated, and simmered exotic ingredients until we came up with delicious spring rolls on one occasion and Thai chicken on another.

> Most people can look back over the years and identify a time and place at which their lives changed significantly. Whether by accident or design, these are the moments when, because of a readiness within us and a collaboration with events occurring around us, we are forced to seriously reappraise ourselves and the conditions under which we live and to make certain choices that will affect the rest of our lives.
> ~ Frederick F. Flack

The piece of expertise that I brought to the farm was my knowledge about okra, a traditional southern vegetable that was always part of our field garden as I grew up on the farm. My last day on the farm, I gave Matia a tutorial on the proper time to cut okra. Last I heard, Pat was planning to make gumbo with their small crop. I wished I could be there to help them eat it.

One morning Nicole and I were weeding those notorious carrots, and she began telling me about an incident involving herself and her ten-year-old daughter. They had been walking down the sidewalk and a homeless man picked a flower and tried to give it to them. She pushed the flower aside and walked on. In my ignorance, I told her I did not understand why his behavior insulted her. Nicole explained that he had objectified her and her daughter, which further confused me. "He was treating us like objects. He only did that because we were females. He would not have done that for a man or a boy." I finally understood. My father thought of and treated women like objects. He had raised me to think that I had only one thing to offer a man – my sexuality. That idea dictated how I saw myself in relationship to men. Because my worth was my sexuality, I had to find a man who found it valuable, and when a man found that desirable, I needed to latch onto him because that was my only way of finding self-value in an intimate relationship. As sick as that sounds, I had grown up with that mentality, and I had embraced it throughout my life. It was not something I wanted to believe, and my logical mind rejected it, but that little girl inside me still wanted to find the love she had never received – no matter where that took me.

Later that week, I bought *A Course in Weight Loss*, by Marianne Williamson as a gift for a friend. Because I love Williamson's writing, I decided to read it and substitute the emotional weight I carried on my back and shoulders for the physical weight she refers to in the book. Using this strategy worked amazingly well. The following are letters I wrote as part of one of the lessons:

> *When it is dark enough,*
> *you can see the stars.*
> *~ Ralph Waldo Emerson*

Dear Hungry Little Girl,   June 28

I understand you need to find love. I get it. You never got it as a kid and you are beyond ravenous for it now, but don't you understand – that's not the way to find love. Choosing someone like Dad is not going to get you any further now than it did then. That ship has left and you didn't make it. You'll never have that experience. If Dad could have loved you and expressed that, he would have. But he didn't, and if we find him (someone like Rael), he will still be the same – unable to love in a healthy way.

So get a clue. Quit barking up a tree that offers nothing. You're just trying to make something happen that will never come to pass. The more that you saw that Rael was like Dad, the greater the clue. Quit trailing after creeps like that. They will only treat you badly.

If you want real happiness and love, look within. That's the only place you'll find it. It isn't out there with some creep who looks like Dad.

Love, Pat (Tough Love)

Dear Tough Love,   June 28

I know you are tired of me showing up with people like Wayne and Rael. I know that they look just like Dad, but as you said, I didn't get the love I needed as a child. I wouldn't be acting out like this if I had. So where am I going to get it if you don't give it to me?

Yes, that's me – that little kid standing at the door outside your heart, wanting more than anything to get in, to feel loved, to feel like somebody cares. I'm not going anywhere, so you might as well let me in. Hold me and give me what I've been hungry for all of my life.

I promise I won't go elsewhere if you'll be there for me. I won't take up your life – I'll be your life. I'll be you and you won't have to go somewhere else to find love. Don't you see? I am you. I'm that part of you that has always wanted someone to love you, to embrace you and be there – not because of what you looked like and not for sex, but because of who you are – a precious child of God.

If you'll let me in, I promise I will show you what real happiness is. You'll never have to search for it with someone else. Love me and you'll never be hungry for love because you'll have it.

Signed,
Available to Satisfy What You've Always Been Hungry For – Your Inner Child

After writing this letter, I sat on the couch and did a meditation in which I quietly listened to my inner child. I thought back to the time I started dating Rael, and I knew she was the voice of reason who had shown up in my journal entries. She was the ache in my chest when Rael failed me during my father's and brother's deaths. She was the one who had whispered in my ear to call Ashley and ask her to take me out of the house of insanity. And she was the one who had initiated and seen me through every healing effort: the yoga, the books, the journal writing, the conversations with friends, the therapists' sessions, the house-sitting experience, and this book – the experience of distilling it all down into an organized summary of what had happened. All of it worked together to bring me to this point in my life, ready to embrace my inner child and finally allow her entry to a place she always should have occupied with honor and dignity.

When I felt ready to open my heart, I visualized her stepping up to my chest, and I expected her to melt into me, but there was something in the way. A steel door, a heavy metal barrier kept her from coming in. For a second I slipped back into my helpless victim mode, but I did not stay there. If I had erected this fortress, I had the ability to take it down. Slowly and carefully, I saw a laser torch of love and light cut through the steel door that had been erected in my childhood. It had found its way there in order to protect me when I knew no other way to deal with the negative messages I received as a child; but as an adult, it now served as an obstruction that prevented me from loving myself. Since its inception, it had kept me isolated and loveless, but I had no conscious knowledge of its presence. Now that I saw its existence, I had the power to remove it. As I set the heavy metal door aside, I felt a physical release of its overpowering weight. The burden I had carried for so long had finally disappeared. Everything I had done in order to heal myself culminated in that quiet afternoon on the couch. Since that day, I have felt a freeness and openness in my chest that is new and liberating. I wrote the following letter that same day.

> *I am a creator. I am genuinely me in every relationship, especially with myself. I follow my Inner Guide. I love myself and vow to take care of myself in every situation.*
> *~Pat Grissom (written while doing lesson 13 in Katherine Woodward Thomas from* Calling in "The One"*)*

Dear Inner Child,   June 28

  Thank you for persisting, for keeping on showing up until I finally heard what you had to tell me, for convincing me that I could not get rid of you by continuing to stuff my emotions. By denying you, I was doing exactly what my dad always taught me to do – refusing to feel, refusing to take care of myself. It was my denial of you that created the whole scenario of you going out looking for love in all the wrong places. I love you, and I commit to keeping my heart open to you, always having my heart open to you so you don't have to find another guy who looks like Dad. I commit to staying open to you and loving you, accepting your love and returning it. I commit to remembering to love myself first and foremost.

  Thank you. Thank you. Thank you.

Birds sing after a storm;
why shouldn't people
feel as free to delight in
whatever remains to them?
*   ~ Rose F. Kennedy*

Open the window in the center of our chest, and let spirits fly in and out.
*   ~ Rumi, thirteenth-century Sufi poet*

Family Reflections

When I was fifty-one, the time had come to call Dad on his stuff. We had grown up ignoring his inappropriate behavior, but recent events mandated that his children, now adults in middle age, stop giving him permission to do what he wanted without repercussion or consequences. A year earlier, when Dad was asked to stop volunteering at the church and then the hospital, my siblings and I got together with Mother via a conference call. We collectively decided we couldn't make Dad go for counseling, but that Mother would go. She started seeing Dr. Vine. Initially, my sister Ruth accompanied her, and when she couldn't go, her daughter Lynn, a thirty-year-old, went with Mother. That's when my niece started telling the secrets she had carried since she was six and my father began sexually abusing her. For the past year, Lynn had accepted my parents' offer to cleaning their house for pay. Dad seized the opportunity to again approach her sexually. Lynn refused his advances, but his behavior served as a glaring reminder of the past. Our family intervention hinged on stopping the next generation of abuse. My niece had a six-year-old-child, Erica, and she did not want history to repeat itself.

The day we intended to do the intervention, Dad walked in the house, and like always, Ruth hugged him. Then she told him we had gathered to discuss something. Ruth told Dad that my brothers, Morgan and Matthew, were present with their wives via the speakerphone that sat in the middle of the living room floor. Dad sat in his chair and waited with a clueless expression on his face. Mother sat near him in her chair. Ashley and I huddled next to each other on the couch. Lynn and Ruth sat on the floor, close to the speakerphone. Ruth spoke first, telling Dad in a strained voice that he had done

> *However confused the scene of our life appears, however torn we may be who now do face that scene, it can be faced, and we can go on to the whole.*
> *~Muriel Rukeyser*

things to her as a child that were hurtful and mean, things she would never get over. Dad didn't respond.

Then Lynn, this grown woman, opened her mouth, and she became a six-year-old. The pain she had carried for all those years filled the room. In a little girl's voice, she described my father coming to her bed when she spent the night with them, telling her not to tell Grandmother, and then putting his hands in places they did not belong. Her story revealed the cruel and heartless things he told her to ensure her silence while causing irreparable damage to her self-concept. The revelation of the manipulation and abuse that he fostered on that little girl still brings tears to my eyes as I recount that day.

When Lynn had finished speaking, we turned our attention to Dad. His hands shook as he cleared his throat. "You may think this is funny, but I don't remember any of that." He spouted some crap about being old and needing us to cut him some slack, but by then I couldn't hear him for the ringing in my ears.

My body trembling to contain the rage that boiled within me, I clutched Ashley's hands and said, "I think this is the most unfunny thing I've ever heard. For once I wish you'd take responsibility for what you've done."

Right after our family intervention, everyone except Dad went to Ruth's house, where we had dinner and conferred on how the intervention had gone. We had stood up to Dad, and that felt good, but nothing we did as adults would repair or erase the pain we had grown to accept as normal while growing up.

The next day – Sunday and the Fourth of July – Mother's side of the family had a reunion at the community center of a local park. Before Ashley and I drove to Lubbock for the annual family get-together, I asked Mother if she wanted to come home with me for a couple of weeks. She had accepted my offer prior to the family's intervention. Because of the emotional changes taking place, the idea of Mother getting out of town felt synchronistic.

At the reunion, Dad acted differently. Instead of crowding in

> *There is often in people to whom "the worst" has happened an almost transcendent freedom, for they have faced "the worst" and survived it.*
>
> *~Carol Pearson*

at the head of the line, he helped the children get their plates. His kind and gentle behavior should have warned me that things were amiss. After lunch, Mother told Dad we were leaving. He asked her if she was coming back – probably because she had chosen to join us at Ruth's house the night before rather than stay home with him. Also, he was not used to his children standing up to him. I suspect he thought we were turning Mother against him. Mother assured him that she would be back, and we left, dreading the ten-hour drive. Because I had class in the morning, we could not dally. We arrived in Houston around midnight, but we encountered a wreck, which blocked the freeway. An angel in the form of a middle-aged man began directing traffic down the wrong way of an on-ramp. We wound our way through a number of back streets, looking for an alternative route home. The clock read 2:00 AM as the three of us fell into our beds.

The next morning, I somehow made it to my 7:30 class. At noon, when I returned home, my sister telephoned. She asked if we had checked our phone messages. I told her about the wreck and our delay in getting home, so, no, we had not thought about checking the answering machine. Then she informed me that she had filed charges against Dad after her boyfriend had caught Dad with his hands in Erica's panties. Ironically, what we had attempted to avoid via our intervention with Dad had come to pass – almost as if he was retaliating.

Shocked by this unfathomable occurrence, Mother and I repeatedly discussed the details of the intervention and our time at the reunion – how Dad had responded when we confronted him and his unusual behavior the next day. Time and time again, we analyzed what must have gone through Dad's head to spur him to do such a thing. Mother decided she would sleep in the extra bedroom when she returned home. Ruth encouraged her to stay at my house or to go to one of her other children's homes. When I saw my therapist and told her the events of the past week, she echoed Ruth's sane advice. Stepping back into her marriage would equate to telling Dad once more she supported him, whether or not she slept in the same bed

> *The thought that we are enduring the endurable is one of the things that keeps us going.*
> *~ Molly Haskell*

with him. In time the incident would become just one more of those things he did that was unacceptable but somehow got away with it. I drove home and told Mother what my therapist had said. Sadly, it took an outsider to see the obviously sensible course of action.

While she waded through the legal process of hiring a lawyer and claiming sole residence of their house, Mother stayed with me, then Morgan, and finally a friend. In January the next year, close to their fifty-fourth anniversary, Mother and Dad were legally divorced. It took another six months before he was indicted for indecency with a child and received a ten-year probated sentence.

Suffering has always been with us, does it really matter in what form it comes? All that matters is how we bear it and how we fit it into our lives.
                                                    ~Etty Hillesum

Nuggets of Gold

Any time I go somewhere for an extended stay, one of the first things I will do is find a volunteer group to join. Not knowing people in a new area is challenging, and I don't want to spend my time with just whoever crosses my path. So devoting part of my time to a volunteer group will help me focus on people who see helping others as worthwhile. The local food bank or a project like the farm connects me to good people with whom I already have a great deal in common. Besides, people who volunteer are the nicest sort of people.

It may not feel like anything is happening, but if I keep moving in the right direction, positive progress will unfold at a deep level outside my awareness. I knew I needed to practice yoga. I knew I needed to say my affirmations. I knew it was important to write in my journal and talk with my therapist and my friends, and also read every self-help book I could find. I needed to remain open to what this experience had to teach me. And little by little the pieces began to fall into place – not immediately and not in a way that I ever imagined, but I understand with perfect clarity that everything I had felt compelled to do eventually became part of my healing, part of the gold that I mined from this experience.

Don't compromise yourself.
You are all you've got.
~Janis Joplin

It is never too late to stand up for myself. All my life Mother had silently given credence to whatever my father wanted or decided to do. When he was charged with fondling his great-granddaughter, she had to make a choice. I am eternally grateful that she finally decided to defy him. Her strength in that moment is a legacy she has given to my children and to theirs. Thank you, Mother. Words cannot convey how proud I am of you and how much I consider your choice a gift beyond measure.

Chapter Sixteen
Fall – The Last Few Pieces
Fall into Place

There's only one corner of the universe you can be certain of improving, and that's your own self. ~ Aldous Huxley

Back in Texas, I returned to my regular walking routine. I never went to the park without looking for my flirty friend, but he never showed – probably because I now walked later in the day, as I did not need to get it done before going to work. It was also likely he had moved on in his life – either physically or emotionally. His sad demeanor the last time I had seen him while he cooled down on the park bench lingered in my mind. He had certainly not welcomed me with his usual smile, which I had to admit probably meant he had no real interest in me.

I finalized the rough draft of this book, but there were missing pieces. Once Rael's trial ended, I expected him to return the video footage I had shot in South Africa. His computer had been apprehended when he was arrested for possession of child pornography, but I thought he would get it to me after his case had been decided. Since I did not know the name of the detective to whom April had given the contact information, I called her and left a message on her phone. She called me back, surprised that I had called, and told me that she had seen Detective Howard that morning.

While discussing Rael's case, he had expressed his gratitude that I had given him the contact info. April gave me his phone number.

When I called Detective Howard, he seemed open to sharing what he knew, so I asked him a number of questions. This is a script of our conversation after we got past pleasantries:

Me: I had a video I took in South Africa that I would like to get off Rael's computer. When will it be returned to him?

Detective Howard: He'll never get it back. Eventually, it will be destroyed. So there is no way to get the video off it.

[Note: I later called the district attorney's office that handled Rael's case, and he told me that I would have to go through a lawyer to get a court order. I decided it was not worth more legal expenses.]

Me: Why was Rael arrested again one week after the first arrest?

Detective Howard: I contacted Child Protective Services and asked the agency to send someone to assess the home environment and make sure the kids (Jacob and Madeline) were not in danger. The CPS agent was in the process of interviewing the children with Rael present, when Rael bragged that I had not found all of it. The agent asked what he meant by that, and Rael said that he had saved it on his thumb drive that he takes to and from work. The CPS agent asked what Rael had done with the thumb drive, and he said he destroyed it. So when I found out about that, I rearrested Rael for tampering with evidence.

Me: Was Harmony helpful in the case?

Detective Howard: Yes, she was willing to come to the sentencing aspect of the trial and tell what Rael had done to her as a child. Her evidence was not admissible during the trial since it had been so long since she was abused, but once he was found guilty she was willing to testify before the jury decided his prison term.

Me: Rael told me he only masturbated in front of her. Did he do more than that?

Detective Howard: Oh, God, yes, he did way more than that. Plus, Harmony said there was another child involved.

Me: Harmony's sister?

Detective Howard: No, a neighborhood child. No telling how many other kids he has abused.

Me: Is Harmony receiving help of any kind?

Detective Howard: We've offered her counseling.

Me: Based on your dealings with Rael, what did you think of him?

Detective Howard: I never spoke with him face-to-face. The day that I went to his house to arrest him and collect evidence, I called him and told him to come home. He refused and said he was hiring a lawyer.

Me: How did you know Rael had child pornography?

Detective Howard: We had been tracking him for over a year. When a porn site is shut down, the mailing list is apprehended, and we got his name and address from one of those a couple of years ago.

If we did all the things we are capable of doing we would truly astound ourselves.

~ Thomas Edison

Me: That's when I was with him. I never saw any evidence of child pornography in the home.

Detective Howard: His new wife didn't either.

Me: When I talked to April to find out your phone number, she volunteered that you classify Rael as highly dangerous to children. What prompts you to make that determination?

Detective Howard: There was a study done between 2002 and 2005 that involved men who had been convicted of possession of child pornography, called the *Butner Child Porn* study. That study showed that of the one hundred and fifty-five men who participated in the study, 85% of them admitted to having sexually abused a child – *on average* thirteen-and-a-half children – not times, but that many different children.

Me: Wow, that's scary.

Detective Howard: Yes, it is and that's why I was so adamant that Rael not get probation, like he kept trying to finagle.

Me: I talked to someone who knows Rael and they said that he had told them he expected to be released in fourteen months on probation.

Detective Howard: He'll be up for parole like anybody else. You can look him up on the TDC (Texas Department of Corrections) website and see what his expected parole date is. He may be up for review at that time, but the actual release date will be after that. Plus, we don't make any deals about when they are going to get out on parole. He's in for five years, but he probably won't serve all of that time.

The thing always happens that you really believe in; and the belief in a thing makes it happen.
~ Frank Lloyd Wright

Me: What will happen after he is released?

Detective Howard: He'll have to register as a sex offender, which means anyone can use the Internet to track where he lives. He'll have to see a parole officer once a month. He won't be able to use the Internet unless it is work related and even then it is highly controlled. He won't be able to vote. He can't hold any kind of public office.

Me: Is he officially unemployed at Big Oil?

Detective Howard: Yes, he had to take early retirement.

Me: One last question. Did he take the cruise or was he stopped from going on that?

Detective Howard: Unfortunately, there was nothing we could do to stop him. At that time, he was not convicted, but he won't be able to do that in the future. He'll be prohibited from doing anything with

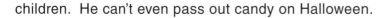

children. He can't even pass out candy on Halloween.

Me: Thanks so much for speaking to me. I appreciate all the information you've shared.

Detective Howard: Any time. If you have more questions, be sure and call back.

After our conversation, I reflected on what Detective Howard had said. His comment about Rael refusing to come home when he was collecting evidence at the house reminded me of the time the policeman stopped us for running a red light and Jacob lay in the backseat, not buckled in. *Refuse to look at them. That's the way you handle that situation.* Those were his words as we drove away. Again, he was refusing to take responsibility. It makes me wonder if he will spend the rest of his life refusing to face the consequences of his actions.

> *Every individual has a place to fill in the world, and is important, in some respect, whether he chooses to be or not.*
> *~ Nathaniel Hawthorne*

In August, at my mother's request, I looked at her finances and realized she could not continue her current spending patterns and remain solvent. After much discussion, she agreed that selling her house and creating a stream of income from it made sense. I called my siblings and they agreed to come when they could and help Mother clean out her house and ready it to put on the market in December.

Throughout the fall, I worked on the manuscript of this book, asking two different sets of readers to give me their impressions. Late October, I happened onto a business card I had picked up three years earlier at a craft fair. It was from Pam, an author who had self-published some of her children's books. Until I examined it closely, I did not realize she billed herself as a publishing consultant. We met, and she laid out a game plan for how we could finish the book.

In November, I drove to Mother's house in Lubbock with the intention of helping her finish readying her house to sell. I brought a hard copy of my manuscript with me, determined to do one more edit before I gave it to Pam. Mother and I staged a huge garage sale, chose a realtor and listed the house, and then we drove back to my house for Christmas.

January – Love Returns in the New Year

Before Mother and I went to church the second Sunday in January, I decided to take a walk. I was on my first lap in the park when I saw my tall, handsome stranger approaching me. Reflexively, I slapped his hand as our paths crossed. We both shouted out a hearty greeting. On the other side of the half-mile loop, we crossed paths once more, and he said, "I'm calculating a hug on the other side."

Thrilled by his boldness, I shouted back, "Okay."

When we met on the other side, he picked me up and hugged me like we were long-lost friends, and in a way I felt we were. I had not seen him in over a year and a half, but I immediately recognized him, although he had lost a considerable amount of weight. While he held me, my feet dangling, I said, "I need to know your name."

"Is that important?" he replied.

"Yes, it is. I can't hug someone and not even know their name."

"It's King," he answered, putting me down.

He joined me as I resumed walking. In a matter of seconds, he divulged that he had lost fifty pounds in the last year, that he had gone through some tough times a while back, and that he typically ran about one hundred miles a week, in large part due to a challenge by other runners whom he interacted with on his Facebook account. When the conversation slowed, I asked what he did, and he said he sold Harley-Davidson motorcycles and that he had one. After telling him I had retired from teaching, I said I was writing a book. He responded that he had written over one hundred and thirty poems. Surprised that he did not inquire about my book, I broached the topic again by mentioning my publishing consultant, which seemed to pique his interest.

Don't surrender your individuality, which is your greatest agent of power, to the customs and conventionalities that have got their life from the great mass…Do you want to be a power in the world? Then be yourself.
~ Ralph Waldo Trine

He gestured toward something behind me, so I turned around to see what he was pointing to. Spontaneously, he gave me another hug, this time with my back against his chest and his arms around my front. Flattered by his lack of inhibition, but also concerned by what kind of first impression I was making, I laughed, not the joyful kind, but that nervous sound I make when I'm not sure things are going as they should. He put me down, but as soon as I turned around, he asked for another hug, which I gave him, this time chest-to-chest. When he turned to go, he said he would see me at the park again sometime soon. Panicky that it would be another year and a half before we happened on each other again, I said I walked erratically since I had retired. I also suggested I needed to give him the information about my publishing consultant. He asked if I had my cell phone with me, and when I said I did not, he asked for my number, which he typed into his phone, calling me and thus leaving his number on my phone. We exchanged last names before he sauntered away.

We have to steer our true life's course. Whatever your calling is in life! The whole purpose of being here is to figure out what that is as soon as possible, so you go about the business of being on track, of not being owned by what your mother said, what society said, whatever people think a woman is supposed to be…when you can exceed other people's expectations and be defined by your own!   ~ Oprah Winfrey

As I walked home, I cursed myself for wearing my lasagna-stained shirt. When I put it on, I had reasoned that it did not matter as I would get it sweaty anyway, and I never saw anyone who cared what I looked like – except I had. King had seen me, and he had hugged me – three times. With the passing of time, his beard had turned almost solid white, but he still looked good. In fact, he looked great after losing weight, and once more I wondered if he was younger than me. I thought about him while I sat in church, when Mother and I went out to eat, and throughout the afternoon as she and I played cards.

In fact, I was still thinking of him when he called that night, saying I had been on his mind all day. Delighted to hear his voice, I admitted that I had also thought of him, giggling when he remarked that he could not get the image and feel of my unbridled breasts out of his mind. When he said this, it occurred to me that I was treading on risky ground, leading with sex rather than friendship, but the instincts were too strong and the flattery he showed me was much too seductive to harness myself with logic and good sense. I remarked that I had worried about the lasagna stain on my shirt, to which he replied that he had not seen that for noticing the swaying of my breasts. It was at this point that I regretted my habit of walking without a bra, but it was an action I could not undo at that point.

When I said I worried that he was younger than me, he asked, "*About* how old are you?"

"I'm *about* fifty-nine," I replied.

King told me that he would be sixty in less than a month. But, he added, even if he were forty, I could be a cougar. Again, I loved the fact that he had thought about me, although I knew leading with sexual attraction wasn't the healthiest start to a relationship. I had never had a guy come on to me who wasn't a setup or someone I met through a dating site, so his attention pleased me. I said we should get to know each other over a drink sometime, to which he replied that he had not drunk alcohol in twenty years because he was a recovering alcoholic. Caught off guard by his forthrightness, I babbled something inane about how good it was that he had "identified" this problem. Even while the words came tumbling out of my mouth, I wondered why I was saying something so asinine.

The next morning, I phoned King after I got out of yoga. He said he needed to call me back, and by the time he did, twenty minutes later, he said he had already eaten, and he had promised his mother, who lived nearby, that he would help her with a mechanical problem. He remarked that his brother still lived at home, but King was the one she called.

He closed the conversation by saying he and I would get together eventually. And he called me "Darling" before he clicked off. His use of this endearment thrilled me and concerned me at the same time.

The next day I told several friends and my daughter about my new love interest. I told Mandy my therapist about King, the hugging, and his remarks about my unbridled breasts. She commented on the attraction of the contrast between a tough guy who sold motorcycles and also wrote poetry. I told her my concern that he seemed mostly interested in sex, and we agreed that I needed to make it clear that I

> *To be what we are, and to become what we are capable of becoming is the only end in life.*
> ~ Robert Louis Stevenson

wanted him to see me first and my body second. The following week when I went in to see Mandy, I had to admit I had not heard from King again, although I had obsessed about him. In fact, I spent an entire morning cruising the Internet in search of facts. From my search, I found out where he lived, that his wife's name was still on the deed to his house, and that he had two children about Ashley's age. As for the wife's name on the deed to the house, I figured it remained there because they had not gone to the expense of taking it off.

Boys will be boys and so will a lot of middle-aged men.   ~ Kin Hubbard

When I searched the county records, I found no sign of a divorce, although I did find the date they married, which was in the early eighties, nearly thirty years ago. I searched obituaries and came up with someone by his wife's name, but she was the same age as she would be now – if she were still alive, which made me think that the computer was too automated and did not stop the age from increasing even though the person had died. Surely she had passed on. That explained why he had looked so sad the time I had approached him over a year and a half ago. When I had seen him in the park a few weeks earlier, he had alluded to a "rough time," which had to be his wife's illness and death.

Two weeks later, King called Saturday evening, wanting to know when I would walk the following day. I told him I might walk, but he wouldn't see me because I was in Lubbock helping my mom move. King said he had been extremely busy, selling ten bikes over the last ten days and running sixty-eight miles in the last three days. I said I would drive back Thursday, and he said he would call me Friday. It wasn't just me obsessing about him. He wanted to see me.

As I drove the six hundred miles back to Houston, I thought of King, fantasizing about this man who sold motorcycles and wrote poetry. Obviously he had suffered a great loss, which totally explained his hesitation when our paths crossed eighteen months earlier. His wavering in starting another relationship was totally understandable, considering what he must have gone through losing his wife in what I suspected was a slow, painful death. When I talked with Ashley as I drove, I told her King had called. She asked if I had found out his marital status, and I said I had not, while agreeing that I should.

At home, I looked for a Facebook account for King's wife. That would prove whether she was still alive. Even I have a Facebook account. I found nothing for her, so I checked his children's Facebook accounts, where I looked for King and his wife under their friends list. She wasn't, but he was, so I made a friend request, and King immediately accepted.

Through the messaging feature, King and I talked about getting together Sunday evening. He asked where he could pick me up and what I wanted to do. Cautious about telling him where I lived, I said the Starbucks close to my house, and I asked if it was too radical to ride his motorcycle on our first date. He said I would have to hold onto him, and I said I planned to. He replied, "Wahoo." When I mentioned my date to Ashley, she asked if I had found out his marital status. I told her all the reasons I thought he was widowed, and at her persistence, I admitted I had not brought it up when I talked to King. Why would he approach me if he wasn't available? Asking him if he was married opened a door that would require me to admit I had been divorced – twice – something a man who had lost his wife, following a long-term marriage could not understand.

Sunday afternoon after I arrived home after attending a play with friends, I changed into snug-fitting jeans and a few layers of shirts since the temperature was dropping, and I wore a bra. I sent King a Facebook message saying I was home and wondered when he wanted to meet. He responded, "Thirty minutes."

The phone rang, and I saw it was Colleen, my friend who has struggled with cancer for the last year and a half. I had to answer it, and I felt compelled to tell her about my date. She laughed and told me she wasn't sure that was a good idea. Right before we hung up, she reminded me about boundaries, that old issue that we constantly discussed – that topic that is huge for both of us.

I arrived at the Starbucks before King, so I sat out front and wondered if I should have followed my desire to let him pick me up at my house. After all, if I was bold enough to ride on his bike, surely

Let us be grateful to people who make us happy; they are the charming gardeners who make our souls blossom.
~ Marcel Proust

I trusted him enough to let him know where I lived. I had mentioned that idea to Ashley, and she had warned me to err on the side of caution. When King drove up, I waved and walked over to where he'd parked. He gave me a big hug and a kiss on the lips. I smelled smoke in his beard, but not on his breath. How could someone run one hundred miles a week and also smoke? It didn't make sense, but I didn't even consider asking him about it.

Before we drove to a Mexican restaurant a couple of miles down the road, he garbed me in a heavy canvas jacket, which he slowly and carefully buttoned. Then he slipped a tube around my neck and leather gloves on my hands. He did not wear a helmet, nor did he offer me one. I climbed on behind him, wrapped my arms around his waist as promised, and enjoyed the feel of the wind in my face. When we reached the restaurant, King took off my gear in the same careful fashion he had put it on me.

After we were seated, he pushed the menu aside and said he usually got the same thing – shrimp enchiladas. I was too distracted by the man who had occupied my thoughts for the last several weeks to concentrate on the options. Having taken far too long to decide, I finally settled on a taco salad with shrimp. I thought about getting a margarita, but I didn't want to get into the whole issue of drinking around an alcoholic, which means I slipped right back into doing what I thought would be acceptable to him – just like I had with Rael.

Eager to promote conversation, I said, "So your mom lives close by?"

He confirmed that, and said his father – who had moved the family from California to Texas, so he could work at NASA – had died twenty-odd years ago. King volunteered that he had left home at sixteen since he and his dad did not get along. I talked about my kids, and he talked about his.

Then he looked me in the eye and said, "I'm going to be upfront with you. I'm still married, and I still live at home. We haven't slept together for years, and I've lived elsewhere, but when she got cancer, I came back and helped her get through it. I took her to all of her

If someone listens, or stretches out a hand or whispers a word of encouragement, or attempts to understand a lonely person, extraordinary things begin to happen.

~ Loretta Firzaris

treatments, and she had a clean bill of health. I moved out again and was making $200 grand a year selling mobile homes, but then she relapsed, so I came back." He shrugged his shoulders.

Open-mouthed, I stared at him. All the rationalization and lies I had told myself floated to the surface of my brain. I was hurt and let down – not so much by him as by me. I had convinced myself he was a widower. I was the one who had ignored every tell-tale sign – her name on the deed to the house, no obituary listing, his hesitation in starting the relationship, his need to call me back when I called him, maybe even the smell of smoke on his beard in some way led back to her. All of it made sense now.

"You look like a ton of bricks just fell on you," he remarked, and took a drink of water.

"I feel like it did." Of course, I couldn't tell him all the things I had made up in my mind or my voyeuristic cruising of the Internet.

We continued talking and little by little what felt like a normal conversation resumed. I mentioned my book again, but he didn't ask me about it. Instead, we quickly shifted to his poetry. I asked him when he started writing it, and he said he was just a kid. King recited the first poem he had composed at age thirteen, and I was amazed by its depth. It described three scenarios in which people had gotten caught in a loop of mindlessly doing something without realizing that they had the freedom to try something different.

It's so easy to fall in love but hard to find someone who will catch you.
~ Anonymous

King had been born deaf and though the doctors were able to facilitate hearing in one ear, he was still deaf in the other one. As a child, he kept to himself, surrounded by a wall of silence. Having grown up with earaches as a kid, I could identify. Not hearing what is going on inflicts a painful state of isolation, especially when it happens to a child.

By the time we left the restaurant, I was ready to ignore the fact that he still lived under the same roof with his wife. He kissed me before we got back on the bike and again after he delivered me to my car. I drove home in a stupor, the whole time fantasizing about how I could make this work. Didn't I deserve to have love and passion in my life?

Right after I got home, King messaged me through his Facebook account, and I immediately responded. The conversation quickly turned sexual, although I expressed clear misgivings about the fact that he was legally tied to someone else. We ended the long conversation with me agreeing to meet him at 3:00 PM in the park the following day, so I could look at the book of his poems he had printed out. Before we signed off, he made repeated pleas that I arrive at the park without a bra, about which I hedged on making a commitment.

I went to bed around ten, and Ashley woke me an hour later when she called as she drove home from work. We talked about how her weekend had gone. The whole time, I avoided telling her that I had seen King. She would want to know about his marital status, and I would either have to lie to her or tell her something I did not want to admit, especially to myself.

> Rather than deny the body, it was elevated to the status of a sexual bargaining chip.
> ~Patricia Foster

After Ashley arrived home, I went back to sleep, but I woke up a couple of hours later, a voice screaming in my head, "What the (beep) do you think you are doing? You just wrote a book about being honest with yourself. Why, why, why would you go there again!?"

It was too similar to the time Rael had told me he had molested his stepdaughter, and I la-la-la-ed my way past the popping red flags and my friends' waving arms of caution. I could justify it as much as I wanted, but truthfully I had headed down an addictive path toward a sick relationship with someone I had no business talking to, much less dating.

The previous several nights, I had returned to my practice of writing love letters to myself and placing them in my big purple gift box. Using my best lavender-colored stationery, the same paper I had been using for my letters to myself, I wrote King a letter explaining why I could not see him again. Nearly finished with the letter, it dawned on me – I could not deliver the letter in person for my resolve would likely crumble when I saw him, especially if he slipped in a few kisses before I got around to handing him the letter. No, I had to type it and send it to him via his Facebook account. Halfway through composing it, I left for my Monday morning yoga class. While in the middle of moving through the poses, I realized both letters were for me, not King. I was the one who needed to understand why I could not pursue this association. All he needed to know was that I would not meet him, and I could not continue the relationship.

After I returned home, I finished the letter – for my sake. A couple of hours prior to our agreed-upon time to meet again, I sent King a message on his Facebook account saying, "In order to stay in integrity with myself, I have to forgo a relationship with you at this time. If you ever find yourself single, I would love to get to know you better. All my best, Pat"

My intention was to post the message and then close the page, but he immediately responded – at first with a sexual overture, but when I did not respond, he began campaigning for a platonic relationship. I said that I doubted his ability to keep it purely a friendship. He stated that he had complete control of his life, to which I replied that I suspected he was using his wife to hide out from becoming emotionally involved with anyone. Of course, he denied it and proceeded to tell me that he multitasked, had a near-140 IQ, had done volunteer work at the Galveston prison system, helping people turn their lives around, and he had learned to stop drinking over twenty years ago.

I told him his counter consisted of intellect, talents, and good deeds, not a reply to my original allegation – he was avoiding emotional commitments. He came back with a reference to Jacob in the *Old Testament* and Captain Dan in *Forrest Gump*. Both of them apparently had overcome huge obstacles and King felt a kinship to them. At that point, I asked him to explain his reasoning, and he said he needed to run an errand. As I signed off and closed the window, I wondered if he would ever understand that he was like one of the characters in the poem he had recited over dinner – imprisoned by his own choices and limited thinking.

I was a mess for the rest of the day. The greatest relief came in admitting my poor judgment to Ashley and several friends, including

> *I think my biggest achievement is that after going through a rather difficult time, I considered myself comparatively sane. I'm proud of that.*
> ~Jacqueline Kennedy Onassis

Colleen, who had reminded me about maintaining boundaries. I thanked her for giving me what I needed, so I could stop before I got too far down my path of dysfunction. The following day, I went to see my therapist and explained what had happened.

Responding to my description of falling off the wagon, Mandy said, "Sounds like you did get pulled along a ways in the mud, but the important thing is you realized that was not where you wanted to stay and you got back on. I'm proud of you." Her reaction helped enormously.

Later that week, I told a group of friends what had happened, and in the process of sharing, I realized that I could interpret the situation two different ways: Number one, I will always attract unhealthy men and relationships into my life. Or, number two, the Universe gave me a valuable test, which I passed. While it was painful to end the relationship, I demonstrated true self-love and nurturing by doing so. I do love myself, and I am able to make hard choices in the name of taking care of me.

Three failures denotes uncommon strength. A weakling had not enough grit to fail thrice. ~ *Minna Antrim*

 **Family Reflections**

Moving is never easy, but having lived over eighty years and having a propensity to not throw anything away complicated the situation for my mother. In the fall, my siblings and I spent several weekends helping her make the transition from her three-bedroom house to a two-bedroom house with little more than half the square footage she'd had. Lots of stuff had to go. From the time I saw her in August until I drove back to Lubbock in November with the intention of helping her complete the task of readying the house to put on the market, Mother had gone from worrying about what she would do with every scrap of paper to flinging photographs in the trash if she could not readily identify them. Without knowing my mother, it is probably hard to appreciate the gigantic strides she had made in a few months' time.

> I discovered I always have choices and sometimes it's only my attitude.
>
> ~Judith M. Knowlton

      Selling her house carried with it a great deal of emotional weight. She had never made a decision of this magnitude on her own. The few times she had moved had been because my dad decided they would, but they always lived within a five-mile radius of his birthplace. Dad moved out of the house Mother now lived in under a court order when she filed for divorce following Dad's arrest for indecency with a child. Dad had been dead for three years when she reluctantly decided to sell the house, but his memory was still largely tied to this home, the only one they had lived in that was not on or close to the land they farmed, the only one that she had been instrumental in selecting. And now, due to finances and the never-ending toll of time and the need to care for a place, she had halfheartedly agreed that she needed to sell it. Where she would live and what she would do with all of her stuff that she could not take with her began to consume her like an incurable disease.

We interviewed three realtors, discussed the pros and cons of each, and then Mother made the final decision, going with the one who had answered her questions most completely. As we looked for housing options, she held out for what she wanted – not the cheapest or the newest or the one closest to her church – all pluses I fervently pointed out. Her final choice was close to her old neighborhood, has a storage room, a garage, and a picture window that looks out over a golf course, which has to be the most scenic view in Lubbock.

When she needed to hire a mover, rather than follow my suggestion to call a number of places and ask them a battery of questions, she talked to a few friends, and then going with her gut instinct, she selected the one who felt right to her. The company she selected did an excellent job, and the final cost was half of what we had originally anticipated.

As I prepared to drive back to Houston, Mother hugged my neck, and then she gave me a beautiful gift. She said, "You know, I feel like I'm just now starting to learn how to make up my own mind. And it feels good." Thank you, Mother, for showing me that it is never too late to accept responsibility for life, that as long as I am alive I will be faced with making choices, and that it is up to me to make up my mind in the way that works best for me – in spite of what others may advocate.

The speed at which any dream may be realized is always a function of how small the miracles have to be in order not to freak out the dreamer.   *~ Mike Dooley from* The Awe-manac

Nuggets of Gold

No matter how painful, it is important that I recognize and stop unhealthy relationships before they become established. I had hoped that processing my experiences with Rael would magically immunize me from attracting another unhealthy situation into my life. A part of me still wants to justify and rationalize my desire to form a relationship with King, but the wise part of me knows that in the long run it would not work – even if he weren't married. Twice, I mentioned writing a book, and twice he ignored me in order to discuss his own writing. He may be empty after years in an emotional vacuum, but his interest in me hinged on sex, and that is not my primary offering. As hard as it is for me to admit, it is my addiction that attracted me to him. Just as an alcoholic will always be an alcoholic, I will always struggle with my codependence. The blessing is that I now recognize it, and while it is a challenge, I have proven to myself that I have enough strength and self-respect to walk away.

  I have known since the beginning of my quest for self-awareness that a lost child resides within me. She is that kid from my youth who never felt heard. Years ago, in a self-help workshop, I made a clay doll replica of her. For years her tiny form faithfully stood next to my computer at work until I retired from teaching. Now, she hangs out on my nightstand. In the process of writing this book, I have finally

> *Man's main task in life is to give birth to himself, to become what he potentially is.*
>   *~Eric Fromm*

figured out why I created her, why I keep her close by, and why she is so precious to me. She represents what I have always yearned for but until now never quite found the wherewithal to give myself – love; love, simply and beautifully unconditional love.

When you are truly clear about what you want, the entire universe stands on tiptoe waiting to assist you in miraculous and amazing ways to manifest your dreams and intentions.
                    ~ Constance Arnold, a radio host

Seeing myself as a victim keeps me in prison. Seeing myself as a creator gives me total control of my life.
                    ~Pat Grissom

    This quote made me think of the countless people, events, and divine inspiration that have come forth to aid me in creating this book. Taking a broader perspective, I realize I orchestrated all of the events from the minute I met Rael until I had the final conversation with King. All of it was an outgrowth of my desire to fill my emptiness, to care for that little girl who felt unloved. I am like the traveler who explores the most remote corners of the earth looking for happiness and returns home to find it there among her friends and family. I fully understand that what I have always wanted cannot be found outside myself. Before I can find love with someone else, I must first love myself.

    Namaste – the light in me sees the light in you.

Cast of Characters

Rael - currently serving a five-year sentence for possession of child pornography in a prison in Central Texas. I'm not sure how old his roommate is.

SJ (Saint Joan) - raising Jacob while his father makes new friends in prison. When she sits on the throne I helped install and looks past the claw-foot tub at the window I built, I'm sure she thinks of me and all I have given her, including a loving husband.

Jacob - enjoying having a sister while he breaks in a new mom.

Me – delighted to have my life back. Eating meat every day of the week, traveling, writing, and extremely grateful for all that this experience has taught me.

Discussion Questions

1. Rael is presented as a charming man initially, but early in the story, Pat begins to find fault with him. Do you immediately agree with her or do you defend him before you start to see his faults? Do you think the author is looking for reasons to criticize and justify why Rael is "bad"? Or do you think his actions and behavior speak loudly enough and the author does not need to discredit him since he does that for himself?

2. Through the first half of the book, Pat is conflicted about her attraction to Rael. What do you see as the underpinning for this clash? Why do you think Pat was unable to end the relationship when Rael told her about his incestuous relationship with his stepdaughter, although she wrestles with that decision in her diary and in her conversations with her friends and therapist? Did you struggle with the decisions Pat made? Did her conundrums remind you of your own struggles or those of friends and family?

3. How does Pat's background, growing up in the '50s and '60s, affect her self-image?   Do you see the influence of pre-and/or post-feminism and how she deals with her intimate relationships with men?

4. Pat says she was addicted to her relationship with Rael. In what ways do you see an addictive quality to their union? How is her addiction for Rael contrary to what one typically considers an addiction? Do you see other compulsions within the context of this book?

5. Soon after she separates from Rael, Pat is inspired to start an organization that aids women's shelters. How does this fit her general personality? Besides the obvious positives that this organization may have for women who are struggling in dysfunctional relationships, who else may benefit?

6. Sex confused with love is a theme addressed in this book. In what ways does this show up beyond the relationship between Rael and SJ? What are the dangers associated with this confusion? How can an individual recognize the difference between sexual attraction and genuine love, especially early in a relationship?

7. Pat and her stepson, Jacob, have a complicated relationship. On the one hand, she says she does not want to mother a young child again; on the other, she commits herself to him – even though she sees herself making choices that will minimize her relationship with her own children. Would Pat have gone through with the relationship without Jacob as part of the mix? How do Pat's mothering instincts figure in to her attraction to Rael?

8. The author's childhood is fed to the reader in snippets. From what we learn about her, how do you see her past haunt her current life? How does the family that Pat attempts to create with Rael and Jacob compare to her family of origin? How does the author's history dictate her actions, both before and after the break-up of her marriage?

9. Pat expresses concern for Jacob's future. He lost his mother at an early age. Then he lost his connection to Pat. Now his father is in prison for a crime that Jacob may not understand. What particular challenges will Jacob face growing up and as an adult?

10. Do you identify with Pat's quest for resolving and/or obliterating the negative core beliefs she developed as a young child? To what extent do childhood experiences shape your adult life?

11. What is your reaction to the title *Too Much Gold to Flush, the Gift of Infidelity*? Does the author live up to her commitment to find the gold in the situation? What truths did you identify with from your own life experiences? What new ideas would you like to incorporate into your day-to-day living? Are there lessons that you gleaned from this story that the author does not discuss?

Acknowledgements

It would require writing another tome to properly thank all the people who contributed to the experiences that brought about this book. Because of space and time, I will confine my thanks to those who had direct input.

I would like to thank Lisa Smith, Dorthy Hawkes, Joann Bruun, Beatrice Harris, Therese Clements, Barbara Montoya, Lynda Hungerford, Mary Bishop, Myrethia Wood, LaVern Watters, Lalor Cadley, Patricia Ross, Lynne Clarke, and Dianne Marion for reading the book in its many drafts and giving me valuable, constructive feedback. Shirin Wright, Ira Van Scoyoc, and Pam Van Scoyoc worked countless hours in the editing, layout, and production process. Thanks to Rodger Marion for his video expertise. The folks at Hurricane Business Recovery Center – Doug Baumann, Chris King, Detra Cunningham, and Elissa Rodriquez – each played a role in making Dedicated to Empowering Women (DEW) a viable vehicle for birthing this book.

My everlasting appreciation goes to Marsha Harris and Deborah Sanders (now deceased), my long-time critique partners. What I received from our weekly sessions years ago reverberates in my mind even today.

I will be forever obliged that SJ contacted Rael, and he eagerly responded. So often the true gifts in life are shrouded in events that look like anything but a present. For me, the insights and truths that I learned about myself through the writing of this book are the real gold to be gleaned from this experience. So while I know SJ and Rael were not intent on enhancing my life, ultimately they did. And I will be eternally grateful.

To the numerous people I encountered during my healing journey, I will always be thankful that Spirit led you to say and do the things that led to the incredible growth I experienced as a result. Thanks also to my friends and family who offered reassurance when I doubted what I had set out to do and a listening ear when I needed to process. Your love and compassion brought me through to the other side. I am grateful to everyone who encouraged me to follow my dream of writing this book. My greatest wish is that it will inspire others to recognize their negative core beliefs, re-write those into empowering affirmations, and follow their passion, knowing that we are each a divine expression of Spirit.

Bibliography

Bourke, Michael L. and Andres E. Hernandez. "The 'Butner Study' Redux: A Report of the Incidence of Hands-on Child Victimization by Child Pornography Offenders." *Journal of Family Violence* 24, 3, 183-191, DOI: 10.1007/s10896-008-9219-y.

Cloud, Henry, and John Townsend. *Boundaries with Kids*. Grandville, MI: Zondervan Publishing Company, 2001.

Downing, Skip. *On Course*, 5th ed. New York: Houghton Mifflin, 2008.

Gibran, Kahlil. *The Prophet*. New York: Alfred A. Knopf, 1923.

Hall, Ron, and Denver Moore. *Same Kind of Different as Me*. Nashville, TN: Thomas Nelson, Inc., 2006.

Quindlen, Anna. *Blessings*. New York: Random House, 2002.

Shimoff, Marci. *Love for No Reason*. New York: Simon and Schuster, 2010.

Stockett, Kathryn. *The Help*. New York: Random House, 2009.

Thomas, Katherine Woodward. *Calling in "The One."* New York: Random House, 2004.

Williamson, Marianne. *A Course in Weight Loss*. Carlsbad, CA: Hay House, 2010.

Williamson, Marianne. *The Gift of Change*. New York: Harper Collins, 2004.

Zadra, Dan. *Five*. Seattle, WA: Compendium, 2008.

What is DEW doing?

If you're reading this page, you already know what a terrific book this is. You also know people it could help.

 Go from victim to victor and let the healing begin with the gift that keeps on giving . . . Forever!

Every single copy of *Too Much Gold to Flush* sold benefits a women's shelter. A full one half, yes 50%, of the purchase price of each book is donated directly to the shelter of your choice.

To schedule an author event, learn more about DEW or to order *Too Much Gold to Flush*, contact Pat at **info@patgrissom.com** or go to **www.patgrissom.com**.

Ordering by Mail

Contact DEW via US Postal Service at:
Dedicated to Empowering Women, LLC
P.O. Box 2235
Friendswood, Texas 77549

Please include:
1. Your shipping address
2. A check or money order for the correct amount
3. To charge, give a phone number. We will call for your credit card information.

Caution: Do not send cash or credit card information through the mail.

Price: $24.99
$1.94 tax (for Texas residents)
$4.99 shipping (inside the US)
$31.92 (Texas residents)
$29.98 (non Texas residents)